THE SWORD
OF JUSTICE

THE SWORD
OF JUSTICE

*Ethics and Coercion in
International Politics*

JAMES A. BARRY

Westport, Connecticut
London

Library of Congress Cataloging-in-Publication Data

Barry, James A.
　　The sword of justice : ethics and coercion in international
politics / James A. Barry.
　　　　p.　　cm.
　　Includes bibliographical references and index.
　　ISBN 0–275–96092–7 (alk. paper)
　　　1. International relations—Moral and ethical aspects.　2. Just
war doctrine.　3. Human rights.　4. Distributive justice.　5. United
States—Foreign relations—Decision-making.　I. Title.
JZ1306.B37　　1998
172′.4—dc21　　　　　　98–24559

British Library Cataloguing in Publication Data is available.

Library of Congress Catalog Card Number: 98–24559
ISBN: 0–275–96092–7

First published in 1998

Praeger Publishers, 88 Post Road West, Westport, CT 06881
An imprint of Greenwood Publishing Group, Inc.

Printed in the United States of America

The paper used in this book complies with the
Permanent Paper Standard issued by the National
Information Standards Organization (Z39.48–1984).

10 9 8 7 6 5 4 3 2 1

Copyright Acknowledgments

The author and publisher gratefully acknowledge permission to quote from the following:

Quotation from Charles Whitehead's "The Solitary," from *The English Poetry Full-Text Database*. Cambridge: Chadwyck-Healey, 1992. Copyright 1992. Used with permission of Chadwyck-Healey, Inc., Alexandria, VA.

An early version of chapter 5 appeared as "Managing Covert Political Action: Insights from Just War Theory," *Studies in Intelligence*, 1992. A revised version was first published as "Covert Action Can Be Just," *Orbis*, Summer 1993, copyright by Foreign Policy Research Institute, Philadelphia, 1993. Used with permission.

This book has been reviewed for security by the Publications Review Board, Central Intelligence Agency. This does not constitute endorsement by the CIA of any statements or opinions therein.

Meanwhile, let be, if aught these words avail,
The sword of Justice laid in Mercy's sheath

Charles Whitehead, "The Solitary" (1849)

Contents

Preface

ETHICS AND COERCION IN INTERNATIONAL POLITICS

The use or threat of force by nation-states is an enduring feature of the international system. Since the Athenian generals at the Melian Conference asserted that "the strong do what they will and the weak suffer what they must" (Thucydides, *Pelopennesian War*), states have tried to coerce other states, and nonstate actors, to bend to their desires.

Running counter to the assertions of Thucydides and the other political realists has been another stream of argument to the effect that force must be replaced by cooperation, and that states should seek noncoercive means to reach accommodation with other actors. Set forth most forcefully by Immanuel Kant, this school of thought advocates a search for "Perpetual Peace" through a gradual end to violence and an increase in international collaboration.

Between the extremes of realism and Kantian idealism is yet another tradition of argumentation. This position accepts the world as it is, full of avarice and ambition, and seeks to temper its excesses by invoking the rule of reason and law. In the Western world, this viewpoint finds its most sophisticated expression in the just-war tradition. Beginning with Augustine and further elaborated by Aquinas, this tradition has deeply influenced modern thinking on warfare and the use of military force. Reflections of the tradition are also evident in Islamic writings on war and peace, and—less explicitly—in the advice given to statesmen by political philosophers and religious leaders in other world cultures.

The "middle way" between international realism and idealism has important insights to offer in other areas of statecraft and international intercourse. In seeking to regulate and challenge, rather than to eliminate, the use of force, the casuistry of the just-war tradition has provided a framework of questions and criteria that have a more general application to situations in which states contemplate the doing of harm, in search of some ostensibly higher good. Statesmen often pose these questions and seek to meet the criteria, but they do so unconsciously, and thus incompletely. The result can be policy disasters that cause harm out of proportion to the good sought.

PLAN OF THIS BOOK

This book explores the relationship between ethical argumentation and the range of coercive measures that states employ. It does this by presenting historical case studies in which the United States has used or envisioned such measures to achieve its goals, and by comparing the actual practice of the United States against the standards established by the just-war framework. Based on the comparison, a number of concrete recommendations are made about specific measures that could strengthen the moral content of policy decisions, and at the same time meet tests of political feasibility in the American system of government.

To improve the ethical quality of decision-making on the use or threat of force is increasingly urgent. International politics is in rapid evolution from the reliance on nation-states that has been its hallmark for more than three centuries to a new, more complex and interrelated set of systems that are as yet poorly understood. The consequentialist approach that focuses on the results of states' actions as a standard of morality is more and more questionable as the "new sciences" of chaos and complexity theory demonstrate that in complex systems, even small actions can have significant and unpredictable consequences. Thus it is necessary to explore new approaches to evaluating the ethical dimensions of actions by states, and by nonstate actors as well.

The book begins with a description of the traditions of ethics and international affairs, with particular attention to the just-war tradition in its classical and modern variants. This chapter serves as a review of the major arguments for those who have studied international ethics or political philosophy, or as an introduction for those readers whose perspective is primarily that of the practitioner. The book then applies the framework of ethical analysis to specific cases that reflect a range of issues: nuclear deterrence, conventional warfare, humanitarian intervention, covert political action, economic sanctions and coercive diplomacy. The final chapter attempts to describe a general approach to reconciling ethical standards and the reality of international coercion, with particular attention to initiatives that the United States might pursue.

The ideas in this book are ancient, but the proposed applications are new. The concept of blending the just-war tradition with contemporary issues has arisen out of both my academic study and my experience in a variety of policy issues. During a government career spanning more than three decades, I have been involved to varying degrees in military policy, arms control, economic analysis and covert political action. At George Mason University, I have had the privilege of teaching courses in American foreign policy, national security decision-making, international management, and ethics and international affairs. In preparing for these classes, I have had the opportunity to ponder the ethical dimensions of some of the policy issues in which I participated. This reflection has convinced me that it is possible to improve the ethical content of policy decisions by improving the process of making decisions, and that the key to this improvement is to ask the kinds of difficult questions required by the just-war tradition.

This book, then, has both educational and operational objectives. It is my hope that it will be useful in upper-level undergraduate and graduate courses in international politics, foreign policy and applied ethics. Beyond that objective, I hope that some current and potential policy makers will read the book as well, and take the opportunity to ponder how some of the tenets of moderation that this book suggests can be integrated into the policy process.

USING THIS BOOK IN THE CLASSROOM

This book has been designed to form an integral part of a university course in ethics and international politics. Typically, such courses deal with the three major recurring moral issues in international relations: war and peace, human rights and distributive justice. This book can make a contribution to understanding all three.

The cases and commentary in this book should be used in conjunction with both primary and secondary source readings on international relations and ethical theory. Many of these are identified in the bibliography. An excellent foundation text is Terry Nardin and David Mapel, eds., *Traditions of International Ethics*. This useful summary of the traditions of ethical argumentation should be supplemented by readings from the principal authors in the most important traditions. Selections should include classical realists (Thucydides, Machiavelli, Hobbes), modern realists (Weber, Kennan, Morgenthau et al.), utilitarians (Bentham, Mill), liberals (Kant) and the advocates of natural law (Aristotle, Aquinas). In addition, it is helpful to use a secondary text that surveys the substantive issues in ethics and international affairs, such as Stanley Hoffman's *Duties Beyond Borders*.

With these readings as a basis, students can explore the ethical dimensions of the use of force by using Michael Walzer's *Just and Unjust Wars*. A grasp of the fundamentals of Walzer's legalist paradigm will prepare them to discuss the cases in this book and how that paradigm, as well as the broader just-war tradition, can inform decisions about the range of coercive measures employed by states. The cases also contain a number of details about policy issues and decision-making that are not explicitly analyzed in this book, but can usefully be discussed in the classroom.

In addition to the cases presented here, there are others that can expand students' understanding. The Carnegie Council on Ethics and International Affairs has a very useful series of cases, including discussions of the U.S. intervention in Grenada, the Reagan administration's program against Nicaragua, the dilemma of doing business in South Africa under apartheid, human rights abuses in Guatemala and terrorism in Northern Ireland. Other cases are available from the John F. Kennedy School of Government at Harvard and from the Pew Case Program at Georgetown University. Films and novels can be useful stimulants to class discussion; I have used *Henry V* to illustrate the ethical dilemmas of warfare. Graham Greene's *The Quiet American* is a classic treatment of the ethics of insurgency, and Doris Lessing's *The Good Terrorist* explores the psychology of violence and manipulation.

USING THIS BOOK FOR POLICY EVALUATION

Beyond its educational objectives, this book can also be used for evaluating proposed approaches to international issues. The first chapter provides a brief summary for policy makers of the principal schools of thought on force and coercion in international politics. It suggests that the most appropriate approach is to evaluate policy proposals by using the "middle way" described in the just-war tradition. The evaluation process would be as follows:

First, describe the current situation, including the central issue; a brief outline of how the issue arose; an identification of the key actors, their objectives and influence; the alternative courses of action available; and the decision-making procedure that will be employed.

Second, identify a case in this book that has similarities to the issue being considered. The cases herein include a variety of coercive measures: nuclear threats, conventional war, humanitarian intervention, covert action, economic sanctions and coercive diplomacy. They also cover the major regions of the world: the former Soviet Union, the Middle East, Africa, Latin America and Asia. Enumerate the key similarities and differences between the case and the current issue.[1]

Third, review the middle section of the book's discussion of the analogous case. This provides commentary by critics on the historical events and may stimulate ideas about the ethical dilemmas of the current situation.

Fourth, look at the final section of the analogous case. The end of each chapter provides a set of suggestions or guidelines for improving policy choices. The specific areas covered are the following:

- Chapter 2: Managing nuclear deterrence and dealing with proliferation of weapons of mass destruction

- Chapter 3: Deciding to use conventional military force, the conduct of conventional warfare and improving the decision process

- Chapter 4: Making decisions on humanitarian intervention, with specific suggestions on information sharing, contingency planning and decision processes

- Chapter 5: Deciding to use covert political action, including a series of key questions that should be answered before using secret methods

- Chapter 6: Employing economic sanctions and deciding whether or not to trade with a country that abuses human rights

- Chapter 7: Using coercive diplomacy, a mixture of "carrots" and "sticks," to induce compliance with a policy objective.

Finally, review the suggestions in chapter 8 regarding overall policy objectives, specific cases and criteria for selecting key decision makers.

ACKNOWLEDGMENTS

A number of people and organizations have been important to the development of my thinking about ethics and international affairs. The philosophy faculty at Georgetown University, especially Louis Dupre, first awakened my interest in ethical issues. Other Georgetown scholars, especially Francis Winters and John Langan, helped me to clarify the application of ethical reasoning to international issues. Joel Rosenthal and Matthew Mattern of the Carnegie Council on Ethics and International Affairs have provided, through their seminars and journal, a forum for dialogue among students of international ethics. Members of the Department of Public and International Affairs at George Mason, especially Louise White and Frances Harbour, have provided a stimulating atmosphere for intellectual growth. And the many officials with whom I have worked, especially Directors of Central Intelligence William Colby, Robert Gates and William Casey, have helped me to gain first hand insights into the complexities of the policy process. The CIA's Publications Review Board provided an expeditious security review of this book. On the opposite end of the spectrum, the National Security Archive has done an outstanding job of stimulating the release of government information for policy research, and proved to be an invaluable source of data..

Finally, I want to thank my children, Jimmy, Tim and Caitlin, and especially my wife, Vicki, for her support and collaboration.

NOTE

1. On the uses and misuses of analogies in decision-making, see Ernest May and Richard Neustadt, *Thinking in Time* (New York: Free Press, 1986), especially chapters 3–5.

Ethics and Coercion:
A Framework for Evaluation

INTRODUCTION: DEFINITIONS AND METHODS

This book is about balance and moderation. In that sense, its approach is arguably antithetical to its topic: coercion in the realm of international politics. It is a truism that politics is largely about extremes. A mythical Texas politician is said to have remarked, "Ain't nothin' in the middle of the road but yellow stripes and dead armadillos!" Politicians who opt for the center find themselves boxed in by the passionate arguments of extremists. And coercion is typically seen as a weapon of extremists bent on forcing their will on others.

It is the premise of this book that there is no inherent conflict between the notion of coercive tactics in international politics and an ethic of moderation. The argument is that coercion may be justifiable under many circumstances, and even obligatory under some restrictive conditions. In order to use coercion ethically, however, policy makers must negotiate a series of difficult hurdles that will press them toward prudence and moderation, especially when the means that they contemplate involve particularly harmful or intrusive measures. These hurdles are articulated in the various ethical traditions regarding international politics, in the form of questions, criteria and norms for decision-making. The purpose of this introductory chapter is to clarify the terms and the criteria set forth by political thinkers and moral philosophers, and thus to provide a framework for analyzing the historical cases that follow.

Power and Coercion

The key organizing concept of this analysis is coercion. Philosophers and sociologists have put forward a number of definitions of this term, some broader or narrower than others. All involve some type of exploitation of a power relationship among actors. Power in this context is taken to mean the capacity to control or influence.[1] In a very broad sense, power can come from organizational relationships, either formal or informal; from expertise or reputation; from control of resources or information; or from alliances or associations.[2] In international relations, we typically think of power as deriving from resources: military, economic or political. It is not always easy to measure, however, since military or economic potential may be constrained by politics, or one element or another may not be usable in concrete circumstances.[3]

In the most general sense, coercion involves the exercise of power among the participants in a relationship.[4] According to the *Dictionary of the Social Sciences*. "Coercion signifies . . . the imposition of external regulation and control upon persons, by threat or use of force and power."[5] Coercion can be thought of as having two aspects or "prongs." There is the aspect of a proposal: A coerces B by threatening certain consequences if B does not act in a particular way. The other aspect is that of choice: B must choose how to respond to A's coercive proposal.[6] Coercion is opposed to freedom; indeed, the definition of one is necessarily related to the other. But they are not simply opposing notions. Coercion is an action, while freedom is a condition. Thus one coerces, but one is (or is not) free.[7] If freedom is generally conceived of as a desirable condition, for individuals or for nations, then it follows that coercion is in some sense bad.[8]

But in what sense? Coercion has moral impact in the sense that it creates circumstances in which a party is faced with the choice of yielding to the threat of superior power or acting contrary to practical reason. Coercion is different from simple brute force. Coerced individuals are forced to act. Individuals subjected to force are acted upon. Thus, coercion is an infringement of an actor's right to individual choice, not in the sense that choice is withdrawn but in that it is constrained and restricted.[9]

Because coercion violates freedom, it is a socially undesirable means of interaction. Therefore, most philosophers hold that it that must be justified.[10] In a domestic political setting, the justification can be said to reside in the collective responsibility of the state to maintain order. Social contract theorists suggest that this justification is implicit in the consent of the governed to the formation of the governing regime.[11] This is most obvious in the assent of citizens to the right of society to create and enforce laws that regulate criminal behavior. But this right cannot, under this reasoning, be extended to justify the coercion of law-abiding citizens, even if their behavior is not pleasing to the state.

COERCION IN INTERNATIONAL RELATIONS

The framework for justification of coercion in international relations is less clear than in the domestic setting. The basic definition and principle remain the same: coercion involves the threat of force to influence another's decision, and that threat involves an infringement on freedom. In the international context, the freedom in question is the sovereign right of a state to determine its own policies. In the broadest sense, international coercion involves influence through the use of external means: military power, economic might or legal strictures.[12] Coercion operates by affecting the factors that influence the target state's choice of strategies and policies. Thus, coercion, by whatever means employed, is opposed to the notion of sovereignty that is the central organizing principle of the nation-state system.

A very broad range of potential threats is available to states for coercive purposes: the use of military force, including weapons of mass destruction as well as conventional forces; the withholding of trade or economic aid; and political interference, overt or covert. All carry negative consequences for the threatened party, but these can vary widely in their effect, and thus presumably in their moral importance. Coercion is not limited to the threat of force, but can include situations in which force is being used to exact specific concessions, or in which greater force is held in abeyance to influence behavior. Thus coercion does not cease with the onset of war, but continues to be an element of waging warfare.

But does coercion in international politics carry the same negative moral weight as in domestic affairs or in relationships among individuals? Clearly there are major differences. Despite the growth in the number and influence of international political organizations in the past half-century, there is no international equivalent of the domestic political order with a clearly defined authority characterized by a monopoly on the legitimate use of force. And there is no universally recognized legal or moral authority that can rule on the legitimacy of coercive actions by one state against another.[13]

Given this absence of a legal or ethical consensus for evaluating coercive actions, it is not surprising that there is no consensus on their moral standing. Indeed, there is little discussion by moral philosophers or political theorists about the morality of coercion as a specific international concern. There is a significant literature, however, on the general problem of ethical standards and international affairs, as well as on the use of force by states. From this, we can deduce how various ethical traditions might approach the problem of evaluating coercive actions in the international arena.

THE ETHICAL ARGUMENTS: TWO EXTREMES

There are a number of traditions of argumentation in international ethics, of which two, realism and Kantian idealism, are particularly relevant to evaluating coercion. These traditions are traditions of dialogue and debate rather than unchanging doctrines.[14] Thus, deductions about how the general issue of coercion might be viewed is a legitimate extension of the framework, vocabulary and structure of their ethical argumentation.

Pre-Twentieth-Century Realism

The oldest of the Western traditions in international ethics is realism. It is part of that broad grouping of ethical traditions that is consequentialist or teleological, arguing that the ethical content of actions is to be evaluated by their consequences. The realist view proceeds from the assumption that the international system is anarchic and that states, like individuals, will be driven to ensure their safety and maximize their influence through whatever means are necessary, including force. The realist view was first articulated systematically by Thucydides in his history of the Peloponnesian

War, a long-standing conflict between the Greek city-states of Athens and Sparta. According to Thucydides, this conflict was inevitable because Athens sought to increase its power (as all states do, in Thucydides' view), and thus Sparta was compelled to go to war to preserve its own independence of action. For Thucydides, as for later realists, the system of states was seen as anarchic, with the result that nations had to act in their own self-interest even when this led to war, bloodshed and harm to other states or peoples. There was, in his view, no higher morality for states or statesmen.

One of the most famous passages in Thucydides' history is the "Melian Conference." The island nation of Melos was an ally of Sparta. When the Athenians decided to take the island, they first sent a delegation to negotiate. The Athenian envoys clearly articulated Thucydides' view of the international system and the imperatives facing states:

For ourselves, we shall not trouble you with specious pretenses—either of how we have a right to our empire because we overthrew the Mede or are now attacking you because of wrong that you have done us—and make a long speech which would not be believed . . . since you know as well as we do that right, as the world goes, is only in question between equals in power, while the strong do what they can and the weak suffer what they must. . . . And it is not as if we were the first to make this law, or to act upon it when made: we found it existing before us and shall leave it to exist ever after us.[15]

Thus, for Thucydides, the conflict among states was a natural and eternal aspect of human existence. And there was no question of right in this conflict; he expected that the strong would coerce the weak, and that the weak would acquiesce. Thucydides noted one important qualification to this view. Following the slaughter of the Melians, Athenian society entered a period of moral decay in which self-interest and factionalism undermined the democratic system on which Athens prided itself. What Thucydides seems to have been saying is that a state like Athens that conducts its external affairs in a manner inconsistent with its avowed internal values is at great risk.

The next significant contribution to the realist tradition was that of Niccolò Machiavelli. Machiavelli is the best-known of the so-called classical realists—so well-known that his name has become synonymous with cynical political realism. Machiavelli's most famous work, *The Prince*, is basically an instruction manual for rulers. It is perhaps the purest form of realism, for Machiavelli held that the anarchic nature of the international system absolves the ruler from any obligation to act ethically. In one of his most quoted passages, the Renaissance counselor suggested that violence should be the principal tool of statecraft: "A prince, then, must have no other object nor any other thought, nor specialize in any other art than in the institutions and discipline of war, because this is the only art that is expected of one who commands, and it is by such virtue that it maintains not only those who are born princes but often permits men from private conditaion to rise to that rank."[16]

Machiavelli's argument was practical and historical. He admired the great empires of history and was critical of monarchs who failed to recognize and respond to threats to their security. For Machiavelli, as for Thucydides, it is the anarchic nature of the international system that dictates the actions of states. Princes must be "prudent," alert to challenges from abroad and ready to attack first if necessary. He offered detailed advice, based on historical examples, on how to create and train armies, and how to maintain the support of the people for foreign adventures.

As Steven Forde has noted, in Machiavelli's view, international politics has its own laws, which have nothing to do with morality. Indeed, according to Machiavelli, moral or "ideological" goals interfere with the primary goal, the security of the state and its ruler.[17]

Nowadays the term "Machiavellian" is often used to describe a leader who is particularly manipulative and contemptible. For such a leader, coercion, if not violence, will be the principal method of control. But while Machiavelli said that the prince should be prepared to manipulate his subjects to gain their support, he did not counsel that rulers should be indiscriminately evil. Rather, he argued on historical grounds that prudent statecraft dictates that coercion, violence and deception should be used when necessary, but not necessarily continuously or even frequently.

It fell to Thomas Hobbes to provide a systematic philosophical rationale for the realist tradition. Hobbes postulated a "state of nature," in which people engaged in unbridled competition, and life was "nasty, brutish and short." (Hobbes didn't actually believe that this was a stage in human history; rather he found it a useful way to describe human nature.) What was Hobbes's solution to this situation? He thought that the only answer was for people to turn over power to a sovereign, a "Leviathan" as he called it. The coercive power of this sovereign would then keep in check those human instincts that led to conflict in the state of nature. But Hobbes did not believe that a "Leviathan" could be created at the international level. That is, although people would "contract" to form societies for their own protection, the societies themselves would exist in a perpetual state of anarchy and war. Hobbes did not necessarily mean that there would be constant warfare, but rather that states would be inclined in that direction.[18]   Under these conditions, Hobbes believed, states would be justified in using whatever means were necessary, including coercion and violence, for their own self-preservation.

But Hobbes, like Thucydides, was a paradoxical character. He seems to have believed in universal ethical principles (otherwise he'd not argue so strongly for a Leviathan to protect people), but he said that these principles are simply set aside in the nasty world of international affairs. Thus we could say that Hobbes accepted a code of ethics but believed that states are not bound by it. Indeed, if he saw any moral duty for states at all, it was the duty to be well-armed and prepared to defend (and expand) self-interest.

Twentieth-Century Realism

Realism has resurfaced over the centuries in the writings of scholars and the practices of states. In the twentieth century there have been a number of prominent realists who took the threads of the tradition and wove them into a modern fabric. Many of these wrote in reaction to what they perceived as a failure of "moralism" following the collapse of the League of Nations and Woodrow Wilson's notion of "collective security" among states. This section deals briefly with three influential modern realists: Hans Morgenthau, Reinhold Niebuhr and George Kennan.[19]

In 1948, Morgenthau published a book, *Politics Among Nations*, that became a classic textbook in international relations.[20] Several editions were published, but it was the 1954 edition that, in its opening pages, best described the basic principles of modern realism:

1. Political realism, like society in general, is governed by objective laws that have their roots in human nature.

2. The main signpost that helps political realism to find its way through the landscape of international politics is the concept of national interest defined in terms of power.

3. Realism does not endow its concept of interest defined as power with a meaning that is fixed once and for all.

4. Political realism is aware of the moral significance of political action.

5. Political realism refuses to identify the moral aspirations of a particular nation with the moral laws that govern the universe.

6. The political realist maintains the autonomy of the political sphere, as the economist, the lawyer and the moralist maintain theirs.

Morgenthau's attitude toward morality and international affairs may seem to be contradictory, but what he was saying appears to be this: objective conditions dictate that states act to increase their national power. These actions have moral consequences, but individual nations are not in a position to judge them because they are blinded by self-interest. Nevertheless, nations must act; they cannot stand aside passively from the political sphere. Nations must pursue their interests through the use of power, coercing other nations to accept their objectives and using violence when national interests so dictate. This is regrettable, even tragic, but it is inevitable.

Morgenthau's tragic worldview was made even more explicit by the Christian theologian Reinhold Niebuhr. His attitude is made clear by considering the titles of two of his books: *Moral Man and Immoral Society* and *The Children of Light and the Children of Darkness.*[21] Niebuhr called himself a "Christian realist." He based his philosophy on the writings of the fourth-century Christian Saint Augustine, as well as on his understanding of modern politics.

Niebuhr believed that humanity was inevitably flawed, and that pure reason and rationality could neither explain everything nor serve as an adequate guide to action. He argued against Marxists, utilitarians and political liberals who believed in the possibility of "scientific" approaches to politics. Niebuhr distrusted moral rhetoric from politicians, believing that moral factors meant nothing when divorced from self-interest. As a Christian, he disliked the use of force, but considered it justifiable if used precisely and quickly for realistic aims.

George Kennan was both a social thinker and a political practitioner. He is best remembered for the "Long Telegram" that he sent from his post as a political counselor in Moscow shortly after the end of World War II. (The telegram was edited into an article and appeared in the journal *Foreign Affairs*, under the pseudonym "X".) In his analysis of Soviet behavior, Kennan recommended that the United States and its allies act to contain the USSR's tendency to expand its territory and export its Marxist philosophy. This policy of "containment" became the basis of the United States' military and political strategy during the Cold War.

Kennan's view was that the challenge from the Soviet Union was primarily political and long-term. Others in the Truman administration (primarily Paul Nitze, who headed the State Department's Policy Planning Staff) saw it as military and urgent. This latter view led to a rapid buildup of military forces and an aggressive use of both overt and covert political action by the United States, policies that Kennan found uncomfortable.

In general, Kennan, like Niebuhr, was opposed to moral crusades. He often criticized what he called the "moralistic-legalistic" approach to foreign affairs. He believed that the United States in particular was prone to using moralistic language as a "cover" for actions pursued in the selfish interest. He was particularly skeptical of the use of secret intelligence services to influence events abroad clandestinely.[22]

Most of the modern realists, then, held an ambivalent view of the nature of international politics and morality. In the words of historian Joel Rosenthal:

The realist world view was dominated by a sense of the tragic. The political realists had few illusions about the possibilities of humanity; they recognized the controlling nature of selfishness and egoism, and believed that such forces were inescapable. Reacting against the Enlightenment faith in the perfectibility of man, the realist held to a quasi-religious image of man as a flawed being aspiring toward perfection but never quite reaching it.[23]

For the modern realists, nations acted in their own self-interest, but this was seen not as a blessing but as a curse.

Kantian Idealism

Realism has an uncomfortable feel, even to many realists. Thucydides, Niebuhr, Kennan, and even Morgenthau and Machiavelli, were aware that human beings have an innate sense that moral principles ought to be followed. Thus, while they argued that the international sphere is somehow different from other aspects of human intercourse, they were uneasy about this fact. Coercion is a reality of international life, but for the realists it would somehow be "better" if it could be employed sparingly, and in keeping with the domestic values of societies.

At the opposite pole from the realists is one of the other venerable traditions of international ethics, Kant's global idealism. Kant belongs to that group of ethical traditions that is deontological (from the Greek *deon*, meaning "duty"), emphasizing positive moral obligations rather than the consequences of action. For Kant, ethical obligations were based on universal principles, principles that are understood innately.

Kant's ethics were grounded in his epistemology, his theory of reality and its relationship to human knowledge. His investigation began with human experience of the world and sought to deduce general, a priori principles that govern the way in which human beings perceive this experience. Having discovered these so-called categories of knowing, Kant then turned to their application in practical circumstances and human action. It was here that he set forth his primary ethical principle, the "categorical imperative."[24] For Kant, moral principles were pure and universal, not empirical. According to him, "the basis of obligation must not be sought in the nature of man, or in the circumstances of the world in which he is placed, but a priori simply in the conceptions of pure reason."[25] Thus, in contrast to the view of the realists, Kant held the condition of international politics to be irrelevant to moral calculations; rather, he insisted that all human decisions are subject to the universal requirement of the categorical imperative, and that this imperative could be understood innately by reason.[26]

Kant had two alternative formulations of the categorical imperative. The first was always to act so that your action could become a general law of humanity. The second, which he considered equivalent to the first, was that human beings should always be considered ends in themselves, never simply means to other ends.[27] These obligations did not admit of exceptions, for Kant was a radical deontologist. He went so far as to say that actions must not merely be in accordance with the imperatives of duty, but also must be done for the sake of duty in order to have moral value.

When he attempted to translate this approach into the realm of international politics, Kant created a moral argument directly in contradiction to that of the realists. Rather than accepting coercion as a fact of international life, he argued that it must be replaced by a program of "perpetual peace." While recognizing that "practical statesmen" would be skeptical of this program, Kant nevertheless put forward a series of "articles" that he described as preliminary to a state of eternal peace between states. These included the following:

1. No treaty of peace shall be held to be such, which is made with the secret reservation of the material for a future war.

2. No state having an independent existence, whether it be small or great, may be acquired by another state through inheritance, exchange, purchase or gift.

3. Standing armies shall gradually disappear.

4. No debts shall be contracted in connection with the foreign affairs of the state.

5. No state shall interfere by force in the constitution and government of another state.

6. No state at war with another shall permit such acts of warfare as must make mutual confidence impossible in time of future peace: such as the employment of assassins, of poisoners, the violation of articles of surrender, the instigation of treason in the state against which it is making war, etc.[28]

To achieve these conditions, Kant admitted, would require a radical transformation of the international system. Thus he counseled that states should be republican in nature, with respect for the freedom and equality of all citizens; that international law should be based on a federation of free states; and that the interactions of states should proceed on the basis of cosmopolitanism and hospitality.[29]

In Kant's view, coercion could never be acceptable as the norm of states' behavior because it cannot become a universal moral law, and because it treats people as ends to the states' objectives. "The hiring of men to kill and be killed . . . cannot be reconciled with the rights of humanity as represented in our own person."[30] But there were exceptions to this prohibition on the threat of force, even for Kant. For example, he argued that while forcible interference in another state is generally to be prohibited, a state under conditions of internal insurrection is not actually a state at all, but rather is swept up in anarchy. Under this circumstance, an outside state could render assistance to a separatist party without violating the principle of noninterference.[31]

This exception aside, Kant stands in stark opposition to the realists. He refused to accept coercion as the natural state of affairs and insisted that individuals, from common people to statesmen, will recognize that only a situation of perpetual peace is acceptable, if they will only search their hearts. While it is easy to dismiss Kant's arguments as hopeless idealism, they have profoundly influenced modern liberal internationalism.[32] Many of the arguments we will encounter in subsequent cases are founded on notions of universal human values, international obligation and the sanctity of individual human life. The challenge is to marry such idealistic notions with the practical reality of international decision-making.

SEEKING A MIDDLE WAY

The search for a middle way between rampant realism and impractical idealism has continued for centuries. Philosophers from both the consequentialist and the deontological schools have attempted to ameliorate the more radical aspects of their traditions by insisting that, in some sense, both consequences and duties matter, that actors should be responsible both for the outcomes of their actions and for the obligations that they intend to pursue.

Utilitarianism

One such attempt to find a middle ground is found in that group of consequentialist thinkers in the utilitarian tradition. Utilitarianism has two basic premises: that well-being or "utility" is the only genuine good; and that the only test of an action is its consequences, measured in terms "the greatest good for the greatest number." Thus, utilitarianism seeks to avoid the realists' tendency toward selfish maximization of power, and to replace it with a more cosmopolitan vision of the common good. John Stuart Mill put it this way: "Utilitarianism, or the Greatest-happiness Principle, holds that actions are right in proportion as they tend to promote happiness, wrong as they tend to produce the reverse of happiness. . . . [P]leasure and freedom from pain are the only things desirable as ends."[33]

Does this mean that utilitarians are hedonists, recklessly seeking bodily pleasure and comfort? Certainly not, according to Mill. He argued that mental pleasures are clearly superior to bodily pleasures, and that humans have an innate capacity for noble feelings that should be nurtured. Further, he said, "the standard [of utility] is not the agent's own greatest happiness, but the greatest amount of happiness altogether."[34]

How does one know whether an action produces the "greatest good for the greatest number?" The utilitarians spend enormous energy (not to mention reams of paper) trying to come up with methods for assessing utility. One of Mill's predecessors, Jeremy Bentham, developed a "felicific calculus," which proposed seven factors that should be taken into account in judging right or wrong, including the intensity, duration and number of people subjected to pleasure or pain.[35] In short, the utilitarians sought a "scientific" basis for making ethical judgments. The modern bureaucratic approach to policy-making, with its emphasis on assessing the pros and cons of alternative policies, and on the costs and benefits of each, is a logical extension of utilitarianism, though its ethical assumptions are often not made explicit.

What about international politics in the thinking of utilitarians? Fundamentally, utilitarians are cosmopolitan; the logical extension of their Greatest-happiness Principle requires nations to act to maximize the happiness of humanity as a whole, and not merely in their selfish interest. Bentham and Mill thought, for example, that national self-determination—the right of every nation to choose its own form of government—was likely to promote the general good. Mill was skeptical of intervention by one nation in the affairs of another, on very practical grounds: interventions are expensive, their prospects are uncertain and nations often find it difficult to extricate themselves, as the United States did in Vietnam.[36]

With respect to coercion in international affairs, utilitarians would draw conclusions based on the outcome of states' actions. But this would not necessarily be a simple, case-by-case assessment. One school of thought, "act utilitarianism," would indeed focus on particular consequences of particular acts, seeking to determine if the good accruing from the action outweighed the harm done. But another influential group of thinkers, so-called "rule utilitarians," come closer to deontologists in their approach. Rather than examining only individual cases, rule utilitarians would apply the utilitarian criteria to general rules or principles of conduct.[37] Thus, they would likely review the classes of coercive actions, such as military threats or economic sanctions, and ask whether utility would be maximized by general observance of these practices. Presumably, they would seek to discourage the types of actions most likely to reduce utility for significant numbers of people.

But Mill and his contemporaries were by no means twentieth-century liberals. Like even "enlightened" thinkers of their times, they were imperialists and racists. Thus, Mill argued against intervention in "civilized" nations, but defended the right of the great powers to colonize "barbarian" nations. Modern utilitarians struggle to shake off this legacy.

Aristotle and Pursuit of the Mean

Centuries before the utilitarians attempted to find a scientific middle ground for ethical judgments, Aristotle was counseling the path of moderation. In contrast to the realists and the idealists who focused on the ethics of policy choices, Aristotle grounded his ethics in an assessment of the character and conduct of individuals. He believed that all entities had a common aim of self-realization, and that for human beings this involved the complete fulfillment of their distinguishing characteristic, the ability to reason. Thus, the goal of human life was to have a rational approach toward balancing the various feelings, desires and appetites that comprise human existence.[38]

For Aristotle, this was accomplished by seeking the "golden mean," by avoiding extremes. Human beings were, in his view, constantly buffeted by conflicting forces. "It is possible, for example, to feel fear, confidence, desire, anger, pity, and pleasure and pain generally, too much or too little; and both of these are wrong."[39] Virtue, for Aristotle, consisted in achieving a mean among these forces.

In his *Ethics*, Aristotle listed a number of "excesses" and "deficiencies" in personal conduct, as well as the mean that balanced them. For example, courage was the mean between rashness and cowardice; temperance, between licentiousness and insensibility; truthfulness, between boastfulness and understatement.[40] He also offered practical advice about how to achieve the mean: first, to avoid the more erroneous of the extremes; second, to be aware of and avoid the errors to which we as individuals are most susceptible; and third, to guard especially against the seductive attraction of pleasures.[41]

Aristotle's approach was, above all, practical. While acknowledging that there are theoretically "right" approaches to particular situations, Aristotle was also conscious that mere humans simply lack the capacity to choose the right in every complex encounter with the world. Thus, he counseled that prudence, or practical wisdom, is a skill that must be practiced. For him, prudence—in the sense of balance and wisdom rather than hesitancy or shallow cleverness—was the highest political virtue. It involved managing the day-to-day activities of the state with regard to both the good aims of the statesman and the complexities of political reality.[42] To do this, he recommended that the political leader seek to acquire, by practice as well as study, certain habits of mind and explicit techniques to enhance balance and judgment.[43] These included the following:

- Deliberateness: This is the capacity to deliberate well, connecting ends with means and balancing competing goods. The statesman who seeks practical wisdom must recognize the gravity of situations and the existence of moral dilemmas. Thus, Aristotle cautioned against rushing to action without a pause to examine the ethical considerations at stake.

- Self-control: Aristotle recognized that there is an element of self-interest in every policy decision. He counseled that personal pleasure and pain are potentially corrupting. The prudent decision maker, then, is aware of his or her ambitions and limitations. Such individuals try to avoid passionate attachments to their policy and personal preferences, and seek to recognize and overcome bias.

- Good sense: Aristotle equated this habit of character with a sympathetic understanding of the impact of one's actions on others. This comprised both a correct judgment of fairness and equity, and capacity to forgive, to put oneself in the place of the other. For the statesman, this entailed the ability to act fairly toward other states, to be magnanimous in victory as well as fair.

- Knowledge of particulars: Recognizing that prudence is practical, not theoretical, Aristotle put great stress on the need for statesmen to have an accurate understanding of the details of issues. While admitting that human beings are constrained in their ability to master all of the particulars of a situation, he argued that a prudent statesman makes a major effort to be aware of as many relevant details as possible.

- Experience: In this regard, Aristotle considered experience to be the "leavening agent" essential to developing prudence. The experienced decision maker is aware of complexity and of the unexpected consequences of political choices. Such an individual will be open to changing situations and flexible in policy decisions. Experience also gives a sense of proportion to the situations that policy makers face.

- Good ends: For Aristotle, none of these qualities merit the appellation of prudence unless they are directed to good ends. Without just intentions, a statesman can at best be clever. The clever person is "capable of carrying out the actions conducive to our proposed aim, and of achieving that aim. Then if that aim is a noble one, the cleverness is praiseworthy; but if the aim is ignoble, the cleverness is unscrupulousness."[44]

Thomas Aquinas elaborated and expanded on the Aristotelian notion of normative prudence. He added further qualities that decision makers should cultivate in order to be wise in a practical sense.[45] These include the following:

- Memory: According to Aquinas, the ability to make judgments about the future depends critically on a knowledge of the past. Thus the prudent statesman studies history and has the capacity to recollect past events honestly and fully.

- Intelligence: Aquinas put great stress on the relationship of intelligence and intuitive insight to normative prudence. He was guided in this by the concept of right reason, the ability to connect particular circumstances to the applicable moral principle.

- Teachableness: Because human reasoning is fallible, it was also important to Aquinas that statesmen cultivate the capacity to learn from others. This involves both a willingness to seek the opinions of others and an openness to criticism by them.

- Prevision and Circumspection: Through intuitive understanding and input from others, prudent statesmen acquire the ability for prevision, paying attention to the consequences of their action (or inaction). And circumspection gives them the capacity to discern how specific circumstances affect the applicability of moral principles.

- Caution: The prudent statesman, for Aquinas, was also cautious. This does not imply hesitancy, but rather an awareness of the existence of evil in the world. This requires an attentiveness to the subtle attractions of evil, as well as a skepticism regarding absolute claims to rectitude.

- Acumen: The statesman who cultivates these attributes, as well as those suggested by Aristotle, will perforce develop the quality of acumen. This is a capacity for deciding on the spot, for avoiding indecisiveness in reaching correct judgments under conditions of urgency.

Thus, the statesman can be both deliberate, giving due weight to relevant considerations, and decisive, acting before the time for action passes.

NATURAL LAW AND THE JUST-WAR TRADITION

Aristotle was no pacifist. He referred to politics and warfare as "pre-eminent in nobility and grandeur among practical activities" when directed to noble ends.[46] Political activity and warfare were to be undertaken for some common advantage of the community, in accordance with principles of justice. And the notion of political justice requires that members of the community be equal and free to act voluntarily. Thus Aristotle was realistic in his outlook toward violence and coercion, but insisted that the virtuous leader will be moderate in the use of these methods, employing them in pursuit of the common good.

Aristotle's stress on aligning human reason and correct judgment, mediated by Saint Augustine and the early fathers of the Catholic Church, developed into the natural law tradition of international ethics that was made explicit by Aquinas and other scholars, including Francisco Suárez and Francisco de Vitoria.[47] This tradition is commonly categorized as deontological because of its stress on universal moral principles, but it is also firmly in the Aristotelian tradition in its awareness of the practical consequences of moral choice.

Aquinas held that there are certain basic principles of morality and practical reason that are naturally known by human beings because they flow from their own essential human nature. He called these laws, because they entail obligation. He thus rejected the notion of legal positivism, which held that laws arise only from agreements among people, rather than having an innate and independent character. Such laws govern all of human reason, deliberation and choice, and are discoverable through study and rigorous, unrelenting logical inquiry.[48]

Aquinas, Suárez and Vitoria made great efforts to codify natural law as it applied to human affairs, including politics and international relations. This proved to be exceedingly difficult because of the complex relationships among general moral principles and concrete political circumstances. Among areas of agreement, however, was a common stress on the importance of an actor's intentions. This puts the natural law advocates squarely at odds with the consequentialist traditions, for which the only relevant moral consideration is the effect of the action.

The application of the natural law tradition to international affairs reached its apogee in its approach to assessing the moral dimensions of war. This was an attempt to apply the principles of right reason to that most damaging of human actions, violence between states. For Aristotle and his contemporaries, war was a fact of international life, though he had reservations about its legitimate employment.[49] With the establishment of Christianity in the Roman Empire, early Christian thinkers faced a serious dilemma: on the one hand, their religion was opposed to violence; on the other, there was at least an occasional need to use violent force to protect the rights of others. For Saint Augustine, writing in the late fourth and early fifth centuries as the Roman Empire was crumbling, this was an intractable problem arising from the sinful nature of humanity. His solution was an idealistic one—to wage war and love the enemy simultaneously![50]

Augustine tried to resolve this dilemma by developing the concept of a "just war." While never part of official Catholic doctrine, the notion of just war has become part of the lexicon of both churchmen and statesmen. As conceived by Augustine, wars could be divided into those that are unjust and those that are just. Unjust wars are those that arise from a desire to do harm, lust for power or riches, or imperial aspirations.[51] He was particularly critical of what he called the "vice of restless ambition" and of leaders who "account the lust of sovereignty a sufficient ground for war," because this "disturbs and consumes the human race with frightful ills."[52] For Augustine, a war was just only if it was waged to avenge injustices or to make up for a violation of rights. But even then, it was an action to be undertaken reluctantly, and with full knowledge of the horrible consequences of violence. He wrote:

The wise man will wage just wars . . . for if they were not just he would not wage them. . . . For it is the wrong-doing of the opposing party which compels the wise man to wage just wars; and this wrong-doing, even though it gave rise to no war, would still be a matter of grief to man because it is man's wrong-doing. Let every one, then, who thinks with pain on all these great evils, so horrible, so ruthless, acknowledge that this is misery.[53]

It fell to Aquinas to expand more systematically on the ways of resolving Augustine's dilemma. In doing so, he focused on both intentions and consequences. He also introduced the notion of authority, arguing that decisions on war and peace were the province of duly constituted governments only. His framework was elaborated by Vitoria and Suárez, who also focused on the need to explore peaceful alternatives, to have achievable aims and to balance force with objectives.

These scholars developed an approach that is often called "just-war theory," a set of guidelines for going to war (the so-called *jus ad bellum*) and for the conduct of hostilities (*jus in bello*).[54] (This book uses the term "just-war tradition" rather than "theory" to emphasize the evolutionary nature of the approach.) Aquinas specified three conditions for the decision to go to war: the action must be ordered by proper authority, the cause must be just and the authority must have a right intention of promoting good or avoiding evil.[55] (Traditionally, there were three conditions that were said to constitute a "just cause": responding to aggression, retaking something wrongfully taken and punishing wrongdoing. Modern commentators, however, have focused primarily on the first of these justifications.) Later authorities added three further criteria: the action must be a last resort and all peaceful alternatives must have been exhausted; there must be a reasonable probability of success; and the evil and damage that the war entails must be proportionate to the injury it is designed to avert or the injustice that occasions it.[56]

Once these conditions are met, the belligerent is subject to two further constraints in seeking his military objectives: his actions must be discriminate, that is, directed against the opponent's military forces, not against innocent people; and the means of combat must be proportionate to the just ends envisioned and must be under the control of a competent authority.[57]

The first of these constraints has been further refined, under the "principle of double effect," to encompass situations in which injury to innocent parties is unavoidable. This principle was formulated by Aquinas as follows: "There is nothing to hinder one act having two effects, of which one only is the intention of the agent, while the other is beside his intention. But moral acts receive their species from what is intended, not from what is beside the intention, as that is accidental."[58]

Under this principle, then, a belligerent may, if there is good reason, be justified in permitting incidental evil effects. The conditions governing this, however, are held by most commentators to be exceedingly strict. For example, the action taken must not be evil in itself; the good effect, and not the evil effect, must be intended; and the good effect must not arise out of the evil effect, but both must arise simultaneously from the action taken.[59]

While the just-war tradition is identified primarily with Catholic scholars, all three monotheistic traditions—Christianity, Islam and Judaism—contain elements of the framework.[60] Though there is controversy about whether the Western notion of a just war exists in Islamic ethics, some authorities see a parallel between that concept and the Islamic notion of jihad or "holy war." [61] Islam also recognizes moral constraints on military conduct, including the principle of discrimination and limiting harm to the innocent.[62] Similarly, the Jewish tradition contains notions of "permitted" wars, as well as of noncombatant immunity. The tradition also evidences great interest in the process by which nations decide to go to war.[63]

Applying Just-War Criteria

The just-war tradition, then, poses tough questions for states contemplating the use of force. But there are no easy answers, and the tradition does not try to offer any. War-related questions are concrete and specific to particular situations. The notion of legitimate authority, for example, does not specify precisely what that authority is. For an individual state, presumably its own constitutional provisions apply. But what of the state that maintains its position by internal repression? And what role, if any, do emerging international institutions play in the decision process? Today, most commentators argue that only a legitimate government may legitimately wage war, and both practical reality and moral prudence dictate that international support—usually in the form of a United Nations resolution—is at least highly desirable.[64]

Similarly, questions of just cause can be complex and the answers uncertain. One key issue is that of preventive or preemptive attack. How much evidence does a nation need to justify going to war to forestall military action by an enemy? Is force justified to rescue a state's nationals abroad, to counter terrorist groups or to retaliate for economic sanctions?[65]

And there are important questions as well about the rules governing the conduct of war. Many of these have been incorporated into positive international law, but uncertainties remain. In particular, the development of modern weapons of mass destruction—especially nuclear weapons—has raised questions about the principles of proportionality and discrimination. Are nuclear weapons, with their devastating power, inherently disproportionate to any just-war aim? And, regardless of whether nuclear weapons are used, is modern warfare so destructive that the principle of protecting noncombatants simply cannot be maintained? The first of these issues is explored in chapter 2 and the second in chapter 3.

The Legalist Paradigm

These considerations have led to a reawakening of interest in the just-war tradition and its applicability to modern international conflict.[66] In the most rigorously developed modern version of this tradition, Michael Walzer has argued that the justification for international use of force derives from a "legalist paradigm," which he describes in the following six propositions:

1. There exists an international society of independent states.

2. This international society has a law that establishes the rights of its members— above all, the rights of territorial integrity and political sovereignty.

3. Any use of force or imminent threat of force by one state against the political sovereignty or territorial integrity of another constitutes aggression and is a criminal act.

4. Aggression justifies two kinds of violent response: a war of self-defense by the victim and a war of law enforcement by the victim and any other member of international society.

5. Nothing but aggression can justify war.

6. Once the aggressor state has been militarily repulsed, it can also be punished.[67]

Recognizing that a strict application of these propositions may endanger states, prevent self-determination of peoples or permit unjust action of states toward their populations, Walzer proposed four "revisions" to the paradigm:

1. States may use military force in the face of threats of war whenever the failure to do so would seriously risk their territorial integrity or political independence.[68]

2-4. States can be invaded and wars justly begun to assist secessionist movements (once they have demonstrated their representative character), to balance the prior intervention of other powers and to rescue peoples threatened with massacre.[69]

Walzer further refined this last exception to permit "humanitarian intervention" as a response not only to massacre but also to acts "that shock the moral conscience of mankind."[70]

Walzer's paradigm has been criticized for being both too permissive and too restrictive.[71] Pierre Laberge identified those who criticize it as too permissive, as promoting an "ethics of peace," and those who see it as too restrictive, as favoring an "ethics of human rights."[72]

Those who argue that Walzer is too permissive seize on the option of humanitarian intervention and argue that it is rarely, if ever, actually humanitarian. Citing the examples of India's intervention in Bangladesh, France's incursion into the Central African Empire and Vietnam's invasion of Cambodia, Stanley Hoffman argued that the stated ends of humanitarian intervention are "likely to be too saintly to be believed," while the real ends are likely to be ambiguous.[73] Jack Donnelly noted that unilateral intervention, even when ostensibly for humanitarian purposes, is the instrument of the strong against the weak, and that the strong are more likely to be motivated by self-interest than by altruism.[74] This argument was stated even more forcefully by some pacifist commentators. They cited the "selectivity, inconsistency, even capriciousness of applying [humanitarian] grounds for intervention," and cautioned that the other five criteria of just-war theory (just intention, competent authority, last resort, probability of success and proportionality) are often neglected.[75]

Walzer would, to some extent, share these reservations. He noted that he has not found a pure case of humanitarian intervention, but only "mixed cases where the humanitarian motive is one among several."[76] Nevertheless, he would leave the door open to such interventions when they can relieve intolerable human suffering.

Other critics, however, would open the door even wider. These commentators have generally faulted Walzer for being excessively "statist" and insufficiently cosmopolitan in his viewpoint. In essence, these critics believe that Walzer's positivist approach to the law of warfare (the view that international law is based on the consent of states) leaves inadequate room for genuine humanitarian action. Gerald Doppelt, for example, criticized Walzer for requiring the citizens of a country with an oppressive government to forgo external military assistance in the name of preserving "self-determination."[77] He held that some human rights are more basic to international humanity that those that derive, in Walzer's view, from the explicit or tacit contract of government in a nation-state.[78] Charles Beitz argued that there is no reason to accept the "inevitable compromises and . . . frequent brutality" that Walzer acknowledges can exist in oppressive states. Beitz would lower the threshold for intervention in the case of significant human rights abuses, on the grounds that "It does no service to politics to defend it, no matter what its nature."[79] David Luban stated the cosmopolitan argument directly: "The entitlement to intervene derives from the cosmopolitan character of human rights; one intervenes, then, on behalf of socially basic human rights, for it is these which enable people to enjoy their political rights. Walzer's hands-off approach, on the other hand, waiting for the day when the nation unites, simply yields to guns and tanks."[80]

In response to the critics, Walzer acknowledged that, according to his paradigm, some states may be presumptively legitimate in international society, but guilty of such heinous crimes that they are illegitimate at home.[81] Moreover, he conceded that "If rights don't require us to intervene, then it is difficult to see why they should be called rights."[82] Thus, he reiterated that interventions are justified in cases of massacre or enslavement because there is then no "fit" between the government and the community of citizens.[83] Nevertheless, Walzer was fundamentally defending the Westphalian system and the rights of states. He did not assert an obligation to intervene in the event of massive rights abuses, but merely a right to waive the normal prohibition against such intervention.[84]

Walzer also investigated the *jus in bello*, the regime covering the conduct of war. He stressed the importance of coherent aims and the duty of the soldier to fight well. Critics contended that Walzer went too far in defending the state's right to use extreme measures in cases of supreme military necessity, in particular in his defense of Britain's strategic bombing campaign against Germany in World War II.[85] He was also criticized for his treatment of the principle of discrimination and noncombatant immunity. Walzer posited what he called the "war convention" to govern the conduct of military operations. The first principle of this convention was that soldiers, either implicitly or explicitly, agree to enter into military duty and thus become legitimate targets of violence.[86] The second principle asserted that noncombatants, who have not made such a choice, cannot be attacked at any time because they retain their individual right of immunity.[87] The exception, according to Walzer, is when noncombatants are subjected to violence that is ancillary to legitimate military operations, under the principle of double effect.[88] Critics contended that this stress on consent overriding immunity is confusing, especially when applied to specific military operations such as siege and blockade, or to situations in which combatant status is unclear, especially guerrilla warfare.[89]

Just-War Guidelines and International Coercion

Despite the criticism of the just-war tradition and its modern variant, the legalist paradigm, the arguments have much to recommend them. First, the structure and vocabulary of the just-war tradition are in common use, not only among scholars but also among policy makers. As noted in subsequent chapters, U.S. policy makers have used just-war concepts in explaining and justifying nuclear deterrence, conventional war, covert action and humanitarian operations. Second, the just-war framework avoids the extremes of both unbridled realism and naive idealism. It neither countenances the state's unfettered right to use force nor relegates it to an uncertain future of perpetual peace. Third, while acknowledging the validity of the utilitarian's attempt to measure consequences, just-war theory avoids simply counting up the numbers of people affected and leaving the minority to suffer.

In sum, the approaches recommended by Aristotle, Aquinas and Walzer simply make sense. It is reasonable to insist that policy makers deliberate about the use of force in a manner that is sympathetic, knowledgeable and forward-looking. And it is certainly common sense to insist that policies that harm or restrict freedom through coercion be undertaken only by legitimate authorities, for good causes, with right intentions and a reasonable probability of success, and only when other measures are unlikely to be effective. Just as reasonable are the requirements that such policies be proportionate to the aims they seek, and that they do not do unnecessary harm to the innocent. In short, it makes eminent sense to hold policy makers who contemplate harmful acts to standards of justice and practical wisdom.

FROM THEORY TO PRACTICE

Practical wisdom requires practice. Unfortunately, most readers of this book will not become senior policy makers and have the opportunity to hone the skills that Aristotle, Aquinas and other advocates of normative prudence recommended. Instead, they will have to be content with developing these attributes by studying and evaluating the actions of others, statesmen who have faced difficult moral choices and—for good or ill—decided how to resolve them.

Just-war proponents acknowledge that the field of international politics is a particularly challenging one for moral reasoning. Conclusions about policy and practice hinge not only on moral principles but also on facts and experience.[90] The cases in subsequent chapters illustrate these difficulties, and provide an opportunity for the study and reflection necessary to sharpen moral reasoning. They describe specific historical events in which leaders employed or contemplated various techniques of coercion to influence international politics. And they seek to blend the empirical facts of each situation with the moral principles that are illuminated by the just-war tradition and the criteria of normative prudence.

In reviewing these cases, we shall encounter examples of moral reasoning from all of the traditions described in this chapter—realism, idealism, utilitarianism, the just-war tradition and Aristotelian notions of prudence. We will employ one central criterion in evaluating these arguments. All of the cases deal in some way with coercion, the use or threat of force. Thus they all entail the notion of harm, either real or threatened. Harm to human beings is acknowledged by all of the traditions to be undesirable; even realists lament the fact that international anarchy and human nature lead to conflict and damage. Thus, we will require that harm be justified in each case. The burden of proof will be assumed to fall on the argument that advocates the greater harm to those states or individuals who are the targets of coercion.

The cases include the full range of coercive actions employed by states in the modern world. Chapter 2 deals with the threat of nuclear war and the moral efficacy of nuclear deterrence. It explores this issue by examining the debate on the morality of nuclear deterrence that took place in Ronald Reagan's first term between members of his administration and the American Catholic bishops. Chapter 3 examines the 1991 Persian Gulf War as an example of the contemporary use of large-scale armed force. In addition to exploring the just-war criteria as they apply to the initiation and conduct of the war, this chapter looks at President Bush's decision-making through the lens of Aristotelian normative prudence. Chapter 4 seeks to extend the inquiry and to ask not only whether coercion can be justified but also whether it may sometimes be an international obligation. It does this by looking in detail at the threat of genocide in the small African country of Burundi and examining the international community's duties from both the just war perspective and the utilitarian notion of a duty of beneficence. Chapter 5 probes the dark side of international coercion by examining the United States' covert interventions in Chile from the just-war perspective. It also looks briefly at more recent uses of covert action and develops some key considerations regarding decisions on secret intervention. Chapter 6 explores ethical criteria for economic sanctions, a frequently used method of coercion short of military force. It looks at the economic embargo placed on Castro's Cuba by the United States and its evolution over time, from the just-war tradition's criteria of authority, proportionality and discrimination. Chapter 7 draws on the work of Alexander George to examine the concept of coercive diplomacy, the combined use of threats and inducements as an alternative to the use of force.[91] The case examined is that of the United States' effort to halt the North Korean nuclear weapons program through a combination of incentives and implied threats.

Chapter 8 integrates the insights from the various cases. It concludes that while violence and coercion continue to characterize the international system, there is also evidence of growing moral sophistication in the actions of policy makers and the attitudes of citizens. The use of just-war criteria, either explicitly or implicitly, in justifying policy decisions suggests that even a tradition that dates back some 1,600 years can apply to the dilemmas of modern warfare and that it can illuminate the use of coercive instruments other than war. The conclusion is that the just-war principles—just cause, right intention, proper authority, last resort, probability of success, proportionality and discrimination—if properly understood, have a broad application to the modern era and to a range of cases in which states employ coercive measures.

The analysis also suggests that it is possible to generalize the criteria of the just-war tradition into a set of principles to guide both decision makers in their actions and citizens in their evaluation of national leaders and international policies. Thus, making these criteria explicit in the policy process is likely to strengthen both the ethical foundation and the effectiveness of policy choices. To do so, policy makers must accept the need and cultivate the quality of prudence by practicing the skills Aristotle and Aquinas recommended, particularly deliberateness, good sense, teachableness and caution. And citizens must evaluate and select their leaders based on an understanding of their moral sophistication and integrity. The qualities that leaders must seek, and the questions that citizens must ask, are exceedingly difficult and increasingly important.

NOTES

1. John M. Rothgeb, Jr., *Defining Power: Influence and Force in the Contemporary International System* (New York: St. Martin's Press, 1993), p. 21.

2. Curtis W. Cook, Phillip L. Hunsacker and Robert E. Coffee, *Management and Organizational Behavior* (Chicago: Irwin, 1997), pp. 427–33.

3. Rothgeb, *Defining Power*, p. 19.

4. Alan S. Rosenbaum, *Coercion and Autonomy* (New York: Greenwood Press, 1986), p. 3.

5. Quoted in J. Roland Pennock, "Coercion: An Overview," in *Coercion*, J. Roland Pennock and John W. Chapman, eds. (Chicago and New York: Atherton, 1972), p. 1.

6. Alan Wertheimer, *Coercion* (Princeton: Princeton University Press, 1988), p. 5.

7. Ibid., p. 6.

8. Ibid., p. 9.

9. Mark Fowler, "Coercion and Practical Reason," *Social Theory and Practice* 8, no. 3 (Fall 1982): 331.

10. Timo Airaksinen, "An Analysis of Coercion," *Journal of Peace Research* 25, no. 3 (September 1988): 213.

11. Fowler, "Coercion and Practical Reason," p. 338.

12. Donald McIntosh, "Coercion and International Politics," in Pennock and Chapman, *Coercion*, p. 244.

13. Ibid., p. 257.

14. Terry Nardin and David Mapel, eds., *Traditions of International Ethics* (Cambridge: Cambridge University Press, 1992), p. 1.

15. Thucydides, *The Peloponnesian War*, trans. John H. Finley, Jr. (New York: Modern Library, 1951), pp. 331–37.

16. Niccolò Machiavelli, *The Prince*, trans. Paul Sonnini (Atlantic Highlands, NJ: Humanities Press International, 1996), p. 81.

17. Stephen Forde, "Classical Realism," in Nardin and Mapel, *Traditions of International Ethics*, p. 66.

18. Ibid., pp. 75–77.

19. This section is derived largely from Joel H. Rosenthal *Righteous Realists* (Baton Rouge: Louisiana State University Press, 1991).

20. Hans Morgenthau, *Politics Among Nations: The Struggle for Power and Peace* (New York: Alfred A. Knopf, 1954).

21. Reinhold Niebuhr, *Moral Man and Immoral Society: A Study in Ethics and Politics* (New York: Scribner's, 1932); *The Children of Light and the Children of Darkness* (New York: Scribner's, 1944).

22. George Kennan, "Morality and Foreign Policy," *Foreign Affairs* 64 (Winter 1985/86): 214.

23. Rosenthal, *Righteous Realists*, p. 7.

24. Thomas Donaldson, "Kant's Global Rationalism," in Nardin and Mapel, *Traditions of International Ethics*, pp. 140–41.

25. Immanuel Kant, "Theory of Ethics," in *Kant: Selections*, ed. Theodore M. Greene (NewYork: Scribner's, 1957), p. 269.

26. Ibid., p. 284.

27. Ibid., p. 281.

28. Immanuel Kant, *Perpetual Peace*, ed. Lewis White Beck (New York: Liberal Arts Press, 1957), pp. 3–9.

29. Ibid., pp. 10–12.

30. Ibid., p. 5.

31. Ibid., p. 7.

32. Michael Joseph Smith, "Liberalism and International Reform," in Nardin and Mapel, *Traditions of International Ethics*, pp. 201–24.

33. John Stuart Mill, "On Utilitarianism," in *The Philosophy of John Stuart Mill*, ed. Marshall Cohen (New York: Modern Library, 1961), p. 330.

34. Ibid., p. 335.

35. Anthony Ellis, "Utilitarianism and International Ethics," in Nardin and Mapel, *Traditions of International Ethics*, p. 161.

36. Ibid., p. 166.

37. Ibid., p. 170.

38. S. E. Frost, Jr., *Basic Teachings of the Great Philosophers* (New York: Doubleday, 1962), p. 85.

39. Aristotle, *Ethics*, trans. J.A.K. Thompson (London: Penguin Books, 1953), p. 101.

40. Ibid., p. 104.

41. Ibid., p. 109.

42. Alberto R. Coll, "Normative Prudence as a Tradition of Statecraft," *Ethics and International Affairs* 5 (1991): 36.

43. Ibid., pp. 37–40.

44. Aristotle, *Ethics*, pp. 222–23

45. Coll, "Normative Prudence as a Tradition of Statecraft," pp. 40–44.

46. Aristotle, *Ethics*, p. 330.

47. Joseph Boyle, "Natural Law and International Ethics," in Nardin and Mapel, *Traditions of International Ethics*, p. 113.

48. Ibid.

49. Richard J. Regan, *Just War: Principles and Cases* (Washington, DC: Catholic University Press, 1996), p. 16.

50. Ibid., p. 17.

51. La Civiltà Cattolica, "Modern War and the Christian Conscience," in *But Was It Just? Reflections on the Morality of the Persian Gulf War*, ed. David E. Decosse (New York: Doubleday, 1992), p. 114.

52. Augustine, *The City of God*, trans. Marcus Dods (New York: Random House, 1950), p. 86.

53. Ibid., p. 683.

54. National Conference of Catholic Bishops, *The Challenge of Peace: God's Promise and Our Response* (Washington, DC: U.S. Catholic Conference, 1983), pp. 25–29.

55. Thomas Aquinas, *Summa Theologica*, trans. Joseph Rickaby, S.J. (London: Burns and Gates, 1892), Question XL, Article I.

56. National Council of Catholic Bishops, *The Challenge of Peace*, pp. 29–32.

57. Aquinas, *Summa Theologica*, Q. XLI, Art. I.

58. Ibid., Q. XLIV, Art. VII.

59. Paul Ramsey, *War and the Christian Conscience* (Durham, NC: Duke University Press, 1969), pp. 47–48.

60. Bassam Tibi, "War and Peace in Islam," in *The Ethics of War and Peace: Religious and Secular Perspectives*, ed. Terry Nardin (Princeton: Princeton University Press, 1996), p. 133.

61. Sohail H. Hashmi, "Interpreting Islamic Ethics," in Nardin, *The Ethics of War and Peace*, p. 165. Tibi takes the opposing view. See "War and Peace in Islam," p. 131.

62. Hashmi, "Interpreting Islamic Ethics," p. 163.

63. Michael Walzer, "War and Peace in the Jewish Tradition," in Nardin, *The Ethics of War and Peace*, pp. 111–12.

64. Terry Nardin, "The Comparative Ethics of War and Peace," in Nardin, *The Ethics of War and Peace*, pp. 253–58.

65. Ibid., pp. 260–62.

66. See, for example, W.L. LaCroix, *War and International Ethics: Tradition and Today* (Lanham, MD: University Press of America, 1988).

67. Michael Walzer, *Just and Unjust Wars*, 2nd ed. (New York: Basic Books, 1992), pp. 61–62.

68. Ibid., p. 85.

69. Ibid., p. 108.

70. Ibid., p. 107.

71. Stanley Hoffman, *Duties Beyond Borders* (Syracuse, NY: Syracuse University Press, 1981), p. 64.

72. Pierre Laberge, "Humanitarian Intervention: Three Ethical Positions," *Ethics and International Affairs* 9 (1995): 15.

73. Hoffman, *Duties Beyond Borders*, p. 70.

74. Jack Donnelly, "Human Rights: The Impact of International Action," *International Journal* 43, no. 2 (Spring 1988): 252.

75. Robert L. Phillips and Duane L. Cady, *Humanitarian Intervention: Just War vs Pacifism* (Boston: Rowman and Littlefield, 1996), p. 54.

76. Walzer, *Just and Unjust Wars*, p. 101.

77. Phillips and Cady, *Humanitarian Intervention*, p. 54.

78. Gerald Doppelt, "Statism Without Foundations," *Philosophy and Public Affairs* 9, no. 4 (Summer 1980): 402.

79. Charles Beitz, "Nonintervention and Communal Integrity," *Philosophy and Public Affairs* 9, no. 4 (Summer 1980): 391.

80. David Luban, "The Romance of the Nation-State," *Philosophy and Public Affairs* 9, no. 4 (Summer 1980): 397.

81. Michael Walzer, "The Moral Standing of States," *Philosophy and Public Affairs* 9, no.3 (Spring 1980): 214.

82. Ibid., p. 223.

83. Ibid., p. 217.

84. Seyom Brown, "On Deciding to Use Force in the Post Cold War Era: Ethical Considerations," paper presented at the Conference on Ethics, Security and the New World Order, National Defense University, February 11–12, 1993, p. 16.

85. Michael Joseph Smith, "Growing Up with *Just and Unjust Wars*," *Ethics and International Affairs* 11 (1997): 9.

86. Walzer, *Just and Unjust Wars*, p. 138.

87. Ibid., p. 151.

88. Ibid., pp. 151–53.

89. Theodore J. Koontz, "Noncombatant Immunity in *Just and Unjust Wars*," *Ethics and International Affairs* 11 (1997): 81.

90. Boyle, "Natural Law and International Ethics," p. 115.

91. Alexander L. George, *Forceful Persuasion: Coercive Diplomacy as an Alternative to War* (Washington, DC: United States Institute of Peace, 1991), p. 5. See also Alexander L. George and William E. Simons, eds., *The Limits of Coercive Diplomacy* (Boulder, CO: Westview Press, 1994).

2

The Ethics of Nuclear Deterrence:
The Reagan Administration Versus
the American Catholic Bishops

THE NUCLEAR DEBATE

When Ronald Reagan came to office in January 1981, he was determined to reverse what he saw as a precipitous decline in American strategic nuclear security. Prodded by conservative groups such as the Committee on the Present Danger, and aided by young activists from the Madison Group, Reagan set out to expand and modernize United States nuclear forces to meet a perceived Soviet threat to the stability of nuclear deterrence.

Reagan was aware that he would have to move carefully. He knew that the enormous increase in nuclear weapons over the past two decades had awakened antinuclear political movements, primarily in Europe but increasingly in the United States. But he was secure in the belief that his own leadership, coupled with support from anticommunist forces, including those in the conservative Christian churches, would provide the momentum needed to reverse Soviet gains.

But Reagan did not count on opposition from another religious quarter. Early in his presidency, he faced an unprecedented onslaught from the hierarchy of the Roman Catholic Church of the United States—the largest single religious group in the country, and one with enormous influence on a key constituency that had helped to elect Reagan in 1980. And the American Catholic bishops confronted Reagan with a potentially devastating argument. They claimed not only that some of his specific policy proposals were flawed, but also that the theory of nuclear deterrence that had guided the United States since the first nuclear test was at best morally questionable.

This chapter reviews the moral arguments that were made by both the Catholic bishops and the Reagan administration during the debates of 1982 and 1983. The debates provide an unusually detailed picture of how politicians and religious leaders framed nuclear issues, and thus illuminate the complexity of ethical argumentation on perhaps the most profound moral question of the modern era—how to avert nuclear destruction of the entire planet.

THE STRATEGIC IMBALANCE

To Ronald Reagan and his nuclear strategists, there was no doubt in the early 1980s that the United States was in serious danger. A Soviet military buildup, dating from the early 1960s, had reversed U.S. strategic superiority and heightened fear that the USSR could convert that superiority into political, or even military, gains.

The figures spoke for themselves.[1] U.S. military expenditures had declined significantly since the withdrawal from Vietnam, while the Soviet defense budget was estimated to have increased by 3–4 percent each year since the 1970s. While the bulk of these expenditures went for the large conventional forces that opposed NATO and China, it was estimated that the USSR outspent the United States on strategic nuclear forces by a factor of about 3 to 1.

Trends in the forces themselves paralleled the spending patterns. By the early 1980s, the United States had reduced the number of weapons in its nuclear arsenal by over 25 percent from the peak of the mid-1960s, while the USSR had greatly expanded its holdings. By the time that Reagan assumed office, the Soviet Union had some 6,000 reentry vehicles (warheads) on its intercontinental ballistic missiles (ICBMs), compared with about 2,000 for the United States. The Soviets also had 950 nuclear missiles on 62 submarines, compared with 656 missiles on 41 vessels in the U.S. fleet. The United States had deployed no new strategic bomber aircraft since the early 1960s, while the USSR had produced well over 200 Backfire bombers, and was preparing to introduce another model nicknamed the Blackjack.[2] The net result of these trends was that, to Reagan administration officials, the strategic situation was dangerously unbalanced. They feared that the Soviets could exploit an emerging "window of vulnerability" in U.S. forces, and undermine nuclear deterrence.

THE THEORY OF DETERRENCE

Why, since both the United States and the Soviet Union possessed enough nuclear firepower to destroy civilization, were Reagan and his colleagues so concerned about the numbers? The answer is that they, and virtually all defense analysts during the Cold War, were thoroughly indoctrinated in theories of nuclear deterrence in which the numbers and capabilities of weapons were intimately connected to both political and military stability in the world.

The theory had been developed in the 1950s by a group of "defense intellectuals" who came to be known as the "Wizards of Armageddon."[3] These thinkers, including Bernard Brodie, Herman Kahn, John von Neumann, and Thomas Schelling, drew on concepts from economics and advanced mathematics to develop ways of "thinking about the unthinkable" uses of nuclear weapons.

The theory of deterrence went roughly like this: Assume that there are two "sides," each possessing nuclear weapons. If one side can absorb a nuclear strike from the other, and still have enough weapons left to retaliate in a way that will cause unacceptable damage to the opponent, then the first side will effectively be "deterred" from initiating nuclear war. This deceptively simple proposition, however, raised a host of complex questions. What would a potential nuclear aggressor consider "unacceptable" damage from a retaliatory strike? Would the side that suffered the attack have the political will to retaliate? Would it be able to communicate with its forces and order the counterstrike? Would the military commanders comply with an order to unleash nuclear conflict? What would happen if there were a nuclear accident or an unauthorized attack? In the fog of war, would the sides then behave in the abstractly rational manner that the theory of deterrence required?

There were two aspects of this theory that were particularly relevant to the ethical debates of the early 1980s. The first was the notion of "stable deterrence." This concept meant that deterrence was effective when both sides knew that they could not achieve their aims by initiating nuclear war—that the costs to themselves would be unacceptable. This meant that it was in the interest of both parties to maintain a rough "balance of terror" in which neither was capable of conducting a disarming first strike that would render the opponent's nuclear arsenal incapable of retaliation. This called for restraint in the development and deployment of nuclear arms, so that neither side gained a strategic advantage. To the Reagan administration in the early 1980s, the USSR had massively violated the principle of restraint, and was on the verge of upsetting the balance. Not only had the USSR continued to increase its forces, but it had developed new missiles with multiple independently targetable reentry vehicles (MIRVs), great destructive power and high accuracy, posing a potential threat to the United States' land-based missile force—the backbone of the U.S. deterrent.

This concept of stability included both offensive nuclear forces and defenses against them. Deterrence strategists held that stability could be undermined not only if a side acquired the ability to destroy the opponent's retaliatory forces, but also if it had a defensive shield that could limit or even prevent damage to itself. Thus, particular restraint in the development of strategic defenses, especially antiballistic missile (ABM) defense, was an inherent part of the theory. This concept would be sorely tested by the Reagan administration's military initiatives and the ensuing moral debate. And in the early 1980s, there were fears that the USSR was working on programs that could ultimately lead to a nationwide defense against nuclear-tipped ballistic missiles, to the great consternation of Reagan administration nuclear planners.

The second noteworthy aspect of the theory of deterrence was its moral neutrality. The theory was typically described in morally neutral terms such as "sides" and "moves" in a surreal game. In the early 1980s, both administration officials and religious leaders objected to this image of moral neutrality, but for very different reasons. Reagan and his colleagues thought it wrong to exclude the character of the Soviet Union, the "evil empire," from discussions of nuclear policy, while skeptics, including many from religious groups, were more concerned about the moral content of U.S. policy. This concern was heightened by rhetoric emanating from the administration about programs to make nuclear war "winnable," a concept that was anathema to deterrence theorists and church officials alike.[4]

Thus, trends in nuclear forces awakened great attention and concern in the early 1980s. Looking at the numbers and capabilities of Soviet weapons, administration planners envisioned a world in which the USSR would use its preponderance of force to exact political concessions from fearful U.S. allies, and even from the United States itself. And critics of the administration feared that the United States was embarking on a new phase in the nuclear arms race, with the potential to usher in a period of profound instability and greatly to increase the risk of war.

CONTROLLING NUCLEAR ARMS

The administration was aware that the theory of deterrence had been tested severely in 1962, when the USSR attempted to place nuclear-armed ballistic missiles in Cuba.[5] Although Soviet Premier Khrushchev asserted that the objective was to protect Cuba against a U.S. attack, the Kennedy administration believed that the Soviets were seeking a capability to launch nuclear strikes against the United States, and reacted by initiating a naval blockade of Cuba.[6] Although the Soviets withdrew the missiles, many thought that the world had been brought to the brink of nuclear war.

The Cuban missile crisis had two very different results. The first was a determination by the USSR to build up its nuclear forces on Soviet territory to match, and if possible to exceed, U.S. capabilities. The second was to increase political pressure to control nuclear arms. Efforts at nuclear arms control had been dormant since the failure of the Baruch plan to internationalize control of atomic weapons during the Truman administration. Under Kennedy, these efforts accelerated, and led during the Kennedy, Johnson and Nixon administrations to treaties that limited nuclear testing in the atmosphere, and prohibited deployment of nuclear weapons in outer space and on the seabed.[7]

The crowning achievement of the Nixon administration in arms control was the successful conclusion of the Strategic Arms Limitation Talks (SALT) in 1972. The negotiations led to two treaties between the United States and the Soviet Union: the Interim Agreement on Strategic Offensive Arms and the ABM Treaty.[8] The first required the parties, among other provisions, to forgo construction of new fixed ICBM launchers and to limit the number of submarine-launched ballistic missile (SLBM) launchers to the number operational or under construction when the agreement was signed. It imposed no limits on intercontinental bombers. The second treaty limited each side to two ABM deployment areas (reduced to one in subsequent negotiations), prohibited nationwide strategic defenses and—in a provision that would become highly controversial in the Reagan years—ruled out development, testing or deployment of space-based defenses.

The SALT precedent had shown that even a conservative Republican president could not sidestep political pressure to control nuclear arms. Indeed, it had become essential for presidents to justify any proposed initiative to upgrade or expand nuclear arsenals in terms of the putative effect on arms control. When Democrat Jimmy Carter tried to pursue this dual-track strategy, however, he ran into serious difficulties.

Faced with unequivocal evidence of a Soviet strategic buildup, Carter undertook a modernization of U.S. forces, including the Stealth bomber, but his efforts to enhance land-based ICBM forces fell victim to political circumstances. In attempting to reduce the vulnerability of these forces, Carter investigated mobile launch systems. While not specifically prohibited by the SALT Interim Agreement, mobile ICBMs raised serious questions in the arms control environment, and the United States had issued a unilateral statement opposing them. (Mobile ICBMs can be difficult to locate from satellites, which makes them less vulnerable to attack, and more difficult to count; thus they complicate the verification of limits on nuclear delivery systems.) When his mobile ICBM proposals aroused opposition from arms control advocates in his own party, Carter came up with a new scheme, deploying ICBMs close together in "dense packs." Nuclear strategists thought that this would decrease vulnerability because incoming nuclear weapons would have to be aimed so close together that they would destroy each other in flight, a phenomenon known as "fratricide." While appealing to the specialists, this concept made no sense to politicians and ordinary citizens, and thus Carter's modernization plans continued to be frustrated.

Carter fared little better in his arms control efforts. Early in his tenure, he decided to propose deep reductions in strategic arms to the USSR. His idea was rejected out of hand by the Soviets, who considered it an attempt to overturn the agreement that had been reached with President Ford in Vladivostok. When Carter was finally able to negotiate a SALT II agreement, he was unable to persuade the Senate to give its advice and consent to ratification because of deteriorating political conditions in the wake of the Soviet invasion of Afghanistan.[9] In addition, opponents of SALT II argued that it codified Soviet strategic superiority. During the 1980 campaign, candidate Reagan called SALT II "fatally flawed."

THE REAGAN ADMINISTRATION AND ARMS CONTROL

Like his predecessors, Reagan pursued both strategic modernization and arms control simultaneously, but his administration gave the appearance of being more committed to the former. Key members of the Reagan defense team were highly skeptical of Soviet intentions and accused the USSR not only of exploiting previous arms control agreements but also of violating some of their provisions.[10] Assistant Secretary of Defense Richard Perle, a major figure in arms control policy, referred to the "unrelenting buildup of Soviet nuclear forces" and to the "enlarging pattern of Soviet violations of the most important arms control agreements."[11] Secretary of State George Shultz argued that in relations with the USSR and in arms control negotiations, "diplomacy alone will not succeed." Modernization of strategic forces was required, in his view, not only to enhance security but also because "No arms control negotiation can succeed in conditions of inequality."[12]

The result of this attitude was that the administration moved deliberately on arms control policy. The president resisted growing pressures for a freeze in deployment of nuclear weapons. In February 1981 he asserted:

A freeze would reward the Soviet Union for its enormous and unparalleled military buildup. It would prevent the essential and long overdue modernization of United States and allied defenses and would leave our aging forces increasingly vulnerable. And an honest freeze would require extensive prior negotiations on the systems and numbers to be limited and on the measures to ensure effective verification and compliance. And the kind of a freeze that has been suggested would be virtually impossible to verify. Such a major effort would divert us completely from our current negotiations on achieving substantial reductions.[13]

Reagan also rejected the notion, advanced by former policy officials including Kennedy's secretary of defense, Robert McNamara, that the United States should reject the first use of nuclear weapons as a key element of its military strategy.[14] Administration planners argued that a "no first use" pledge would reduce the credibility of the Western deterrent and give greater political weight to the USSR's preponderance of conventional military forces in Europe.

ENTER THE BISHOPS

While the Reagan administration approached issues of nuclear policy from strategic and political perspectives, the American Catholic bishops argued from the perspectives of theology and ethics. When they issued their pastoral letter, *The Challenge of Peace: God's Promise and Our Response,* the bishops were continuing a dialogue about war and peace that stretched back to the time of Saint Augustine.[15] Moreover, their preoccupation with nuclear policy was not new; Catholic commentators had pondered the enormity of the issue since the dawn of the atomic age.[16]

The initiative to promulgate a pastoral letter came from Auxiliary Bishop P. Francis Murphy of Baltimore, a member of Pax Christi, an international Catholic peace organization.[17] In August 1980, he proposed that the bishops undertake to summarize for Catholics the teachings of the church on war and peace, and to develop educational efforts on the issue. When the National Council of Catholic Bishops met in November of that year, Reagan had been elected following a vigorous campaign against his predecessor's arms control efforts. Growing concern about nuclear issues galvanized opinion among the bishops, and the conference agreed to the preparation of a study that would be debated at its meeting in November 1982.

Conference president Archbishop John Roche of Saint Paul-Minneapolis appointed a leading moderate and former president, Archbishop Joseph Bernardin of Cincinnati, to lead the effort. Bernardin selected a varied group to develop the study, including Auxiliary Bishop Thomas Gumbleton, president of Pax Christi, and Auxiliary Bishop John O'Connor, a member of the "military ordinariate" that supervised Catholic chaplains in the armed forces. The committee chose Father J. Bryan Hehir, associate secretary of the U.S. Catholic Conference and a noted authority on ethics and international affairs, for the staff, as well as his assistant, a retired Foreign Service officer named Edward Doherty. They asked Yale University political scientist Bruce Russett to take on the task of preparing an integrated draft of the study.

The committee decided to include a discussion of the Catholic scriptural teachings on war and peace, to carry out an ethical analysis in the just-war framework and to consult widely with experts on nuclear strategy and arms control. These included former defense secretaries James Schlesinger and Harold Brown, and SALT negotiator Gerard Smith. Schlesinger and Brown particularly impressed the committee. They asserted that nuclear war had to be avoided at all costs, and encouraged the Catholic bishops to take a stand. At one point in the meeting with Brown, O'Connor asked if nuclear strategy was not just "rationalizing insanity," to which Brown replied in the affirmative.[18]

Early in its work, the committee began meetings with officials of the Reagan administration. The first session with State Department officials went badly, with the diplomats chiding the bishops for their idealism. Subsequent meetings with Defense Secretary Caspar Weinberger and Arms Control and Disarmament Agency director Eugene Rostow went more smoothly, but the information they supplied was disturbing to the committee. Weinberger confirmed that in his view, there could be no such thing as a limited nuclear war, a point made by other specialists as well. Of more concern was his assertion that there could be no substantial negotiations on limiting strategic arms until the United States restored parity with the USSR, a process that he estimated would take eight years!

The committee prepared a first draft for discussion at the November 1981 conference meeting. The draft called deterrence a "sinful situation" but noted that the use of nuclear weapons would be an even greater evil. It proposed a number of arms control measures, including rejection of first use of nuclear weapons and a freeze on the testing, production and deployment of new strategic systems. Administration officials, including the president, reacted sharply, accusing the bishops of ignoring Reagan's initiatives to reduce nuclear arms, especially the proposed Strategic Arms Reduction Talks (START), the successor to the SALT process. Deputy Secretary of State Lawrence Eagleberger wrote to Bernardin to argue that a freeze would lock in Soviet advantages in critical areas. The administration also cited statements by the pope on the morality of deterrence that were less critical than the bishops'.

Over the next year, the committee refined its draft. The administration followed the process warily, cognizant of the criticisms that were likely to emerge from the debate at the bishops' November 1982 conference meeting. As the time for debate neared, administration officials decided to engage the issues publicly, in the form of a letter from William Clark, Reagan's national security adviser, to Bernardin. Although intended for distribution to the bishops, the letter was leaked by administration officials and published in the *New York Times*.

Clark's arguments included the following:

- U.S. policy is not to use any force, nuclear or nonnuclear, except to deter and defend against aggression.

- The bishops' letter ignored both the facts and the impact of the Soviet military buildup, which in the administration's view goes beyond defensive needs.

- Despite the administration's earlier suggestions to the bishops, the letter does not give adequate weight to recent U.S. arms control initiatives, including the START proposal, the offer to eliminate all Intermediate-range Nuclear Force (INF) missiles, the talks on Mutual and Balanced Force Reductions in Europe and proposals to limit biological weapons.

- The U.S. strategy of deterrence is not an end in itself, but a means to prevent war and preserve American values, including freedom of conscience and respect for life.

- Pope John Paul II had said that deterrence could be considered morally acceptable as a step on the way to progressive disarmament.[19]

While the administration disagreed with the bishops' stance, many others did not.
A Gallup Poll just after the November 1982 conference found 82 percent of Catholics
favoring a bilateral freeze. In addition, 24 prominent former government officials,
including former Director of Central Intelligence William Colby and SALT negotiator
Gerard Smith, supported the bishops' letter. Bolstered by these developments, the
bishops endorsed the basic thrust of the report, and ordered further consultation and
revision.

OTHER CRITICS

But there were others who criticized both the process and the findings of the
American bishops' study, and many were within their own church. Notable among the
critics were the Catholic hierarchies in some European countries, who objected to the
draft letter's language on deterrence. The French bishops, for example, defended
France's possession of nuclear arms, and argued that there is a moral difference
between the deterrent threat to use nuclear weapons and their actual use.[20] The
German bishops couched their analysis in Augustinian terms, emphasizing the
continuing presence of evil in the world. It fell to governments, they argued, to protect
innocent people from this evil—by persuasion if possible, but by force if necessary.[21]
Indeed, in 1982 it appeared to one scholar that a "collegial consensus" on nuclear
issues among Catholic authorities seemed highly unlikely, with the English and
Scottish bishops moving toward a definitive rejection of nuclear war, whereas the
bishops of continental Europe were more supportive of the current Western military
strategy that emphasized a "flexible response" to Soviet aggression, including possible
use of nuclear weapons.[22]

In presenting these more flexible views on deterrence, the European bishops were
reflecting in part the concerns of their congregations and their governments.
Europeans of all political beliefs were aware that if a nuclear war were to be fought
it would likely begin in Europe. They wanted to deter such a war at all costs.
Moreover, they were concerned that if nuclear deterrence were to be abandoned, the
cost of providing a conventional military deterrent would fall primarily to European
countries, requiring a massive reallocation of resources.

Some critics, both within the Catholic Church and elsewhere, tried to portray the
American bishops' view of deterrence as at odds with that of Pope John Paul II, as
Clark had attempted to do. The pope's view had been put forward most clearly in an
address to the United Nations Special Session on Disarmament on June 11, 1982.
The statement, read by the Vatican representative, Cardinal Casaroli, said: "In current
conditions, 'deterrence' based on balance, certainly not as an end in itself, but as a
stage on the way towards a progressive disarmament, can still be judged morally
acceptable. Nonetheless, in order to preserve peace, it is indispensable not to be
satisfied with this minimum, which is always susceptible to the real danger of
explosion."[23]

In January 1983, the committee traveled to Rome, where they reviewed Vatican
reactions to the draft of the pastoral letter. The meetings included a private session
between Bernardin, recently elevated to the rank of cardinal, and the pope. There was

discussion of the European and American perspectives, particularly on the "no first use" issue, and the pastoral's language was altered to reflect this. Bernardin was satisfied, however, that there was no papal objection to the letter's conclusions about deterrence policy. Though the American bishops went further in their recommendations, they were not out of step with the Church's ultimate teaching authority.

Work on revising the draft letter proceeded. A significant change was that the language was altered to substitute a proposed "curb" on new nuclear programs for the "halt" that had appeared in the second draft. While the committee held that either formulation was consistent with a nuclear freeze, there was concern that the bishops would be seen as giving in to the administration.

REAGAN'S WILD CARD

While the bishops were preparing for the final debate, Reagan dramatically shifted the terms of discussion. On March 23, 1983, he proposed a massive, space-based system of strategic defenses as a step to making nuclear weapons obsolete. The proposal apparently developed out of discussions with former military officers and nuclear scientists, notably Edward Teller. Key Reagan advisers, including Secretary of State Shultz, had been kept in the dark.[24] Critics immediately decried the proposal as a violation of the ABM treaty as well as a technical and strategic impossibility. Disputes broke out within the administration about how to explain and implement the president's plan. Among his close confidantes, however, there was a general understanding that the president was serious in his desire for a nonnuclear world. As Shultz put it, "President Reagan was consistently committed to his personal vision of a world without nuclear weapons. His advisors were determined to turn him away from that course."[25]

For the next several years, a battle royal raged within the administration, between the administration and outside critics, and between U.S. and Soviet officials, about the Strategic Defense Initiative (SDI). Opponents called it "Star Wars" and, much to Reagan's displeasure, the name stuck. Critics of the proposal—including the Soviets—claimed that it would undermine deterrence by giving the United States the ability to "ride out" a Soviet nuclear strike and then destroy the USSR in retaliation. Reagan responded by offering to share the benefits of SDI with the Soviet Union and other countries, but the skeptics were unconvinced.

When the bishops met at Chicago in May 1983 for a final discussion of the pastoral letter, polls continued to show support for a nuclear freeze among both Catholics and the general population. Reflecting this, the "peace forces" in the hierarchy proposed restoration of the "halt" language, as well as the second draft's stronger language on "no first use." These proposals were but a tiny part of the more than 500 amendments proposed, most of which called for strengthening the draft. Proposals to weaken the language, primarily from conservative Bishop O'Connor, were handily defeated, and the "halt" formulation was reinstated by an overwhelming margin. In the end, the Chicago meeting significantly strengthened the document. On the critical issue of deterrence, the final document quoted John Paul's 1982 statement but went on to make its own arguments about the conditions under which deterrence could be justified as a transitional strategy.

THE BISHOPS' CONCLUSIONS

When the process was complete, the bishops spoke clearly and forcefully. Consistent with the just-war tradition, their final report emphasized the sanctity of human life and the moral responsibility to preserve it. In assessing nuclear policy, they employed the criteria of just cause, just intention, proper authority, last resort, probability of success, proportionality and discrimination.

How did Western nuclear policy and deterrence measure up to these criteria? In summary, the bishops concluded that any actual use of nuclear weapons would be uncontrollable, disproportionate and indiscriminate, and that there was no realistic prospect of victory in a nuclear war. Thus they were extremely doubtful that resort to even a limited nuclear war could be justified; highly skeptical that nuclear war could be fought under the conditions laid down by the just-war tradition; and concerned about the moral implications of nuclear deterrence.

Resort to War

The American Catholic bishops were adamant that any use of nuclear weapons is immoral. In one of the most widely quoted passages of their pastoral letter they asserted, "We do not perceive any situation in which the deliberate initiation of nuclear war, on however restricted a scale, can be morally justified."[26] They drew this conclusion because, in their view, nuclear war violates key provisions of the *jus ad bellum*, the criteria for deciding to go to war. The bishops doubted, for example, that in nuclear war there can be reasonable hope of success in bringing about justice and peace. Having studied the literature on control of nuclear warfare and heard testimony from military and civilian officials involved in nuclear strategy, the bishops proclaimed themselves highly skeptical that nuclear war can be limited or that national authorities can maintain effective control of their forces. They also expressed concern that the number of casualties, even in a "limited" war, would be disproportionately high, and that the long-term effects of nuclear war would be serious and unpredictable.[27]

Conduct of War

The American Catholic bishops were even more skeptical that nuclear war could be conducted under the prescribed rules of discrimination and proportionality. Their pastoral letter concluded that nuclear warfare directed against cities would result in the indiscriminate destruction of vast areas and their populations. They were not reassured by assertions that it is not U.S. policy to target civilian populations per se. Such statements, they noted, "Do not resolve . . . another very troublesome moral problem, namely that an attack on military targets or militarily significant industrial targets could involve 'indirect' (i.e., unintended) but massive civilian casualties."[28] Such casualties, according to the bishops, could not be considered consistent with the requirement of proportionality, whether or not they were intended.

The Morality of Deterrence

Having condemned nuclear war, the bishops turned their attention to the policy of deterrence. This is a serious moral dilemma because, in their ethical tradition, an intention to commit an evil act is held to be morally indistinguishable from the act itself. Nuclear deterrence requires the intention to carry out, under certain conditions, an attack that is at best morally questionable. Moreover, one side must act and communicate in such a way that the other believes that such an attack will occur. Do not such actions and signals, in themselves, constitute morally questionable behavior?

The final version of the pastoral letter accepted the necessity of deterrence, but added strict conditions:

- Deterrence is justifiable only in conjunction with resolute determination to pursue arms control and disarmament.

- Deterrence must be based on a balance of forces, and efforts to achieve superiority are to be condemned.

- No use of nuclear weapons which would violate the principles of discrimination or proportionality may be intended in a strategy of deterrence.[29]

The American bishops also expressed concern for the stability of deterrence. They opposed weapon systems that may create the impression in an opponent's mind that a disarming first strike is being planned. They defined such weapons as those that not only have a capacity for "prompt hard target kill" but also are vulnerable to attack themselves, and thus are unsuitable for retaliatory use. They noted that some considered the Reagan administration's proposed MX ICBM and the Pershing II intermediate-range ballistic missile (IRBM) to be in this category, though they did not, as some administration supporters alleged, condemn these weapons outright.[30]

The American bishops asserted that proposed weapon systems, as well as proposed changes in doctrine, must contribute to progressive disarmament. They acknowledged that highly accurate weapons might minimize civilian casualties, but argued that any program to develop such weapons must be accompanied by efforts to minimize risk of escalation. They considered counterforce targeting (aiming nuclear weapons at the opponent's nuclear weapons) to be preferable to counterpopulation targeting, but not if it threatens the stability of deterrence or if it is joined with a strategy that seeks to plan for protracted nuclear war or to "prevail" in nuclear conflict.[31]

Ultimately, the bishops proposed that nuclear strategy be replaced by a policy of mutual deterrence based on a conventional force balance. They acknowledged that the costs of such efforts would be high, especially in western Europe—a point clearly made by the European hierarchy in commenting on the pastoral letter. Nevertheless, the American bishops were so concerned about the potentially devastating consequences of nuclear war that they considered it morally preferable to pay the large economic and social costs that such a change in strategy would entail.[32]

In line with this conclusion—that nuclear deterrence must gradually be replaced by a conventional balance and ultimately by disarmament—the bishops set forth a number of specific proposals. Their recommendations were far more comprehensive than those of any previous group of churchmen. They included the following:

• An immediate, bilateral, verifiable agreement to halt the testing, production and deployment of new nuclear weapon systems

• Deep reductions in existing nuclear arsenals

• Negotiation of a comprehensive treaty to ban tests of nuclear weapons

• Removal of short-range nuclear weapons, and nuclear stockpiles, from areas in which they could be overrun

• Strengthening of command and control over nuclear forces to prevent inadvertent or unauthorized use

• Ratification by the United States of the Threshold Test Ban Treaty

• Measures to decrease the threat of any war, and East–West meetings at all levels, including regular, carefully prepared summits.[33]

The tone of the bishops' letter was somber and moderate. Its content, however, left no doubt that they were skeptical of the Reagan administration's intentions. They feared the president's anticommunist rhetoric, and doubted that he was serious about implementing the arms control initiatives that they considered essential to a conditioned acceptance of deterrence.

ARMS CONTROL TAKES CENTER STAGE

These concerns turned out to be exaggerated. One concrete result of Reagan's "Star Wars" speech was to prod the Soviets into comprehensive nuclear negotiations. They walked out of the INF negotiations in November 1983 to protest U.S. deployment of new intermediate-range missiles in Europe. When Gorbachev became general secretary of the Soviet Communist Party, however, he quickly resumed talks on a wide range of nuclear issues. The new negotiations included reductions in strategic offensive arms within a new framework that Reagan, in a symbolic gesture to disarmament advocates, had renamed the Strategic Arms Reduction Talks (START).

In December 1987, Reagan and Gorbachev signed a treaty that called for elimination of INF missiles, and later a START treaty that required reductions in strategic nuclear forces. A START II treaty was signed under President George Bush, further reducing strategic forces to 3,500 on each side. Many observers credit Reagan's SDI for these results. They argue that the Soviets were so concerned about the possibility that U.S. technology could provide effective defenses that they preferred deep cuts in their own forces to a defensive arms race.[34]

Since the signing of the second START agreement, further progress has been made on the bishops' nuclear agenda. A comprehensive ban on nuclear testing has been negotiated. Although the Russian Duma (parliament) has yet to ratify the START II treaty, work has begun on even deeper reductions. There is serious discussion among current and former officials, including the former head of U.S. strategic forces and the former commander of NATO's European forces, about reductions to a few hundred weapons and the eventual elimination of nuclear forces worldwide.[35] In a very real sense, the bishops' agenda for nuclear arms reductions has been implemented by the political leaders of whom they were so skeptical.

When the American bishops wrote their 1983 letter, nuclear issues dominated the debate on international ethics. Subsequent progress in arms control, which many attribute to Reagan's vision of a nuclear-free world, has resulted in a sharp decline in such discussion. While other dangers continue, the risk of nuclear holocaust seems more remote than it did in the early Reagan years. Who, then, prevailed in the 1983 debate? Did the bishops turn the tide with their just-war arguments? Or did Reagan successfully capture the moral high ground with his consequentialist arguments about using a military buildup to effect arms control agreements, and thus emerge the victor? To explore this further, we now examine some of the moral arguments that emerged after publication of the bishops' letter.

NUCLEAR ETHICS

In venturing into the field of nuclear ethics, the American Catholic bishops were entering a conceptual minefield. Commentary that followed the letter's publication—from philosophers as well as politicians—illustrated the complexity of the issues. The bishops were attacked as unrealistic and inconsistent. The debate involved what one commentator called a clash between a "rhetoric of morality" and a "rhetoric of manipulation."[36]

Assessing the Debate

The bishops employed the logical methods and rhetoric of Aquinas and others in the Scholastic tradition. They assumed the priority of moral principles over other types of argumentation. They then described these moral principles, identified the ethical issues at stake, enumerated factual considerations bearing on the issues and deduced the implications.

Members of the Reagan administration, their surrogates and conservative scholars attacked the bishops as unrealistic and dangerous. But they did not directly argue with the bishops' reasoning. Instead, they shifted the ground to focus on matters more under their control.[37] They asserted that the administration had no choice but to confront the ethical dilemma of deterrence directly, as a fact of international politics, and thus was required both to maintain a strong deterrent and to pursue arms control negotiations. They sidestepped the bishops' charge that the current posture of deterrence was morally suspect, and complained that the pastoral letter ignored the administration's arms control initiatives. Using a realist argument, Weinberger asserted that the burden of proof was on the bishops, because history has shown that nuclear deterrence has kept the peace.[38] Weinberger and other spokesmen also sought to associate the bishops (inaccurately) with those who advocated unilateral nuclear disarmament.[39]

Other conservative commentators attacked the bishops' methodology and premises more directly. They took a consequentialist approach and argued that the real issues were not the specifics of nuclear strategy, but rather "how power and the restrained use of force may be related to the achievement of a tranquil and well-ordered international political community."[40] This classic realist argument proceeds from the assumption that international politics is an autonomous sphere, that the international system is anarchic and that the challenge for states is to find ways to exercise power to advance their interests in an orderly manner.[41] In this view, international stability in the nuclear era requires a continuing reliance on deterrence; moreover, precipitate reductions of nuclear arsenals could actually cause instability, because—in the realists' view—unscrupulous nuclear powers could cheat on arms control agreements and achieve the ability to wage nuclear war. The problem, then, is not the existence of nuclear capabilities but the pervasive fact of international aggression. One realist commentator put it this way: "Aggressors, not weapons, cause war, and aggressors are wont to initiate offense . . . when they perceive that the costs of war are substantially outweighed by their gains."[42]

A more subtle argument was that the bishops' letter was inconsistent, particularly in its treatment of deterrence. This criticism rested on the juxtaposition of four aspects of the pastoral:

- That the bishops were highly skeptical that any use of nuclear weapons could be justified

- That they accepted the principle that, if an act is wrong, intending to carry it out is also wrong

- That the strategy of nuclear deterrence involves a threat to use nuclear weapons

- That they nevertheless grant a moral acceptance of deterrence, albeit a conditional one.[43]

This is a serious charge, not only because of its policy implications, but also because it strikes at the heart of the bishops' advantage in the debate, the rigor of their ethical argumentation. Some critics charged that the pastoral, taken as a whole, was considerably more pacifist than the conclusion on deterrence would suggest. They attributed this to political reasons, citing the range of views within the Catholic Church and the composition of the drafting committee. In effect, these critics argued, the American bishops were initially influenced largely by the pacifist elements in their midst, but ultimately had to accommodate the more conservative views of their European counterparts, especially of Pope John Paul II, who had already judged deterrence to be acceptable as an interim step toward disarmament. Moreover, in this view, the American Catholic Church—long a supporter of U.S. military programs—feared that carrying the logic of the argument to its pacifist conclusion would reduce its influence with mainstream church members.[44]

One response to the criticism of inconsistency is to employ the principle of double effect in defense of deterrence. The bishops did not do this specifically, but an argument to this effect could be framed as follows:

- Nuclear deterrence is not intrinsically evil. It does not violate the principle of immunity as long as innocent people are not targeted directly.

- Deterrence has two effects: that it deters nuclear attack and avoids significant hostility; and that it entails a significant risk of actual use of nuclear weapons, which would be morally unjustifiable.

- Only the first (good) effect is intended in a strategy of deterrence.

- The second (bad) effect does not arise out of the good effect, but rather is coincident with it.

- The good effect is commensurate with the bad effect.[45]

This argument is consistent with just-war theory but is not completely convincing, given the profound uncertainty about the ability to control nuclear weapons and their devastating consequences. Moreover, it relies on assumptions about intentions that can only be deduced, never demonstrated. These intentions, in addition, may very well differ across cultures and among individual leaders. In this regard, the realists have a point in asserting that aggressors are different from those who intend peace and stability.

In the final analysis, the bishops' arguments on deterrence are weighty and sensible, but not completely compelling. And there is undoubtedly merit to the view that so large and diverse a body as the National Council of Catholic Bishops was subject to both internal and external political pressures. Nevertheless, their intervention in a realm previously dominated by strategists and politicians decisively shifted public and scholarly dialogue on nuclear strategy. Following publication of their letter and Reagan's attempt to take the moral high ground with his Strategic Defense Initiative, the ethical analysis of nuclear issues continued to evolve and became increasingly sophisticated.

Subsequent Arguments

During Reagan's second administration, with progress being made in arms control negotiations and research proceeding on strategic defenses, Harvard University political scientist Joseph Nye published a small book called *Nuclear Ethics*.[46] While remaining generally within the just-war tradition, Nye effectively integrated technological and political considerations to develop a set of "maxims" of nuclear ethics:

- Self-defense is a just but limited cause.

- Never treat nuclear weapons as normal weapons.

- Minimize harm to innocent people.

- Reduce risks of nuclear war in the near term.

- Reduce reliance on nuclear weapons over time.[47]

These maxims provided concise, if somewhat simplified, tests for evaluating policy choices on nuclear weapons. For example, the first principle counseled moderation in defense policy, especially when that policy relies largely on nuclear deterrence. Nye cautioned against the simple justification of new weapon systems or employment policies on the grounds that they strengthen deterrence. Rather, he suggested, the nuclear age requires that states avoid hubris and self-centeredness. He particularly urged abandonment of the tendency to see one's own actions as inherently contributing to order and stability, and those of others as destabilizing or evil. In short, his first maxim was a plea for prudent restrictions on a foreign policy that rests on nuclear deterrence.[48]

Nye's second maxim cautioned against technological deception. While acknowledging that it may be possible to construct small, accurate nuclear weapons and to use them in a way that greatly limits their destructive effects, he argued that the political and strategic implications of using nuclear weapons will always be profoundly different from those that arise in conventional war. He was somewhat less skeptical than the bishops about the possibility for limiting nuclear war. But he was wary of initiatives to "strengthen" deterrence by enhancing the potential for fighting limited nuclear wars. He argued that it is appropriate to have plans for limiting nuclear use, but these should be for the purpose of minimizing devastation should deterrence fail rather than for enhancing deterrence itself.

Nye next dealt with the specifics of selecting targets for nuclear weapons to minimize harm to the innocent. He rejected the deliberate targeting of civilian populations, but was also concerned that targeting of the opponent's nuclear forces could increase pressure for their early use in a conflict, and thus undermine deterrence. Nye agonized over this issue, and ultimately was unable to come up with an adequate solution to the targeting dilemma. The basic problem, in his view, lay in the inherent difficulty of predicting the consequences of any employment policy. In vague language that reveals his moral uncertainty, Nye noted: "In situations where consequential analysis is so uncertain, we might make the choice by invoking our sense of integrity about reducing the direct threat of harm to innocents, preferring a counter-combatant targeting doctrine. . . . But the ethical problems of nuclear deterrence cannot be solved by adjustments of targeting doctrine alone."[49]

With regard to reducing the risk of nuclear war, Nye noted that some element of risk is inherent in the concept of deterrence. He distinguished three basic intellectual approaches to deterrence. "Hawks" argue that the best way to avoid nuclear war is to undertake programs that strengthen deterrence by maintaining an effective retaliatory capability, even if that entails some overinsurance. "Doves" emphasize the risk of irrational behavior in a crisis and recommend trying to reassure the adversary by reducing armaments. "Owls" are conscious of the nonrational elements of crises, but emphasize the need to control military actions and to terminate war at the lowest possible level of destruction. Nye observed that all three views have an inherent logic but also entail risks: the hawks risk provoking unintended reactions, the doves risk appeasing aggression and the owls risk paralysis in a crisis.[50]

Nye's own recommendations are largely "owlish" but contain concepts from the doves and hawks as well. To avoid nuclear war in the near term he suggested the following:

- Maintaining a credible nuclear deterrent

- Improving conventional deterrence

- Enhancing crisis stability

- Reducing the impact of accidents

- Preventing and managing crises

- Invigorating non-proliferation efforts

- Limiting misperceptions

- Pursuing arms control negotiations.[51]

It would be hard to argue with most of these principles. Unfortunately, however, this is due to their lack of specificity with respect to specific policy initiatives. This ambiguity leaves ample room for the hawks, doves and owls to fight over particular policies and programs, each claiming to be adhering to principles that will reduce the risk of nuclear war.

Finally, Nye counseled reducing reliance on nuclear weapons over time. He assumed that deterrence might someday fail, and thus saw a need to reduce both the likelihood and the potential impact of such failures. He rejected utopian solutions based on international cooperation, and was also skeptical of President Reagan's assertion that strategic defenses would provide the means to eliminate nuclear weapons. He criticized Reagan's view that defenses are a "moral imperative" as based on faulty reasoning, in particular the failure to acknowledge that a true escape from deterrence would require leakproof defenses not only against ballistic missiles but also against bombers and cruise missiles. Such defenses, he argued, were highly unlikely. Thus defenses might enhance deterrence but could not replace it.[52]

Nye put more hope in political and social paths to reducing reliance on nuclear weapons than in technological ones, though he acknowledged the desirability of continuing research on defensive systems as long as they do not increase the risk of nuclear conflict. Political and social change, he argued, is the key factor in the long-range future. Presciently anticipating the end of the Cold War, Nye noted that "sometimes political relations between states can change quite quickly."[53] In the interim, he suggested, there is value in "prolonged strategic discussions; holding talks at a high level on force structure and stabilization measures; and efforts to consider crisis prevention techniques, not necessarily in the expectation of signing formal agreements, but as a means of enhancing transparency and communications."[54]

Nye acknowledged that these maxims of "just deterrence" cannot solve all nuclear dilemmas. But he did suggest that they will be valuable to leaders who must make key decisions on nuclear strategy, sometimes very quickly, as well as to citizens who must evaluate their nations' policies.[55]

ETHICS AND NUCLEAR WEAPONS IN THE TWENTY-FIRST CENTURY

In the past decade, many of the policies suggested by the bishops, and some of the political and social changes recommended by Nye, have come about. Is it now possible to integrate the ethical insights from the American Catholic bishops with the criticism of their realist opponents and Nye's thoughtful analysis to develop an approach to evaluating nuclear policies in the post-Cold War era?

In the decade and a half since the bishops and the Reagan administration engaged in debate, conditions have changed in ways that both facilitate and complicate the development of an ethical approach to nuclear policy. The Soviet Union is no more, and although Russia remains a nuclear power of substantial significance, it is largely preoccupied with internal political and economic survival. Treaties among the United States, Russia and the other nuclear successor states have reduced the number of deployed nuclear weapons by an order of magnitude from the peak levels of the 1980s. High-level dialogue on military issues is now routine, and officers of the former Communist states regularly attend senior military schools in the West and serve on planning staffs with their former adversaries. The United States and Russia have altered their declaratory nuclear policies, and assert that their missiles have been "detargeted" to inhibit a rapid nuclear strike. The number of nuclear delivery systems on alert status has also been sharply reduced.

On the other hand, the deactivation of nuclear weapons and the cancellation of nuclear programs has created concern about diversion of nuclear materials and the knowledge of former Soviet nuclear scientists to other states or even to subnational terrorist groups. Proliferation of nuclear weapons, recently underscored by nuclear tests in India and Pakistan, remains a major concern, despite the existence of international treaties prohibiting it. And the United States and its allies continue to fear proliferation of delivery systems for nuclear weapons, and of other weapons of mass destruction, in "rogue states" such as Iraq, Iran, Libya and North Korea.

Given these changed conditions, the bishops' arguments seem dated. But the basic thrust of their judgments, and of Joseph Nye's, remains valid. Nuclear weapons are different. Any use of nuclear weapons is so dangerous as to be unacceptable, and reliance on the implicit or explicit threat of nuclear retaliation is intolerable as a long-term strategy. There are still more than enough nuclear weapons available to destroy civilization as we know it. Despite improvements in command and control systems, and improved trust among the Western powers and the successor states to the USSR, there remains a risk of accidental use of nuclear weapons, or their deliberate employment by regional powers or subnational groups.

The realists' concerns about aggressors may apply more to the rogue states than they ever did to the Soviet Union. Thus, the recommendations made by Nye and the bishops must be tempered by the realization that some current or potential nuclear powers operate within a political and psychological, not to mention ethical, framework that is very different from that of the Cold War period. It was difficult enough to discern what constituted stabilizing or destabilizing behavior in an essentially bipolar nuclear standoff. To make such judgments in a world of many nuclear powers would be truly mind-boggling.

Thus, despite the fact that there is now much less discussion about ethics and nuclear weapons than in the Reagan years, the urgency of reducing reliance on nuclear threats is, if anything, even greater. A number of Nye's proposed steps have been, or are being, achieved. These include progress in arms control between East and West, improved crisis management procedures and reductions in situations that could lead to nuclear accidents. But other tasks, especially controlling the proliferation of weapons of mass destruction and reducing misperceptions, remain daunting challenges.

In the past, the ethical debate on nuclear issues, and the policy choices regarding them, have been the province of the major nuclear powers. The United States played an invaluable role in providing leadership on nuclear arms control issues, and American church authorities and others in the West were essential to fostering moral awareness of the impact of the nuclear age. It is now time to broaden the debate to include other powers and other ethical traditions. In this, U.S. leadership will again be essential, and the American Catholic bishops could usefully turn their attention again to the nuclear dilemma.

This would be a propitious time for dialogue on nuclear issues. The START II Treaty is stalled in the Russian legislature. And President Clinton has established a new nuclear arms policy that contains positive elements but raises new questions. According to press reports, the secret directive jettisons the Reagan administration objective that the United States must "prevail" even in a protracted nuclear war. Instead, Clinton has ordered that the aim of nuclear forces is to deter through threatening a devastating response, an apparent return to the Eisenhower policy of "massive retaliation." In addition, the directive permits use of unclear weapons against powers that use chemical or biological weapons, a highly controversial proposition among military planners.[56] Such a policy, critics note, could "weaken the taboo that restrains other nuclear powers . . . doing far more to imperil America's global security than to advance it."[57] It also awakens serious moral concerns about America's intentions regarding nuclear employment.

WINNERS AND LOSERS

Who won the debate? Both sides can rightly claim victory. The bishops certainly increased public awareness of nuclear issues, increased political pressure on the administration and helped to stimulate policy choices that have effected major changes in the nuclear environment. But the Reagan administration and its successors were the ones who successfully implemented those changes. While the bishops and Ronald

Reagan differed profoundly over specific policies, and while each was skeptical of the other's arguments and proposals, in the end they shared the goal of a managed transition to a world less threatened by nuclear holocaust. To their successors falls the task of designing and implementing the next steps on what Pope John Paul II called the way to progressive nuclear disarmament.

NOTES

1. The data on Soviet and U.S. military forces and expenditures are drawn from Sven F. Kraemer, "Toward a Responsible Policy," in *Ethics and Nuclear Arms*, ed. Raymond English (Washington: Ethics and Public Policy Center, 1985), pp. 19–24, 45–51.

2. There was controversy about whether the Backfire bomber would actually be used on operational missions against the United States. Most intelligence analysts thought the aircraft could not strike U.S. territory and return to Soviet bases, but other analysts, and Reagan administration officials, thought that the USSR would have no hesitation about sacrificing pilots and aircraft on one-way missions in a nuclear war.

3. Fred Kaplan, *The Wizards of Armageddon* (New York: Simon & Schuster, 1983).

4. One noteworthy commentator in the administration was a former defense industry official named T. K. Jones, whose views on surviving nuclear attack were described in Robert Scheer, *With Enough Shovels: Reagan, Bush and Nuclear War* (New York: Random House, 1982).

5. For a penetrating analysis of the Soviet gambit and the U.S. response, see Graham Allison, *Essence of Decision: Explaining the Cuban Missile Crisis* (Boston: Little, Brown, 1971).

6. Strobe Talbott, ed., *Khrushchev Remembers* (Boston: Little, Brown, 1970), p. 495.

7. James A. Barry, "The Seabed Arms Control Issue, 1967–1971: A Superpower Symbiosis?" in *International Law Studies*, vol. 61, Richard B. Lillich and John Norton Moore, eds., (Newport, RI: U.S. Naval War College, 1980).

8. John Newhouse, *Cold Dawn: The Story of SALT* (New York: Holt, Rinehart and Winston, 1973), provides a comprehensive account of the negotiations as well as the texts of the treaties.

9. Ernest May and Richard Neustadt, *Thinking in Time: The Uses of History for Decision Makers* (New York: Free Press, 1986), pp. 111–33.

10. Strobe Talbott, *Deadly Gambits* (New York: Alfred A. Knopf, 1984), describes the infighting in the Reagan administration over nuclear arms control.

11. Richard Perle, "Abutere Patentia Nostra" (address to the Conference on Communism and Liberal Democracy, London, March 18–20, 1985), *Survey* 29, no. 1 (Spring 1985): 88–95.

12. Speech given on December 9, 1984, before the convocation of Yeshiva University, New York.

13. Ronald Reagan, "Address to the Nation on the Economy, February 5, 1981," in Reagan, *Speaking My Mind* (New York: Simon & Schuster, 1990).

14. Robert S. McNamara, "The Military Role of Nuclear Weapons: Perceptions and Misperceptions," *Foreign Affairs* 62, no. 4 (Fall 1983): 57–80.

15. National Conference of Catholic Bishops (hereafter NCCB), *The Challenge of Peace: God's Promise and Our Response. A Pastoral Letter on War and Peace in the Nuclear Age* (Washington, DC: U.S. Catholic Conference, 1983).

16. Notable writings by Catholic authorities on nuclear issues prior to 1983 include Margaret Feeney, *Sword of the Spirit: Just War? Papal Teaching on Nuclear Warfare with a Scientific Commentary* (Hinkley, UK: Walker, 1958); John Courtney Murray, S.J., *Morality and Modern War* (New York: Council on Religion and International Affairs, 1959); *The Documents of*

Vatican II (New York: America Press, 1966); and an encyclical of John XXIII, *Pacem in Terris* (New York: America Press, 1963).

17. Jim Castelli, *The Bishops and the Bomb* (Garden City, NY: Image Books, 1984), contains a detailed description of the politics of the pastoral letter. This book is the primary source for the following section.

18. Ibid., p. 81.

19. William Clark, "Text of Administration's Letter to U.S. Catholic Bishops on Nuclear Policies," *New York Times*, November 17, 1982, sec. B, p. 4.

20. J. M. Cameron, "Nuclear Catholics" in Cameron, *Nuclear Catholics and Other Essays* (Grand Rapids, MI: William Eerdman, 1989), p. 72.

21. James V. Shall, S.J., ed., *The Bishops' Letters: Out of Justice, Peace, Joint Pastoral Letter of the West German Bishops; Winning the Peace, Joint Pastoral Letter of the French Bishops* (San Francisco: Ignatius Press, 1984), p. 9.

22. Francis X. Winters, "After Tension, Detente: A Continuing Chronicle of European Episcopal Views on Nuclear Deterrence," *Theological Studies* 45, no. 2 (Winter 1984): 343.

23. The text appears in *Origins*, 24 June, 1982, p. 107.

24. George P. Shultz, *Turmoil and Triumph: My Years as Secretary of State* (New York: Scribner's, 1993), p. 253. The CIA had been aware of some of the proposals, but not of Reagan's intentions, about a year earlier. See Robert M. Gates, *From the Shadows* (New York: Simon & Schuster, 1996), p. 264.

25. Shultz, *Turmoil and Triumph*, p. 360.

26. NCCB, *The Challenge of Peace*, p. iv.

27. Ibid., pp. 42, 45.

28. Ibid., pp. 52–53.

29. Ibid., p. ii.

30. Ibid., p. 55.

31. Ibid., pp. 52–53.

32. Ibid., p. 62.

33. Ibid., pp 55, 58–59.

34. Gates, *From the Shadows*, p. 539.

35. Andrew J. Goodpaster, *Nuclear Weapons and European Security* (Washington, DC: The Atlantic Council, 1996).

36. Robert L. King, "Rhetoric of Morality, Rhetoric of Manipulation," *Cross Currents* 34, no. 4 (Winter 1984–85): 455–72.

37. Clark, "Text of Administration's Letter;" John Lehman, article in *Wall Street Journal*, November 15, 1982, p. 28; Michael Novak, "Arms and the Church," *Commentary* 37, no. 4 (March 1982): 39.

38. King "Rhetoric of Morality, Rhetoric of Manipulation," p. 467.

39. Ibid., p. 468.

40. Ashley J. Tellis, "Nuclear Arms, Moral Questions, and Religious Issues," *Armed Forces and Society* 13, no. 4 (Summer 1987): 600.

41. Joel H. Rosenthal, *Righteous Realists* (Baton Rouge: Louisiana State University Press, 1991), p. 7.

42. Tellis, "Nuclear Arms, Moral Questions, and Religious Issues," p. 605.

43. James W. McGray, "Nuclear Deterrence: Is the War-and-Peace Pastoral Inconsistent?" *Theological Studies* 46, no. 4 (December 1985): 701–2.

44. Susan Moller Okin, "Taking the Bishops Seriously," *World Politics* 36, no. 4 (July 1984): 528–29.

45. McGray, "Nuclear Deterrence: Is the War-and-Peace Pastoral Inconsistent?" pp. 707–9.

46. Joseph S. Nye, Jr., *Nuclear Ethics* (New York: Free Press, 1986).

47. Ibid., p. 99.
48. Ibid., p. 104.
49. Ibid., pp. 114–15.
50. Ibid., pp. 115–19.
51. Ibid., p. 120.
52. Ibid., p. 125.
53. Ibid., p. 126.
54. Ibid., p. 130.
55. Ibid., p. 132.
56. "Clinton Directive Changes Strategy on Nuclear Arms," *Washington Post*, December 7, 1997.
57. "The Bomb and the Button," *New York Times*, December 9, 1997.

3

Ethics and Military Force:
George Bush and the Persian Gulf War

FROM CRISIS TO WAR

In April 1990, Prince Bandar bin Sultan, an influential member of the Saudi royal family and his country's ambassador to the United States since 1983, received a curious request. His uncle, King Fahd, asked him to travel to Baghdad and meet privately with Iraqi President Saddam Hussein. When Bandar arrived on April 5, Saddam told him that he was concerned about how he was viewed in the West. The United States, he said, had overreacted to Saddam's recent speeches and he wanted Bandar to assure President Bush that Iraq had no intention of attacking Israel. He asked that Bandar obtain assurance from Bush that Israel would not attack Iraq. Saddam went on to say that the "imperialist–Zionist conspiracy" was spreading rumors that he had expansionist ambitions, but that these were false.

Surprised by Saddam's request, Bandar nevertheless agreed to carry the message. Four days later, he met with President Bush. Bush was confused by Saddam's message, but responded, "I don't want anyone to attack anyone. We'll talk to the Israelis." Bandar reported the results of the meeting to his uncle, who passed the information on to Saddam.[1]

The rationale behind Saddam's request became clearer later in the year. During the summer, Saddam began to complain that Kuwait was distorting international oil prices by exceeding the quota established by the Organization of Petroleum Exporting Countries (OPEC). In July, Western intelligence services detected a large-scale redeployment of Iraqi military forces, including the crack divisions of Saddam's Republican Guard, to positions near the Kuwait border.

Bush's Response

The Bush administration was concerned, but not alarmed. Officials reasoned that Saddam was putting pressure on Kuwait but would not necessarily attack. On July 25,

U.S. Ambassador April Glaspie met with Saddam. An account of the meeting has been released by the Iraqi government; the United States has neither confirmed nor denied its accuracy. According to this document, Glaspie told Saddam, "I have a direct instruction from the president to seek better relations with Iraq." Later, in the context of Iraqi complaints about oil prices, Glaspie reportedly said, "I have lived here for years. I admire your extraordinary efforts to rebuild your country. I know you need funds. We understand that and our opinion is that you should have the opportunity to rebuild your country. But we have no opinion on the Arab–Arab conflicts, like your border disagreements with Kuwait."[2]

Glaspie's comments were consistent with U.S. policy established by the Bush administration in 1989. At that time, National Security Adviser Brent Scowcroft had summed up the consensus by saying there was little to be lost by improving relations with Saddam, and that he could be a regional counterweight to Iran, though he was not to be trusted. This ambivalence characterized U.S. actions as the administration encouraged business with Iraq while simultaneously denouncing Saddam's anti-Israeli rhetoric.[3]

Whether or not Saddam took Glaspie's comments as a green light to pursue his ambitions, on August 2 his forces rolled into Kuwait. Just a day before, the Central Intelligence Agency (CIA) had concluded that an invasion was imminent. Some administration officials, including Scowcroft, were surprised by Saddam's action. After consulting with Bush, Scowcroft met with other senior officials and prepared a statement condemning the invasion and calling for immediate withdrawal of the Iraqi forces. A plan was drawn up to freeze Iraqi assets, and preparations were made to deploy F-15 fighter aircraft to Saudi Arabia if the Saudis requested them.

Iraq justified the invasion by pointing both to Kuwait's "threatening posture" regarding oil and to a putative historic injustice that Iraq suffered at the hands of British colonial authorities. In 1921, the British Colonial Office established the border between Iraq and Kuwait, cutting off Iraq's access to the Persian Gulf. In 1961, Iraqi strongman Abdul al-Karim Qassim claimed that Kuwait was part of Iraqi territory. British peacekeeping forces were dispatched, later replaced by an Arab peacekeeping force.[4] Thirty years later, Saddam would resurrect his predecessor's claim that Kuwait was properly the "nineteenth province of Iraq."

The morning after the invasion, President Bush met with reporters shortly before attending a meeting of the National Security Council (NSC). In response to questions, he asserted, "We're not discussing intervention." The NSC meeting focused on economic sanctions and diplomatic activity, as well as on the proposed aircraft deployment. The participants included Bush, Scowcroft, Chairman of the Joint Chiefs of Staff (JCS) Colin Powell, Commander of the United States Central Command General H. Norman Schwarzkopf (CENTCOM had operational responsibility for the Persian Gulf region), Secretary of Defense Dick Cheney and Undersecretary for Policy Paul Wolfowitz, Undersecretary of State Robert Kimmett, Director of Central Intelligence William Webster, Chief of Staff John Sununu, Budget Director Richard Darman and Treasury Secretary Nicholas Brady. They debated, inconclusively, the impact of the invasion on the price and availability of oil. Bush let the conversation drift from military options to an economic embargo. The meeting adjourned without reaching a decision.[5]

Military officials retired to prepare contingency plans. Their concern, and that of other senior decision makers, was primarily with a potential Iraqi threat to Saudi Arabia. Intelligence reports indicated that Saddam's forces were repositioning for a possible incursion into the kingdom, with the likely objective of seizing oil fields. Such a move would be a significantly greater threat to the world oil supply, as well as an attack on the United States' staunchest ally in the region. On August 6, however, President Bush changed the parameters for military planning. He met with British Prime Minister Margaret Thatcher, who pressed him to take a hard line.[6] According to Secretary of State James Baker, Thatcher's exact words were "We simply can't let this stand. We've got to take care of it right now."[7] Already inclined in this direction, Bush told reporters after the meeting, "I view very seriously our determination to reverse this aggression. . . . This will not stand. This will not stand, this aggression against Kuwait."[8]

According to Bob Woodward, JCS Chairman Powell was surprised and concerned by the president's remark. Woodward claims that Powell's reaction was that the president "had six-shooters in both hands and he was blazing away."[9] Powell himself confirms his surprise, but in more moderate tones. He has no doubt that Thatcher influenced Bush's attitude. The decision process, Powell says, "was pure George Bush. He had listened quietly to his advisors. He had consulted by phone with world leaders. And then, taking his own counsel, he had come to this momentous decision and revealed it at the first opportunity."[10]

Bush himself has said that he made up his mind in the first few hours after the invasion that he could not tolerate Saddam's aggression. He has acknowledged that he gave mixed signals about his intentions, and refrained from making them clear even to his closest advisers.

During my press remarks at the outset of the first NSC meeting, I did say that I was not contemplating intervention. . . . I did not intend to rule out the use of force. At that juncture I did not wish explicitly to rule it in. But following the series of meetings, I came to the conclusion that some public comment was needed to make clear my determination that the United States must do whatever might be necessary to reverse the Iraqi aggression. I don't know that I had determined at that point that force would be required, but I had decided that would be up to Saddam.[11]

The NSC met again that evening. Secretary of Defense Cheney was dispatched to Saudi Arabia with the mission of securing an "invitation" to deploy U.S. forces there. Accompanying Cheney were Deputy National Security Adviser Robert Gates, Wolfowitz, Schwarzkopf, two diplomats and a CIA expert. Before the trip, Scowcroft talked with Prince Bandar in an attempt to secure advance permission for deployment, but the prince was noncommittal. Nevertheless, Cheney and his colleagues were pleasantly surprised when King Fahd accepted the proposal on the spot, saying simply, "Okay."[12]

On August 8, Bush announced the deployment in an Oval Office speech. He said that there were four principles that guided his policy:

First, we seek the immediate, unconditional and complete withdrawal of all Iraqi forces from Kuwait. Second, Kuwait's legitimate government must be restored to replace the puppet regime. And third, my administration, as has been the case with every president from President Roosevelt to President Reagan, is committed to the security and stability of the Persian Gulf. And fourth, I am determined to protect the lives of American citizens abroad.[13]

Diplomacy and Force

By this time, adroit diplomacy by Baker had resulted in a United Nations resolution that not only condemned the Iraqi action but also imposed tough economic sanctions.[14] In Washington and the Middle East, military planners began to implement a buildup that would take months. Powell briefed the President on progress in mid-August. Following the briefing, Bush spoke to Pentagon employees and made a direct personal attack on Saddam. Later that month he signed a "finding" authorizing the CIA to conduct covert operations to recruit Iraqi dissidents to overthrow Saddam.[15]

Differences among the military planners began to be evident in September. General Schwarzkopf had organized two related but separate planning efforts, one centered on an air campaign, the other on ground operations. In the end, they were to be united under the concept of an "air-land battle," but at this early stage differing concepts were put forward by military service specialists. Air Force planners, in particular, pressed for reliance on air power, arguing that they could win the war and avoid the casualties that would result from a ground campaign.

In mid-September, the *Washington Post* published a story based on an interview with Air Force Chief of Staff Michael Dugan, "U.S. to Rely on Air Strikes if War Erupts." The paper quoted Dugan as saying that the United States could dislodge the Iraqis through air bombardment alone. He claimed that the best way to hurt Saddam was to target his family, his personal guard and his mistress.[16] Dugan's threat to take the war to downtown Baghdad provoked a storm of controversy, and he was sacked by Cheney the day after the article appeared.[17] But Air Force planners continued to develop lists of targets, including both military and civilian facilities in Baghdad.

By late September 1990, the buildup of forces was well under way. Baker had succeeded in assembling a coalition to support the U.S.-led effort. Great Britain, France and some Arab countries had agreed to provide troops, while other countries provided economic, logistic and political support. In the United States, President Bush had not made clear his ultimate intentions. General Powell, meanwhile, was concerned about the president's apparently growing conviction that military force would have to be used. Consequently, he outlined another option—continuing to rely on economic sanctions backed up by the threat of force—and began to make the rounds discussing it with other senior officials. By this time, there were only seven others who counted. Decision making in the administration was focused in the "Gang of Eight," Bush, Vice President Quayle, Powell, Cheney, Baker, Scowcroft, Gates and Sununu. Of these, Baker, Cheney and Scowcroft were the most important.[18] None was particularly supportive of the sanctions option.

Accounts differ regarding what Powell ultimately told the president. Bob Woodward says that Powell spoke as an advocate of containment, arguing that it would work, although it could require as much as two years. But he did not put it forward as a personal recommendation.[19]   Powell himself characterizes the presentation as a balanced one. He says that he recommended that preparations continue for an offensive as early as January, but noted that sanctions remained a "live option." According to Powell, "I was not advocating either route, war or sanctions, on this day. I simply believed that both options had to be considered fully and fairly." Powell accepts, however, Woodward's characterization of him as a "reluctant warrior":

Guilty. War is a deadly game; and I do not believe in spending the lives of Americans lightly. My responsibility that day was to lay out all the options for the nation's leadership. However, in our democracy it is the President [sic] not generals, who make decisions about going to war. I had done my duty. The sanctions clock was ticking down. If the President was right, if he decided that it must be war, then my job was to make sure we were ready to go in and win.[20]

Powell apparently left the meeting with the president believing that the sanctions option was still open. But within a few days, he received a signal to the contrary when Bush requested a detailed briefing on offensive war plans. The briefing took place on October 10, and revealed that while resources were in place for an air campaign, the coalition's ground forces were not strong enough for a decisive victory.[21] In mid-October, Powell went to see Baker. By this time, the general had taken up the offensive option, and asked for the secretary's support in convincing the president to augment the ground forces and in garnering additional support from coalition partners.[22]

With Baker helping to smooth the way for a force augmentation, Powell asked Schwarzkopf to estimate his needs. The commander's reply was dramatic: "I want the VII Corps." This was the backbone of the United States forces in Europe, and its redeployment would have been unthinkable before the end of the Cold War. Powell promised to make good on the request, and promised additional units as well.[23]

On October 30, Powell briefed the president and members of the Gang of Eight. He told the group that it would take another 200,000 troops—nearly double the authorized deployment—to conduct an offensive against Iraqi forces. According to Powell, the president didn't blink. He asked again if air power could not do the job. When Powell assured him it could not, Bush said, "Okay, do it." The president had decided to go to war.[24]

Bush accompanied his decision with increasingly shrill rhetoric. On December 16, at a taping session for an interview with David Frost that was shown on January 2, Bush referred to an Amnesty International report on Iraqi abuses of human rights in Kuwait. He characterized the situation as "such a clear case of good and—good versus evil. We have such a clear moral case. . . . Nothing of this moral importance since World War II." Bush repeatedly and publicly compared Saddam to Hitler.[25]

In addition, Bush expanded his war aims beyond the liberation of Kuwait. The force buildup and operational plan that he approved on October 31 were intended not merely to force the retreat of Iraq's forces but also to destroy their military capability.

Moreover, Bush specifically wanted to eliminate Saddam's potential for nuclear, chemical and biological warfare.[26]

In addition to military preparations, two important political tasks remained. Bush had to convince both the United Nations and the United States Congress to agree to the use of military force. On November 29, Baker negotiated a compromise that achieved the support of the Soviet Union for a UN resolution authorizing "all necessary means" to force Iraq out of Kuwait.[27] Throughout the day, he held bilateral meetings with other members of the Security Council. When the vote was taken, the tally was 12–2 in favor of the resolution, with Cuba and Yemen in opposition and China (a permanent member that could have exercised a veto) abstaining. The resolution set a deadline of January 15, 1991, for Iraqi withdrawal.[28]

Diplomacy was required at home as well. Powerful members of Congress, including Senate Armed Services Committee chairman Sam Nunn, opposed war without giving sanctions longer to work.[29] Some of Bush's advisers believed that the president did not need formal congressional approval, but Baker argued successfully that such a step was essential for practical and political reasons. According to Baker, "For the most part, the Bush administration strove hard to keep Congress well briefed. George Bush, after all, was a former member of Congress himself, and instinctively understood the wisdom of keeping Congress apprised."[30]

Keeping Congress informed, however, was a different matter than convincing the lawmakers of the wisdom of the war. Congressional opposition turned on differing judgments about the effectiveness of sanctions. Former Chairman of the Joint Chiefs of Staff William Crowe had testified in November before the Senate Armed Services Committee in favor of continuing economic pressure.[31] Several academic experts on sanctions also counseled letting the pressure on Saddam build longer before using military force.[32] But influential members, including Representative Stephen Solarz, argued forcefully that Saddam would never bend to the pressure of sanctions. Moreover, he asserted, "it would appear that the prospects for the success of the sanctions are less likely than the prospects for the collapse of the coalition if we wait for the sanctions to be given more time to work."[33] Executive branch experts were divided. In December, a Special National Intelligence Estimate concluded that once Saddam recognized the potential of the coalition force and the resolve of its members, he would withdraw from Kuwait, but the military intelligence agencies dissented from this view.[34] By January 10, at the height of the congressional debate, CIA Director William Webster testified that "even if the sanctions continue to be enforced for another six or twelve months, economic hardship alone is unlikely to compel Saddam Hussein to retreat from Kuwait or cause regime-threatening popular discontent in Iraq."[35]

Members of Congress also expressed concern about the scale of casualties, the wisdom of going to war for oil or jobs, and their prerogatives under the Constitution. Many of Bush's advisers were convinced that there was no constitutional bar to the use of force on the president's authority, but agreed that congressional support was politically essential. Ultimately, Saddam Hussein himself helped to turn the tide of debate by remaining intransigent, even spurning a last minute offer from Baker to Iraqi Foreign Minister Aziz to resolve the issue peacefully. Aziz characterized Bush's letter to Saddam as "full of threats," and refused to take it to his president.[36] On January 12, 1991, the Senate voted 52–47 to authorize the president to wage war under UN Resolution 678. (The House had earlier approved by a vote of 250–183.)[37]

THE AIR WAR

Despite the consensus among American decision makers that air power alone could not achieve their objectives, air forces were assigned a central and early mission. The war plan, dubbed "Instant Thunder" to distinguish it from the staged escalation "Rolling Thunder" campaign in Vietnam, called for operations to begin with widespread air attacks on a variety of targets in Iraq. According to Schwarzkopf's operations plan, the objectives of the opening phase of the air campaign were "loss of confidence in the [Iraqi] government, the disruption of Iraqi command and control and significant degradation of Iraqi military capabilities."[38] After a week or so, the priorities would shift to "open a window of opportunity for initiating ground offensive operations by confusing and terrorizing Iraqi forces in the [Kuwaiti Theater of Operations] and shifting combat force ratios in favor of friendly forces." One specific goal was to "inflict maximum enemy casualties." Another was to ensure that once the ground campaign began, Iraqi escape routes were blocked to create a "kill zone" north of Kuwait.[39]

To accomplish these goals, the initial targets selected for the air campaign numbered nearly 250. More than one-third of these were identified as command and control, leadership and air defense targets. The most threatening military forces—Saddam's suspected chemical arsenal, his Scud surface-to-surface missiles and his crack Republican Guard divisions—comprised about one-fifth of the targets. (The Scud threat turned out to be less serious than anticipated; the weapons were used only for a few terror attacks on Israeli cities and caused a few score casualties at an American base. The chemical weapons threat never materialized, though some Gulf War veterans may have been affected by chemicals released when coalition forces destroyed munitions storage sites.) The remainder—nearly half of the priority targets—were components of Iraq's military and economic infrastructure, including electrical facilities, oil refineries, railroads, bridges, airfields, ports and military production and storage sites.[40]

While pilots were briefed to avoid unnecessary civilian casualties, the nature of the targets selected inevitably involved risk to noncombatants. One specific bombing objective was attacks on the Iraqi political and military leadership. Official records indicate that there were 60 bombing raids against sites where the coalition thought Iraqi leaders might be hiding. One senior military officer asserted that the coalition was not trying to assassinate Saddam, "but we were trying to kill him."[41]

One particularly controversial raid was conducted on February 13 against the Amariya air raid shelter in Baghdad. Military planners categorized this facility as a command-and-control bunker, as it had been designated by both the CIA and the Defense Intelligence Agency. Apparently, however, the shelter was packed with civilians when it was attacked. General Schwarzkopf maintains that it was a "legitimate military target."[42] Critics of the war condemn the attack as a deliberate killing of civilians.[43]

Another controversial target was a building that had been suspected by U.S. intelligence of harboring a biological warfare facility. Although the indicators were ambiguous, the air campaign planners categorized it as a "potential manufacturing plant" until shortly before the war began, when the Iraqis camouflaged the factory. The planners shifted it to the active target list and the facility was attacked. Subsequently, Iraqi authorities claimed that it was a "baby milk factory." An investigation by the House Intelligence Committee after the war concluded that "we still do not know with absolute certainty whether the plant that was bombed was a biological site or a legitimate baby milk plant."[44]

THE GROUND WAR

By late February 1991, the air campaign had achieved its goals. President Bush issued an ultimatum on February 22, calling on Saddam to capitulate. Two days later, in the early morning, U.S. Marines crossed in force into Kuwait.[45]

The Marines were not in the main attack. Although they would have the privilege of liberating Kuwait City, the principal action would be to the west. In an audacious ploy, Schwarzkopf moved a massive ground force westward and attacked the Iraqis' flank in a "left hook" maneuver. The concept was that the Marines and Arab allies would pin down the Iraqi forces in Kuwait while U.S. and British forces enveloped their right flank. A simulated amphibious attack on Kuwait would deceive the Iraqi high command about the main thrust. The United States VII Corps, commanded by General Frederick Franks and recently redeployed from Germany, would then attack across the Saudi border, trapping the Iraqi forces in a three-way pincer. With the bridges across the Euphrates River knocked out by air raids, the Iraqi ground forces would be pounded into submission.[46]

In some ways, the plan worked too well, while in others, the chaos and fog of war disrupted coalition objectives. The Marines, rather than pinning down the Iraqi forces, acted as a "piston" and shoved them out of Kuwait. At the same time, the planned destruction of the Euphrates bridges was frustrated by the Iraqis' rapid rebuilding of the damaged spans.   Thus, significant numbers of Iraqi soldiers fled north or surrendered (some to news reporters) before the coalition's western forces could trap them. These included the vaunted Republican Guard, who acquitted themselves no better than the other units. Then Franks's VII Corps was slow to advance, causing Schwarzkopf considerable consternation and providing additional opportunities for the Iraqis to escape. By the fifth day of the war, the Iraqi forces were in full retreat, and some 70,000 had been captured by the coalition. Coalition forces advanced so rapidly that some Iraqi soldiers were buried alive in their trenches as their positions were overrun. With Saddam's troops fleeing along a packed "highway of death," Bush and his key advisers decided to propose a cease-fire on February 28.[47] The president was concerned about a public perception that Allied forces were brutalizing their opponents, and felt that he had achieved the aim of getting Saddam's forces out of Kuwait, but Secretary of State Baker acknowledged that the future issues of Saddam's government and the embargo were unfinished. Thus the president achieved the victory he sought, but felt no elation.[48]

PEACE WITHOUT VICTORY

Bush's ambivalence deepened when the cease-fire arrangements were finalized. Lacking detailed guidance from Washington, Schwarzkopf met with his Iraqi counterpart on March 3, 1991, to work out the parameters of the postwar situation. The Iraqi commander requested permission to operate helicopters within southern Iraq to carry government officials where lines of communications had been cut. Schwarzkopf agreed that any military helicopters, including armed ones, would not be attacked. Later, Schwarzkopf regretted his action. In his words, "In the following weeks we discovered what the son of a bitch really had in mind: using helicopter gunships to suppress rebellions in Basra and other cities. By that time it was up to the White House to decide how much the United States wanted to intervene in the internal politics of Iraq."[49]

The White House was not inclined to intervene. On several occasions before and during the war, Bush had called on the Iraqi people and the army to overthrow Saddam, and he had directed the CIA to stir up rebellion among the Kurds in the northern part of Iraq and among the Shiites in the south. But the president decided not to involve U.S. forces in assisting the uprisings. Some Kurdish and Shiite rebel leaders accused the president of betraying them in the aftermath of the war, Bush defended his policy, saying:

The battles between the Kurds and the Baath Party have been going for a long, long time. To solve that problem forever was not part of the United Nations' goals, nor was it the goal of the United States. We deplore killings, of course, but to tie the Kurdish or Shiite problem into the handling of the aggression of Iraq is simply a bit revisionistic. It is disappointing that Saddam Hussein remains in power and is still brutal and powerful. But that in no way diminishes the highly successful effort to stop the aggression against Kuwait.[50]

In the narrow sense that Bush defined the effort, it was successful. Iraqi forces were forced out of Kuwait and the former government was restored. The cost on the coalition side was modest—fewer than 150 U.S. lives were lost. But the casualties to Iraq and Kuwait were much greater. Just how great is difficult to estimate, and the Iraqi government has never released detailed casualty figures. The Pentagon and Schwarzkopf's Central Command estimated that perhaps 100,000 Iraqi soldiers perished, and perhaps 300,000–400,000 were wounded.[51] Other estimates are much lower. George W. S. Kuhn, an independent defense analyst, estimated that some 8,000–18,000 (and perhaps fewer) died. Another analyst, Anthony Cordesman, places the number of casualties at 25,000 killed and 50,000 wounded.[52] A press report suggested that revised administration estimates say 25,000 is a "reasonable" number for Iraqi dead.[53]

Civilian casualty estimates are even more uncertain and controversial. Ramsey Clark asserts that "150,000 minimum civilian deaths in Iraq since the beginning of the war until early 1992 [is] a very conservative number."[54] Other figures, however, are smaller by at least an order of magnitude. Greenpeace estimated fewer than 3,000 civilian deaths from bombing. The U.S. Census Bureau estimated 5,000, and one of its researchers assessed the total at 13,000.[55] A team sent to Baghdad after the war by *The Nation* magazine estimated 3,000 or perhaps fewer civilians had been killed.[56]

Indirect civilian casualties may ultimately be much greater. According to some estimates, the war destroyed some 85 percent of Iraq's electrical grid and set industrial development back 15 to 20 years. Bombing of the infrastructure devastated the civilian economy and disrupted health care services, leaving the population vulnerable to cholera, typhoid and other communicable diseases.[57] Six months after the war ended, an international team sponsored by Harvard University estimated that child mortality was three times the prewar level. The United Nations Children's Fund (UNICEF) predicted that by the end of 1991, some 170,000 Iraqi children would be malnourished and that perhaps half of them would die.[58]

A massive displacement of people resulted from the Gulf War. The Iraqi invasion caused some 380,000 Kuwaitis to flee their country, and in the aftermath of the war up to 400,000 Palestinians who had lived in Kuwait were turned away at the border of their former homeland. On the order of 2 million Kurds fled to Turkey and Iran after Saddam's repression of the uprisings that the Bush administration had urged.[59]

Damage to the environment in the Persian Gulf region was also significant. This resulted both from military operations and from Saddam Hussein's decision to set fire to Kuwaiti oil fields. A comprehensive study of the environmental consequences of the war concluded that "although early predictions of a global environmental disaster in the wake of the Gulf War were proven unfounded . . . much harm was done to the local environment [that] will have both short- and long-term consequences."[60]

WAS IT JUST?

Before, during and after the Gulf War, literally dozens of authors debated whether the resort to war was justified and whether the conflict was fought justly. Remarkable in this debate was the explicit use of the just-war tradition to structure the evaluations. Even pacifists who disagreed with the very notion of a "just war" felt compelled to "play the game" and examine how the tradition illuminated or obscured the decisions about initiating and conducting war.[61]

Bush's Supporters

Some of the commentators praised the war and the Bush administration. George Weigel, president of the Ethics and Public Policy Center and a well-known conservative Catholic theologian, asserted that the war "satisfied the eight classic criteria of the just-war tradition, and in a manner that is quite arguably unprecedented in modern warfare."[62] Though troubled by the "sloppy ending" that left Saddam in power and by the suffering visited on the Shiites and Kurds, Weigel professed to be satisfied that the decision to attack Iraq and its forces met the standards of just cause, just intention, competent authority, last resort, probability of success and proportionality, and that the subsequent military operations were carried out in conformity with the standards of proportionality of means and discrimination.

James Turner Johnson was also convinced that "all of the just war criteria providing guidance on the justified use of force were amply satisfied."[63] Moreover, he asserted that the Gulf War "clearly showed that contemporary warfare may in fact be conducted within the limits imposed by these two just-war principles [discrimination and proportionality]."[64] He praised the coalition forces, and in particular the United States, for their use of "smart" weapons, as well as for having rejected deliberate counter-population bombing.

Paul Baumann, an associate editor of *Commonweal*, agreed that the Gulf War met the just-war criteria of just cause, proper authority, last resort, likely outcome and proportionate means. However, he was skeptical that the "abstract categories" of the tradition can capture the horror and messiness of modern warfare. In Baumann's view, the Bush administration's intentions were just and its conduct of the war honorable, but "the unintended consequences of any war of this size in that part of the world make it a very dubious enterprise."[65] Thus the war was just, but imprudent.

Pacifist and Moderate Critics

These three authorities, however, constituted a minority of those who joined the Gulf War debate. Most commentators found fault with the decision to unleash military force, the manner in which it was used or both. These critics fell into three general groups: pacifists who rejected the just-war tradition as a subterfuge used by nations in their pursuit of realist aims; those who used the tradition to condemn most of the coalition's and the Bush administration's decisions and actions; and those who argued that the war generally conformed to just-war criteria but deviated from them in specific, important ways.

Pacifists attacked on both the political and the philosophical fronts. Former United States Attorney General Ramsey Clark took the lead in forming an unofficial "international commission of inquiry" to investigate the conduct of the war. Composed of scholars, human rights activists and jurists, the commission conducted interviews and on-site investigations, convened an "international war crimes tribunal," issued complaints against the Bush administration and wrote letters to the media. While their charges were not explicitly framed in just-war terms, they conformed in general to the criteria. The Clark Commission condemned the administration for the following:

- Provoking Iraq into conduct intended to justify U.S. military intervention

- Intending to establish a permanent military presence in the Gulf to control its oil resources

- Encouraging and aiding rebel forces in Iraq and causing "fratricidal violence"

- Usurping the constitutional power of Congress to declare war

- Manipulating media coverage to obtain political support for its goals

- Using prohibited weapons capable of mass destruction, inflicting unnecessary casualties

- Intentionally using excessive force against the Iraqi military, killing soldiers seeking to surrender and killing randomly and wantonly

- Indiscriminately using force, including ordering destruction of facilities essential to Iraqi civilian life and intentionally bombing businesses, schools, hospitals, religious sites, shelters, residential areas, homes and government offices.[66]

The commission leveled a number of specific charges. Citing press stories from some small newspapers, they alleged that the administration misled the public about the strength of Iraqi forces in order to justify deployment of 540,000 troops in Saudi Arabia.[67] They also asserted that the bombing of civilian infrastructure was central to the coalition strategy, intended to make postwar Iraq dependent on the West and to increase the efficacy of sanctions.[68] In addition to this overall charge, the commission was particularly critical of the bombing of the Amariya bomb shelter, which it estimated killed 1,500 civilians. In their view, it was "unbelievable that the United States did not know the shelter was being used mostly by women and children."[69]

Clark and his colleagues charged that the United States employed weapons that, because of their destructiveness, were inconsistent with international law. These included fuel-air explosives that create large-scale blast and heat, napalm, cluster bombs (single weapons that contain many "bomblets" and are used, for example, to blast numerous craters in runways) and the GBU-28 "superbomb," an earth-penetrating, high-explosive weapon used against buried shelters.[70] U.S. and coalition forces also, according to the Clark report, conducted assaults on defenseless Iraqi military units that were in the process of surrendering, as well as on retreating units on the "highway of death."[71] In the view of Clark and other commission members, the one-sided figures on military casualties—fewer than 200 on the U.S. side, compared with an estimated 200,000 Iraqi soldiers—confirm that the war violated the principle of proportionality. Moreover, the commission estimated that some 150,000 Iraqi civilians died directly as a result of the conflict, and that many more would die in the future. This, in their view, argues that the war was indiscriminate as well.[72]

Other pacifist commentators also faulted the decision to go to war and the conduct of military operations. Gordon Zahn maintained that "a good case can be made that most, if not all, of the 'just-war' conditions were ignored or violated."[73] Zahn acknowledged that Saddam Hussein's aggression was unjust, but argued that the scale of the response was itself aggressive. He faulted the Bush administration's intentions, noting that the statements of objectives shifted and expanded to include not only the expulsion of Iraqi forces from Kuwait but also the restoration of stability in the region and "kicking Hussein's ass." He also believed that the standard of legitimate authority was flawed by "deceit and manipulation." This included persuading Saudi Arabia to invite U.S. forces, constructing a "facade of international participation" and using crude personal comparisons between Saddam and Hitler to persuade a reluctant Congress to agree to the use of force.[74]

With respect to the conduct of the war, Zahn gave credit to the coalition for its declared intent to discriminate military from civilian targets, and acknowledged that this was accomplished to a commendable extent. He noted, however, the inherent imprecision of much of the weaponry, the decision to mount a full-scale assault on the nation's infrastructure, often within urban areas, and the consequent risk of civilian casualties. Echoing the Clark report, Zahn condemned the use of napalm and fuel-air explosives, and attacks on retreating Iraqi forces.[75]

Zahn was particularly critical of what he saw as a rush to war, without sufficient time to see if other solutions to the problem of Kuwait could be found. He characterized this as "the choice of *certain* evil over *potential* inconveniences that might arise from a continuation of sanctions."[76]

One of the most remarkable theological critiques of the war, clearly bordering on the pacifist position, was an unsigned article published in *La Civiltà Cattolica*, a Jesuit magazine printed in Rome and often linked to official Vatican views. The article noted that the just-war tradition is not, in the final analysis, about "justifying" war but about preventing it if possible, or severely limiting it if not. While acknowledging that the Gulf War may have been fought for a "just" cause, the article asserted that "by its own inexorable logic it led, first of all, to the systematic destruction of Iraq. . . . Thus the liberation of Kuwait was purchased at the price of destroying a country and killing hundreds of thousands of people."[77] It went on to question whether it is still possible to think about modern war as just. "Shouldn't we say instead that 'just wars' can't exist because, even when just causes come into play, the harm [modern] wars do by their very nature is so grave and horrendous?"[78]

There were a number of other commentators who, while rejecting the broad, pacifist condemnation of the Gulf War, nevertheless expressed grave concern about its initiation, its conduct or both.[79] As a group, these commentators were skeptical about the use of the just-war tradition in the case of the Gulf War, regarding it as particularly susceptible to manipulation in support of political goals. They cited the following as examples of the war's deviations from just-war principles:

- Framing the issue too narrowly, and failing to acknowledge the full historical context of the war, in particular the colonial legacy that left Iraq without access to the sea; Western support of Saddam during the Iran–Iraq war; United States ambivalence about Iraqi posturing during the summer of 1990; and the broader dimensions of Arab–Israeli tensions and the Palestinian question

- Expanding the war's aims to include goals beyond meeting Iraqi aggression and achieving military victory, especially the economic crippling of postwar Iraq and ensuring a dominant U.S. position with respect to oil resources

- Assuming that war would inevitably be required to dislodge Saddam's forces, and reluctance to allow enough time for economic sanctions to work

- Rushing to war when not required to do so by the applicable UN resolutions

- Failure to prosecute the war to a decisive end, including overthrowing Saddam Hussein

- Inciting the Shiites and Kurds to rebellion, then abandoning them

• Deliberate adoption of a strategic doctrine that included the targeting of infrastructure, with resultant severe damage to civilian resources.

One novel criticism was that the coalition erred in failing to anticipate and forestall predictable actions by Saddam, including his setting fire to Kuwait's oil fields and creating environmental havoc. The argument was that the coalition shared in the culpability because such actions were a predictable result of the decision to use military force.[80]

The third group of critics comprises authors who noted that in its conduct of the war, the coalition made significant progress toward just-war goals while falling short in some specific respects. Some of these commentators coined new terms to describe the war, including "imperfectly just" and "just but unwise."[81] These critics generally accepted that there were just reasons for going to war against Iraq and believed that, at least at the level of declaratory policy, the coalition attempted to honor the criterion of discrimination. They faulted the United States and its allies, however, for mixed motives (combating aggression as against ensuring access to oil), escalation of objectives, disproportionate casualties (especially at the end of the ground war when the rush to win appeared to have overwhelmed the rules of engagement), actions (as opposed to policy declarations) that put civilians unnecessarily at risk, unnecessarily personalizing the conflict with Saddam Hussein and terminating the war too hastily without a full understanding of the likely consequences. Two prominent Catholic theologians, John Langan and Bryan Hehir, argued that there are continuing uncertainties that make a definitive judgment about the conduct of the war impossible: the lack of reliable information on casualties and the inherent ambiguity of applying the criterion of proportionality to modern warfare. Langan noted, in particular, that the disproportionate casualties on the Iraqi side are not, prima facie, evidence that the standard was violated. Noting how difficult it is to apply rigid standards in the heat of battle, he argued for giving some benefit of the doubt to military commanders.[82]

A NET ASSESSMENT

Although pacifist critics derided the characterization of the Gulf War as "imperfectly just," this is in fact a reasonable reading of the events as they unfolded and have been documented. It seems too mechanical to treat the just-war criteria as a checklist, as Weigel did, and tick off how the coalition conformed to the requirements. In fact, the decision to launch the Gulf War, as all momentous policy decisions must, derived from a mix of motives, and combined justification with rationalization. The politics of going to war dictated that a checklist approach could not be expected, nor was it particularly desirable. Instead of asking whether the war conformed perfectly to the standards, then, should we not explore whether the decision to go to war and the conduct of the war showed some evidence of moral reflection and moral progress?

It appears that the answer on both counts is a qualified yes. Turning back Iraq's aggression was in fact a just cause and meets the most basic standard of Walzer's "legalist paradigm."[83] Moreover, it is reasonable to agree with Walzer that aggression not only should be stopped, but also should be punished, and the destruction of an aggressor's military potential is an appropriate punishment.[84] In the realm of intentions, it is true that the Bush administration's objectives were mixed and that they evolved over the course of the crisis and war. Beyond liberating Kuwait and eliminating Saddam's offensive military potential, the administration sought, appropriately, to send signals to the world about the importance of the rule of law and the unacceptability of aggression. But it also clearly had in mind to secure Western influence over oil, an aim that, while not unjust in itself, raises questions about the West's long-term commitment to peaceful dialogue about control of important economic resources.

The overthrow of Saddam Hussein, which the administration saw as highly desirable if not essential to stability in the region, is an inappropriate war aim. Saddam had done evil, but to label him a Hitler was, as even Bush came to understand, to exaggerate his importance. The responsibility to remove him from office was not that of the United States but of the Iraqi people and government. The basic principle, derived from utilitarian John Stuart Mill, is that the freedom of a political community can be won only by members of that community.[85] While an outside power may aid a revolutionary movement that has established that it is representative, the creation of a revolution by an outsider is a clear violation of sovereignty that goes beyond the legitimate punishment of aggression.

A number of critics complained that the Bush administration used political pressure to influence the United Nations, coalition countries and the U.S. Congress to give it authority for the use of force. This is not surprising; diplomacy and policy-making are inherently political activities. What is important, however, is that the administration used the systems that were in place and persuaded, rather than bypassed, the appropriate authorities. They did this even when, in the view of some presidential advisers, there was no legal requirement to do so.

Similarly, critics who complain that the use of force was not a last resort are wide of the mark. There is nothing in the just-war tradition that requires all other means to be exhausted in sequence. Rather, the potential belligerent must make an informed political decision that only military force will advance the just cause and meet the just intentions. Certainly, many well-informed authorities disputed whether or not economic sanctions would dislodge Saddam's forces. But Solarz's judgment that the coalition would not have been able to sustain sanctions long enough appears to be reasonable and prudent. Moreover, sanctions could not have achieved the other legitimate aim of eliminating Saddam's potential for future aggression.

The decision to use military force was by no means disproportionate to the cause that occasioned it or to the legitimate war aims. Though the casualties fell disproportionately on one side, this was due in large measure to overestimation of Iraqi capabilities and to luck. Thus, the United States may be faulted for an intelligence failure but not for excessive cruelty. Once a just decision has been made to go to war, it is vital that justice prevail. That means winning, and there is nothing in the principle of proportionality that requires a belligerent to barely win. In the Gulf War, the "Powell Doctrine" called for the use of superior force and for pursuing a victory through sound strategic military principles, with military officers making the operational decisions. Thus the coalition forces achieved a resounding, but not disproportionate, victory.

The Bush administration can rightly claim, then, that it did a reasonably good job of meeting the requirements of the *jus ad bellum* and Walzer's legalist paradigm. The victors can be faulted, however, for insufficient attention to the *jus in bello* and what Walzer calls the "war convention," governing the conduct of hostilities. The principal criticism here is that there were more civilian casualties and more damage to Iraq's economic infrastructure than the war aims required. The justification for attacks on the infrastructure depends on the principle of "double effect." This requires, most importantly, that the belligerent's intention is good and that the evil effect is neither one of his ends nor a means to his ends.[86] But it addition, it is essential that the attacker also seek to minimize suffering to the innocent, even if it means higher costs to his own forces.[87] It is on this last test that the coalition fails. The devastation of the Iraqi economy was disproportionate to the legitimate military end of disabling Saddam's command system and military industry. And it was indiscriminate in that there was no attempt to isolate aspects of the infrastructure that were key to military activities while sparing those that served the civilian population. That the systems were complex and interlocking does not relieve the coalition of its responsibility to exercise greater care to protect noncombatants, both those in Iraq at the time of the war and their descendants.

In part, this failure stemmed from the decision to delegate much of the authority for target selection to military planners. Wary of the resentment caused by political interference with military operations in Vietnam, the Bush administration swung in the opposite direction and, with few exceptions, left the military decisions to the military commanders.

Another area for legitimate criticism is the confusing manner in which the war ended. In his autobiography, Powell quoted approvingly from Fred Ikle's book, *Every War Must End*, on the importance of focusing attention on the outcome and having clear ideas about how to conclude a conflict.[88] But in the end, the administration's concern about public perceptions of the violence of the final engagements drove it to halt the conflict precipitately. Moreover, the lack of clear guidance to Schwarzkopf, together with Bush's ill-advised signals to the Shiite and Kurdish rebels, resulted in a tragic loss of life and raised doubts about the administration's goals and commitment.

In the final analysis, the Gulf War reflects progress in meeting the standards of the just-war tradition. Certainly, compared with the Vietnam War or even the Korean War, there was greater adherence to the standards of just cause, competent authority and proportionality. With regard to just intention and last resort, the record is mixed but largely positive, especially when contrasted with the Johnson and Nixon administrations' performance in Southeast Asia. The *jus in bello* standards of proportionality and discrimination are the most problematic, but even here, there was considerable progress from the devastation of Hiroshima, the firebombing of Dresden or the obsessive body counts of Vietnam.

BUSH AS DECISION MAKER AND LEADER

As Aristotle noted, moral behavior is measured not only by policies and activities, but also by process and personal qualities. The key, then, to learning from the Gulf War is to look particularly at those areas in which the decisions or operations fell short of the mark, and ask how improvements in procedure, or greater attention to personal virtues, could improve the outcome. Aristotle and Aquinas provide guidance for this under the rubric of normative prudence. It is instructive, then, to review how the administration made its decisions and to compare the procedure with the suggestions put forth by Aristotle and Aquinas.

According to Robert Gates, who worked closely with five presidents, George Bush was well-versed in foreign affairs and had a particular flair for developing relationships with other leaders. He worked hard and sought opinions from those inside and outside of government. He was capable, despite the views of some of his critics, of bold action. On big issues, Bush preferred small, informal meetings with senior advisers, and he encouraged differing points of view. Most of his senior advisers had similar styles, relying an a close group of aides. He mistrusted the bureaucracy and looked to his key people for new initiatives.[89]

Another senior member of the administration (though not, like Gates, a member of the Gang of Eight) felt that on the Gulf War, the inner circle was too close-knit. There was, in his view, a lack of systematic articulation and weighing of alternatives. There appeared to be little organized debate, and the input of experts from the principals' staffs was not sought.[90]

This tendency to rely on a small group of confidantes was also characteristic of several of Bush's senior advisers. Secretary of State Baker noted that because of what he called the "institutional rigidity" of the Foreign Service's career diplomats, he "preferred to centralize policy authority in a small team of talented, loyal aides, and build outward from them."[91] Woodward described Secretary of Defense Cheney as closed and uncommunicative even with Powell. He quotes the following exchange between Powell and his predecessor as chairman of the joint chiefs, Admiral William Crowe:

Crowe wanted to ask some of his own questions. "Where is Cheney on this?" he asked. Secretary of Defense Dick Cheney was Powell's immediate boss.
   "Beats me," Powell replied.
   "What does that mean?" Crowe asked, lowering his voice.
   "He holds his cards pretty close, as you know," Powell replied.
   Crowe knew that, indeed. His last six months as Chairman had coincided with Cheney's first six as Secretary. He'd seen how unrevealing Cheney usually was.
   "Cheney comes back from the White House and tells nothing," Powell said.[92]

Presidential scholar James Pfiffner noted that Bush's dependence on a small group of close advisers is "not unlike the approach that other presidents have taken during times of war and crisis. John Kennedy had his executive committee during the Cuban missile crisis, and Lyndon Johnson depended on his 'Tuesday lunch group' for advice during the Vietnam War."[93] The problem is that such groups are particularly susceptible to the phenomenon of "groupthink," arising from a false sense of consensus.

In this regard, it is notable that the key decision makers shared a similar worldview. Baker, in particular, saw the conflict with Iraq in starkly realist terms. Like Thucydides, he pondered when "human volition and the wish to maintain peace give way to fate and the necessities demanded to prosecute war."[94] He and his colleagues saw the international system as inherently dangerous, and their role as using their "emotions and intuition" to find the best path through the thicket.[95] Deputy National Security Adviser (and later Director of Central Intelligence) Robert Gates shared the realist perspective; he firmly held to the view that the USSR was an "evil empire," and described the Cold War as a "glorious crusade."[96] Defense Secretary Cheney also had a conservative, realist outlook. When he was in Congress his "pet issues" included aid to the Nicaraguan contras and the threat posed by Soviet submarines.[97] Perhaps the only member of the Gang of Eight to hold a more nuanced view was Colin Powell, the "reluctant warrior." In his memoirs, Powell noted that he was heartened by the "reconciliations taking place around the globe, by a fundamental shift from chronic conflict to negotiated settlements," while taking account of the fact that "this is not going to be a world without war or conflict."[98]

Bush himself shared the realist view, reinforced by a sense of American righteousness. This conceptual framework, according to political psychologist Stephen Wayne, probably developed during Bush's World War II experience and strengthened his conviction that as president, he had a responsibility to combat evil abroad. "Bush saw and rationalized Saddam Hussein as the embodiment of evil," Wayne asserted, "and Hussein's actions as blatant aggression that needed to be reversed."[99] In addition, Wayne believed that Bush's psychological makeup, especially his need to counter perceived challenges to his strength and decisiveness, reinforced his predilection to use military force against Saddam.[100]

National Security Adviser Brent Scowcroft saw this common ideology as a strength of the administration's decision process. "President Bush put together a national security team that was generally like-minded. . . . That was one of the reasons we were effective; because we did have a general consensus. We were all facing in the same direction on national security issues."[101] Debate, according to Scowcroft, centered on means rather than ends. He noted that he and Powell were at opposite poles regarding the military option, but claimed that Powell never made his reservations known directly.[102]

Richard Haass, a political scientist who served as a senior Middle East adviser on Scowcroft's staff, described the administration's decision-making process as "carefully managed." According to Haass, "When I add up all of the meetings . . . there was an extraordinary amount of interaction and of structured consideration."[103] He noted, however, that this structure deteriorated as the war began, and became "messier" at the end. As the conflict drew to a close, the process, according to Haass, "was not quite as deliberative as it might have been because things happened rather suddenly."[104]

THE COUNSEL OF PRUDENCE

While Bush's leadership was resolute and his decision-making free of the internecine conflict that had plagued his predecessors Ronald Reagan and Jimmy Carter, there were clearly ways in which they could have been improved. Aristotle and Aquinas would have praised Bush's experience, knowledge of foreign affairs and selection of experienced advisers. They would have supported his decision to resist Saddam Hussein's aggression, but they would also have been concerned about the possibility of concealed motives. They would have criticized aspects of the decision, and counseled the president in particular to open up his process, to make more of an effort to understand his adversary and to consider more carefully both the immediate and the long-term consequences of his decisions. Among the suggestions Aristotle might have made are the following:

- Deliberateness: While agreeing that the president correctly assessed the gravity of the Gulf crisis, he would have been uncomfortable with Bush's early public statement of intent to reverse the Iraqi invasion. He would have urged a more systematic connecting of ends and means, as well as a period of reflection for the president to examine his own motives and presumptions.

- Self-control: Aristotle also would have urged the president to be more moderate in his public statements and to refrain from personalizing the conflict with Saddam. He would have suggested that Bush reflect on the complex interactions between international order, national interest and personal ambition. He would have urged the president to avoid "passionate attachment" to his initial policy preferences, and to recognize that his self-interest made his outlook inherently biased in favor of rapid, forceful action.

Thomas Aquinas might have suggested that George Bush pay more attention to the following aspects of practical wisdom:

- Memory: Bush would have profited from a deeper study of the history of Iraq and its neighbors, in particular of the colonial legacy, the history of claims regarding Kuwait and the ethnic and religious rivalries in Iraq and the region more broadly. He also could have probed Saddam's personality and the roots of his behavior more deeply, rather than dismissing him as a madman or a Hitler. Had Bush done so, he might have understood his adversary as a man with a narrow worldview, who possessed an unusual drive to control events and a messianic vision.[105] This learning would not have been for the purpose of empathizing with Saddam's aggression, but rather for a more complete understanding of the impact of coalition actions on the Iraqi leader and on the various resistance groups within his country. For example, Bush might have moderated his rhetoric, recognizing that Saddam was psychologically incapable of giving in to his threats, and might have been more cautious in implying American support for the Kurdish and Shiite resistance movements. He might also have anticipated more clearly some of Saddam's desperation moves, such as setting fire to the Kuwaiti oil fields, and found ways to forestall them.

- Teachableness: Probably the most significant suggestion that Aquinas might have given to Bush, as well as to his advisers, would be to cultivate the virtue of *docilitas*, openness to advice and information. Bush and his advisers preferred the comfort of a close working relationship to the messiness of encouraging alternative viewpoints and arguments. It is particularly noteworthy that their process left the examination of alternatives to war incomplete. Pfiffner notes that there are three systematic ways in which "groupthink" can be mitigated: "multiple advocacy," in which individuals or institutions are charged with proposing and defending points of view; creation of a formal policy development process that includes all options, their advantages and their disadvantages; and presidential insistence that all alternatives be examined, as John Kennedy did in the Cuban missile crisis.[106] None of these approaches was used by the Bush administration. The Department of State, the logical agency to recommend diplomacy and sanctions rather than military force, was effectively eliminated from the process because of Secretary of State Baker's views and style. And the one advocate of an alternative to war, Colin Powell, failed to press his case when he realized that the president was leaning decisively toward offensive military operations.

- Acumen: Aquinas probably would not have been surprised at the deterioration of the administration's decision-making toward the end of the war. He would have noted that Bush had failed to cultivate essential elements of normative prudence and was therefore lacking in acumen, the ability to reach rapid, correct judgments under urgent conditions. Thus, at the climax of the conflict, Bush was swayed by political and public relations considerations into calling a hasty cease-fire. He then failed to give adequate instructions to his field commander and urged the Iraqi resistance groups to overthrow Saddam, later leaving them exposed to the Iraqi leader's wrath and remaining might.

THE AFTERMATH

At this writing, Saddam remains in power. The United Nations sanctions are still in place, and Iraq resists disclosure and inspection of its weapons of mass destruction. Another round of warfare was narrowly averted in early 1998, when the UN secretary-general negotiated a modification of the regime for inspecting Iraqi weapons sites as U.S. and British forces were poised to strike. The Kurdish and Shiite rebellions have been crushed. Iraq is still a major irritant to U.S. policy and to the international system, an unfinished piece of business in a strategic region of the globe.

Would it have turned out differently if the Bush administration had adhered more closely to the standards of just-war theory and been more prudent in its decision-making? This is not at all clear, and such a counterfactual analysis would not have been particularly relevant to Aristotle, Augustine or Aquinas. They would have argued that the measure of right in such a situation was in following the duty to use force only when necessary and proportionate to the situation, and to deliberate wisely, with due attention to unpleasant information and advice. Perhaps the political outcome would have been similar, but the cost in human life and ecological devastation could have been lower if the policy process had made more explicit use of the counsels of just-war theory and normative prudence.

Possibly the explanation for Bush's approach to the war was inadvertently telegraphed by Secretary of State Baker. While expressing his admiration for Thucydides' political realism, he cited the Greek scholar's conclusion that the Peloponnesian War was caused by the growth of Athenian power and the fear that engendered in Sparta. Could it be that the cause of the Gulf War, and the reason that it was "imperfectly just," were the growth of Saddam Hussein's power and the (political) fear that engendered in George Bush?

NOTES

1. Bob Woodward, *The Commanders* (New York: Simon & Schuster, 1991), pp. 199–204. The narrative on the evolution of the 1990–91 crisis and war draws heavily on this journalistic account, as well as several other sources. Michael R. Gordon and Bernard E. Trainor, *The Generals' War: The Inside Story of the Conflict in the Gulf* (New York: Little, Brown, 1995), provides a meticulously documented narrative of decision-making and military operations. Several key policy makers and commanders have published memoirs, including James A. Baker, *The Politics of Diplomacy* (New York: G.P. Putnam's Sons, 1995); Robert M. Gates, *From the Shadows* (New York: Simon & Schuster, 1996); Colin L. Powell, *My American Journey* (New York: Random House, 1995); and H. Norman Schwarzkopf, *It Doesn't Take a Hero* (New York: Bantam Books, 1992). Useful histories of the war are Lawrence Freedman and Efraim Karsh, *The Gulf Conflict 1990–91* (Princeton: Princeton University Press, 1993), and U.S. News & World Report, *Triumph Without Victory* (New York: Times Books, 1992). A number of important documents and contemporaneous articles are reproduced in Micah L. Sifry and Christopher Cerf, eds., *The Gulf War Reader: History, Documents, Opinions* (New York: Times Books, 1991). These various sources provide a consistent picture of the general evolution of the crisis but differ in their portrayal of some of the key decisions. In general, I have given the greatest weight to the firsthand accounts and to Gordon and Trainor's book, because they have the benefit of several years of research and draw extensively on primary documents and on-the-record interviews, including correspondence from President Bush and his closest advisers.

2. "The Glaspie Transcript: Saddam Meets the U.S. Ambassador," in Sifry and Cerf, *The Gulf War Reader*, pp. 128–30.

3. Gordon and Trainor, *The Generals' War*, p. 11.

4. Ibid., p. 7.

5. Woodward, *The Commanders*, p. 229.

6. Gordon and Trainor, *The Generals' War*, p. 36.

7. Baker, *The Politics of Diplomacy*, p. 279.

8. Woodward, *The Commanders*, p. 260.

9. Ibid., p. 261.

10. Powell, *My American Journey*, p. 467.

11. Gordon and Trainor, *The Generals' War*, p. 49.

12. Schwarzkopf, *It Doesn't Take a Hero*, p. 305.

13. George Bush, "In Defense of Saudi Arabia," speech given August 8, 1990, in Sifry and Cerf, *The Gulf War Reader*, p. 198.

14. United Nations Resolution 661, August 6, 1990, in U.S. News & World Report, *Triumph Without Victory*, pp. 416–18.

15. Woodward, *The Commanders*, p. 282.

16. Powell, *My American Journey*, p. 467.

17. J. Bryan Hehir, "Baghdad as Target: An Order to Be Refused," *Commonweal* 117, no. 18 (October 26, 1990): 117–18.

18. Powell, *My American Journey*, p. 485.

19. Woodward, *The Commanders*, p. 42.

20. Powell, *My American Journey*, p. 480.

21. Woodward, *The Commanders*, p. 307.

22. Baker, *The Politics of Diplomacy*, p. 302.

23. Woodward, *The Commanders*, p. 301.

24. Powell, *My American Journey*, p. 489.

25. Woodward, *The Commanders*, p. 343.

26. Ibid., pp. 319, 337.

27. Ibid., pp. 334–35.

28. Baker, *The Politics of Diplomacy*, p. 327.

29. Powell, *My American Journey*, p. 493.

30. Baker, *The Politics of Diplomacy*, p. 333.

31. William J. Crowe, Jr., "Give Sanctions a Chance," testimony before the Senate Armed Services Committee, November 28, 1990, in Sifry and Cerf, *The Gulf War Reader*, p.234.

32. Kimberly Elliott, Gary Hufbauer and Jeffrey Schott, "Sanctions Work: The Historical Record," in Sifry and Cerf, *The Gulf War Reader*, pp. 255–59.

33. Stephen J. Solarz, "The Case for Intervention," in Sifry and Cerf, *The Gulf War Reader*, p. 276.

34. Woodward, *The Commanders*, p. 351.

35. U.S. News & World Report, *Triumph Without Victory*, p. 207.

36. Gordon and Trainor, *The Generals' War*, p. 197.

37. Ibid., p. 344; Woodward, *The Commanders*, p. 362.

38. Gordon and Trainor, *The Generals' War*, p. 190.

39. Ibid.

40. Ibid., p. 192.

41. Ibid., p. 314.

42. Schwarzkopf, *It Doesn't Take a Hero*, p. 435.

43. Ramsey Clark, *The Fire This Time: U.S. War Crimes in the Gulf* (New York: Thunder's Mouth Press, 1992), p. 70.

44. Gordon and Trainor, *The Generals' War*, p. 503.

45. Schwarzkopf, *It Doesn't Take a Hero*, p. 451.

46. Ibid., pp. 354–62.

47. Powell, *My American Journey*, pp. 520–21.

48. Gordon and Trainor, *The Generals' War*, p. 416.

49. Schwarzkopf, *It Doesn't Take a Hero*, p. 489.

50. U.S. News & World Report, *Triumph Without Victory*, p. 403.

51. Robert Tucker and David Hendrickson, *The Imperial Temptation* (New York: Council on Foreign Relations, 1992), p. 74.

52. U.S. News & World Report, *Triumph Without Victory*, pp. 406–8.

53. Tucker and Hendrickson, *The Imperial Temptation*, p. 75.

54. Clark, *The Fire This Time*, p. 209.

55. Ibid.

56. U.S. News & World Report, *Triumph Without Victory*, pp. 409–10.

57. Ibid., p. 410.

58. Clark, *The Fire This Time*, p. 211.

59. Tucker and Hendrickson, *The Imperial Temptation*, p. 77.

60. Farouk El-Baz and R. M. Makharita, eds., *The Gulf War and the Environment* (Lausanne, Switzerland: Gordon and Breach Science Publishers, 1994), p. 196.

61. Gordon C. Zahn, "An Infamous Victory," *Commonweal* 118, no. 11 (June 1, 1991): 366.

62. George Weigel, "From Last Resort to End Game," in *But Was It Just? Reflections on the Morality of the Persian Gulf War*, David E. DeCosse, ed. (New York: Doubleday, 1992), p. 29.

63. James Turner Johnson, "Was the Gulf War a Just War?" in *Just War and the Gulf War*, James Turner Johnson and George Weigel, eds. (Washington, DC: Ethics and Public Policy Center, 1991), p. 30.

64. Ibid., p. 33.

65. Paul Baumann, "Limits of the Just War," *Commonweal* 118, no. 5 (March 8, 1991): 150.

66. Clark, *The Fire This Time*, pp. 264–65.

67. Ibid., p. 29.

68. Ibid., pp. 62–64.

69. Ibid., p. 70.

70. Ibid., p. 44.

71. Ibid., p. 53.

72. Ibid., p. 83.

73. Zahn, "An Infamous Victory," p. 366.

74. Ibid., pp. 366–67.

75. Ibid., p. 367.

76. Ibid., p. 368. Italics in original.

77. "Modern War and the Christian Conscience," in DeCosse, *But Was It Just?*, p. 117.

78. Ibid.

79. These include Jean Bethke Elshtain, "Just War as Politics: What the Gulf War Told Us About Contemporary American Life," in DeCosse, *But Was It Just?*, pp 43–60; Stanley Hauerwas, "Whose Just War? Which Peace?" in DeCosse, *But Was It Just?*, pp 83–106; David C. Hendrickson, "In Defense of Realism: A Commentary on *Just and Unjust Wars*," *Ethics and International Affairs* 11 (1997): 19–53; Brien Hallett, "The Just War Tradition: A Reconsideration," in *Engulfed in War: Just War and the Persian Gulf*, Brien Hallett, ed. (Honolulu: University of Hawaii, 1991), pp. 3–20; Meredith L. Kilgore, "Ethics and War in the Persian Gulf," in Hallett, *Engulfed in War*, pp. 79–92; Dennis Menos, *Arms over Diplomacy: Reflections on the Persian Gulf War* (Westport, CT: Praeger, 1992); Jeff McMahan and Robert McKim, "The Just War and the Gulf War," *Canadian Journal of Philosophy* 23, no. 4 (December 1993): 501–41; Sari Nussibeh, "Can Wars Be Just? A Palestinian Viewpoint of the Gulf War," in DeCosse, *But Was It Just?*, pp. 61–82; Jeffrey Record, *Hollow Victory* (New York: Brassey's, 1993); Tucker and Hendrickson, *The Imperial Temptation*; Bruce Watson, "Cardinal John J. O'Connor on the 'Just War' Controversy," in *Military Lessons of the Gulf War*, Bruce W. Watson, ed. (London: Greenhill Books, 1991), pp. 194–201; Donald A. Wells, "Can Modern Wars Be Just," in Hallett, *Engulfed in War*, pp. 21–42; Roger Williamson, "Engulfed in War: On the Ambivalence of the Just War Tradition During the Gulf Crisis," in Hallett, *Engulfed in War*, pp. 45–78; and several participants in a United States Institute of Peace symposium on Christian, Muslim and Jewish attitudes toward force after the Gulf War. The proceedings were published as David R. Smock, ed., *Religious Perspectives on War* (Washington, DC: United States Institute of Peace, 1992).

80. Williamson, "Engulfed in War," pp. 63–65.

81. This group includes: John P. Langan, "An Imperfectly Just War," *Commonweal* 118, no. 11 (June 1, 1991): 361–65; J. Bryan Hehir, "Just Cause? Yes," *Commonweal* 119, no. 4 (February 28, 1992): 8–9; and Kenneth L. Vaux, *Ethics and the Gulf War: Religion, Rhetoric and Righteousness* (Boulder, CO: Westview Press, 1992).

82. Langan, "An Imperfectly Just War," p. 365.

83. Michael Walzer, *Just and Unjust Wars* (New York, Basic Books, 1977), p. 62.

84. Ibid.

85. Ibid., p. 88.

86. Ibid., p. 153.

87. Ibid., p. 155.

88. Powell, *My American Journey*, p. 518.

89. Gates, *From the Shadows*, p. 454.

90. Woodward, *The Commanders*, p. 320.

91. Baker, *The Politics of Diplomacy*, p. 31.

92. Woodward, *The Commanders*, p. 37.

93. James P. Pfiffner, "The Presidency and War Making" in *The Presidency and the Persian Gulf War*, Marcia Lynne Whicker, James P. Pfiffner and Raymond A. Moore, eds. (Westport, CT: Praeger, 1993), p. 7.

94. Baker, *The Politics of Diplomacy*, p. 345.

95. Ibid.

96. Gates, *From the Shadows*, p. 574.

97. Woodward, *The Commanders*, p. 67.

98. Powell, *My American Journey*, p. 605.

99. Stephen J. Wayne, "President Bush Goes to War," in *The Political Psychology of the Gulf War*, Stanley A. Renshon, ed. (Pittsburgh: University of Pittsburgh Press, 1993), p. 39.

100. Ibid., p. 36.

101.   Quoted in David Mervyn, *George Bush and the Guardian Presidency* (New York: St. Martin's Press, 1996), p. 188.

102. Ibid.

103. Ibid., p. 187.

104. Ibid.

105.   Jerrold M. Post, "Saddam Hussein's Leadership During the Gulf Crisis," in Renshon, *The Political Psychology of the Gulf War*, p. 57.

106. Pfiffner, "The Presidency and War Making," pp. 7–8.

4

The Limits of Humanitarian Obligation: The International Community and the Crisis in Burundi

THE TRAGEDY OF BURUNDI

Burundi is a poor, landlocked African country slightly larger than the state of Maryland. It is bordered on the north by Rwanda, on the east by Tanzania and on the west by the Democratic Republic of the Congo (formerly Zaire) and Lake Tanganyika.[1] It is located just south of the equator, in the Central African Rift Valley. Although it has deposits of minerals, Burundi is dependent on its coffee crop for 80 percent of its foreign exchange earnings. More than 90 percent of Burundi's population of about 6 million persons is engaged in subsistence agriculture. The industrial sector is minuscule, with fewer than 100 enterprises employing a little more than 6,000 people. As of the mid-1990s, Burundi's per capita Gross Domestic Product stood at $200, making it the eighth poorest country in the world.

Life in Burundi is, to use Hobbes's famous phrase, "nasty, brutish and short." Crowding is endemic. Burundi's population density of 223 persons per square kilometer is exceeded among the less-developed countries only by Bangladesh, Haiti and several small island nations. Life expectancy is 38 years for men and 42 years for women. Infant mortality is 112 per 1,000. The Center for International Health Information estimates that 20 percent of the urban population is HIV-positive. Half of the rural population lacks access to potable water and adequate sanitation. Murder, destruction of land and property and displacement of population may face those who survive the difficulties posed by the land and the primitive infrastructure.

Burundi is a complex society in which ethnic identities, class status and family connections overlap to create myriad frictions and rivalries. There are three major ethnic groups: the Hutu, a Bantu people, currently about 85 percent of the population, who migrated to the region from about 500 BC to AD 1000; the Tutsi, a people of Ethiopian origin, currently about 14 percent of the population, who came to Burundi beginning in the 14th century; and the Twa, a pygmoid people presumed to be the oldest inhabitants of the area. The classification of persons by ethnic background is complicated and sometimes is obscured by the deliberate manipulation of myths by politicians and intellectuals on all sides of a long-standing ethnic conflict.

Kingdom and Colony

From the time of the Tutsi arrival until its annexation as a colony of Germany in the late 19th century, Burundi was ruled by a succession of independent *mwami*, or kings. Throughout the time of German colonial rule, the emphasis was on military force. Little attention was paid to civil administration. Belgium assumed responsibility for Burundi following World War I, and administered Burundi and Rwanda (then known collectively as Rwanda-Urundi) under a League of Nations mandate. As a protecting power, Belgium was charged primarily with the maintenance of peace and order, and with promoting social progress. Preparing the nation for ultimate independence was not part of the agenda. As had been the case under German rule, Burundi under Belgium was a stratified society with political influence and educational opportunities restricted largely to the Tutsi elite.

Instability in Independence

Following World War II, Rwanda-Urundi became a United Nations Trust Territory. In 1961, limited self-rule was granted to Burundi and elections were scheduled. By June 1961, 23 political parties were officially registered, of which the most important represented two of the most powerful Tutsi clans. Crown Prince Louis Rwagasore, head of the larger Tutsi party, the National Party of Unity and Progress (UPRONA), led it to a landslide victory in legislative elections in September 1961. He was assassinated within a month, a result of a plot by Tutsi opponents. This was the first of no less than six extraconstitutional changes of government in Burundi's postcolonial history.

Within a month of the assassination, the conflict among Tutsi factions erupted into the beginnings of large-scale ethnic conflict. Partly this was related to the general explosion of ethnic tensions that accompanied independence in a number of African countries. Another cause was the reaction of both Burundi's Hutu majority and its Tutsi minority to the overthrow of the monarchy in neighboring Rwanda in January 1961. Finally, an internal crisis in UPRONA following the assassination of Rwagasore exacerbated political tensions.

Through the 1970s and 1980s, Burundi's political instability continued. In 1972, a Hutu-led rebellion erupted in southern Burundi. The details of the plot are complex and confusing. The Hutu claim a Tutsi conspiracy, and the Tutsi maintain that there was outside provocation. But the insurgency sparked a cycle of violence and counterviolence that, by most accounts, left between 50,000 and 100,000 people, mostly Hutu, dead. Military coups occurred in 1976 and 1986. In 1988, a Hutu rebellion broke out in the northern part of the country, leading to the slaughter of tens of thousands. Coup plots were uncovered in 1989 and 1992. Political parties and factions proliferated. UPRONA gained adherents among the Hutu, though it continued to be Tutsi-dominated. The Party for the Liberation of the Hutu People

(PALIPEHUTU), created in the refugee camps in the 1980s, promoted Hutu ascendency. A third group, the Burundi Democratic Front (FRODEBU), was organized in 1983 by a Hutu intellectual and sought to foster an image of openness and nationalism.

Violence in the 1990s

On June 1, 1993, national elections were held, and FRODEBU's Melchior Ndadaye became president, the first Hutu head of state in the nation's history. His predecessor, Major Pierre Buyoya, became the first president of Burundi to leave office voluntarily (and indeed was one of the few in all of postcolonial Africa to do so). From the outset, the Ndadaye government was plagued with problems—a massive influx of returning refugees; vestiges of Tutsi and UPRONA control of the army, the press and the judiciary; and ever-present economic challenges. On October 21, 1993, troops of the Tutsi-dominated army attacked the presidential palace and captured Ndadaye and other senior officials. The president was executed the next day. As the news spread, a spasm of revenge killings took place, with tens of thousands of Tutsi, as well as Hutu supporters of UPRONA, slaughtered.

It was not until February 1994 that an interim government was formed under President Cyprien Ntayamira. In April of that year, he was killed, along with the president of Rwanda, in a suspicious plane crash at Kigali, Rwanda—an event that sparked mass killings in that neighboring country. Following intense political maneuvering, a convention of government was signed by interim President Sylvestre Ntibantunganya and representatives of the major political parties in September 1994. Real power, however, continued to lie with the army and UPRONA.

In the period after the convention was signed, intragovernment rivalry increased, and the violent activities of insurgents and militias multiplied. The sheer number of groups and individuals vying for position in Burundi was bewildering. New Hutu insurgent groups sprang up, of which the most important was the National Committee for the Defense of Democracy (CNDD) and its military arm, the Front for the Defense of Democracy (FDD), under former Interior Minister Leonard Nyangoma. Nyangoma's group carried out numerous attacks on the army and Tutsi civilians, creating a major security problem for the authorities. On the Tutsi side, in addition to the army, new extremist militia groups were formed.

The government of interim President Ntibantunganya faced major challenges in 1995. Violence escalated. Ntibantunganya warned in his 1996 New Year's address that the country was on the verge of collapse. In an address on April 25, Ntibantunganya condemned violence, and announced a major reorganization of the security forces and judicial system. He also renewed the call for a national debate on ending violence and forming a stable system of government[2]

Human Rights Abuses in Burundi

Every conceivable type of human rights abuse was taking place in Burundi in 1996. One reporter estimated that "the massacres may have claimed as many as 100,000 or

200,000 Tutsi lives, possibly a third of all the Tutsi in Burundi."[3] The most frequently cited estimate of killings since the October 1993 coup, however, was "in excess of 100,000." This estimate by Amnesty International[4] was adopted by the U.S. Department of State in its annual human rights report.[5]

Massive numbers of people were displaced by the violence in Burundi. In a speech to a regional gathering in Burundi in February 1995, the UN high commissioner for refugees referred to "the massive internal and external displacement of 3.8 million people," including refugees from both Rwanda and Burundi.[6] Amnesty International in 1995 estimated that a total of 700,000 refugees from Rwanda and Burundi were in Zaire, and another 1,000,000 in Tanzania.[7] Of these, some 200,000 were said to be from Burundi.[8] The UN secretary-general, citing assessments from the field, referred in May 1996 to more than 300,000 displaced persons. The report, noting the difficulty of such estimates and characterizing them as conservative guesses, went on to state that more than 140,000 Burundian refugees were in Zaire, and that 10,000 had fled from Burundi to Tanzania so far in 1996.[9] The refugee camps became safe havens for tens of thousands of insurgents, including Nyangoma's FDD. Major attacks from Zaire into Burundi and Rwanda were conducted in the spring of 1996, as were incursions from Rwanda into Zaire.

The International Response

After the 1993 coup, the international community sent a steady stream of envoys to assess the situation in Burundi. Following the 1994 genocide in Rwanda, concern about Burundi rose, and the United Nations began to urge planning for an international intervention force. In February 1996, Secretary-General Boutros Boutros-Ghali issued a pessimistic report that took the international community to task. "It is unrealistic," he said, "to expect a handful of small-scale measures to have any real impact on the fundamental problems of Burundi." In this report Boutros-Ghali set forth for the first time the details of a potential humanitarian intervention force. His proposed force included some 25,000 troops deployed by air and sea, including parachute, motorized and mechanized units; light tanks; artillery and combat engineers; and logistic and administrative units. He also called for close air support and attack helicopters.[10] Boutros-Ghali made it clear that his intention was that the force could be deployed over the objections of the Burundi government. Its purpose was to prevent human rights abuses from erupting into a threat to international peace, as authorized under Article VII of the UN Charter. The intervention would later be replaced by a peacekeeping force authorized under Article VI, with the agreement of Burundi's government and opposition forces. Western leaders indicated general support for an intervention, but the planning became mired in squabbling between the United States and France and among U.S. government agencies.

African leaders became increasingly concerned, and, frustrated by the inability and unwillingness of the factions in Burundi to come to a political accommodation, took action to resolve the conflict. The most significant regional initiative was led by former Tanzanian President Julius Nyerere. In 1996, two rounds of negotiations were conducted at Mwanza, Tanzania, involving the 12 parties that had signed the convention of government, but not Nyangoma and the CNDD. Disagreements about the scope and focus of the discussions led to failure of the talks, as well as to subsequent attempts to promote dialogue among the warring factions. Subsequently, Nyerere became more and more pessimistic, and on several occasions talked publicly about the need for intervention.[11]

Another Military Coup

In late June and July 1996, after a brief period of cautious optimism, the situation in Burundi began to deteriorate rapidly. At the end of June, in Arusha, Tanzania, Burundi's leaders and regional heads of state called for outside intervention. In a rare show of unanimity, the president and the prime minister both joined the call, and agreed that a technical committee, chaired by Tanzania, would work out the details. Once this became known in Burundi, however, extremist leaders there denounced the proposal, and their followers erupted in violent demonstrations. The army expelled thousands of Rwandan refugees from camps in Burundi, charging that they were supporting Hutu rebels. In reaction, Nyangoma's insurgents massacred some 300 civilians.

At the memorial services for the victims on July 24, Ntibantunganya was stoned, and later took refuge at the residence of the American ambassador, where he remained for nearly a year. At that point, party leader Charles Mukasi declared that UPRONA had withdrawn from the government, and that the convention of government was void. FRODEBU officials subsequently echoed this assertion, but others maintained that the convention could not be dissolved without concurrence of all the parties. While outside powers declared that they would not recognize any government that came to power by force, and renewed planning for an intervention, the situation inside Burundi became increasingly chaotic.

On July 25, the army took control. All political activities were suspended. Major Buyoya, who had been maneuvering behind the scenes since his defeat in the 1993 elections, was named president. A day after assuming power, Buyoya offered to talk with the rebels if they would renounce force. But CNDD representatives dismissed the offer and pledged to step up their fight. In response, Tutsi youth rushed to join militias.

The international community condemned the coup, but action was slow in coming. Consultations about contingency planning continued, but no nation volunteered to take the leadership role. The United States had begun to accelerate contingency planning even before the coup, and sent military planners to East Africa in mid-July. Immediately following the July 25 coup, the U.S. State Department stated again that the United States would not recognize any government that came to power by force. The White House press spokesman said that the United States would propose an international humanitarian mission at the United Nations, but—according to knowledgeable diplomats—U.S. planning continued to be hampered by internal disagreements over the size and cost of an intervention force. Other nations in a position to lead an intervention, France and Belgium, stayed on the sidelines. Belgium alerted troops, but only to evacuate its nationals in Burundi. Only Zambia, Malawi and Chad offered soldiers for an international force. A leading African affairs analyst noted, "The international community is divided. There isn't the concerted effort to say: 'All right, we move in.'"

The most tangible response to the coup came from regional leaders. On July 31, at a meeting at Arusha, the neighboring states agreed to clamp economic sanctions on Burundi, in an effort to restore a semblance of democracy. According to officials who attended the meeting, the objective of the sanctions was to give Buyoya an incentive to enter into negotiations with his rivals, and a rationale that he could use with his Tutsi supporters to explain such a change in policy. But if the Arusha parties thought they could induce a change in policy so directly, they were mistaken. Buyoya took cosmetic measures, including appointment of a Hutu prime minister and dismissal of the army chief of staff who had been implicated in the 1993 coup, but he remained firmly in control of the political machinery. Buyoya offered to talk to the CNDD, but only if they first laid down their arms—a condition that he surely knew was unacceptable.

The basic dilemma facing the international community was that while sanctions might eventually induce Buyoya to move toward negotiations, the ensuing economic hardship could in the meantime increase the propensity for violence. A month after the coup, Amnesty International released an estimate that some 6,000 Burundians had been killed since Buyoya took power. U.S. officials were skeptical of the figures, but reiterated their condemnation of the violence. Boutros-Ghali was more alarmed, warning that the international community had to be prepared for the possibility of genocide and expressing concern about the limited success in gaining financial and military commitments for an intervention force.

On September 28, officials of the Clinton administration announced a plan to organize, train and equip an African intervention force of 10,000 troops, and to assist in its deployment to trouble spots such as Burundi. The plan called for a $25 million investment in 1997, about half of which would be funded by the United States and half by its European allies. Assistant Secretary of State George Moose embarked on a trip to Europe and Africa to drum up support. Support in the Republican-controlled Congress was lacking, however, and some observers considered the size and timing of the effort to be too little and too late.[12]

In early October, Secretary of State Warren Christopher traveled to Africa, culminating a series of visits to the continent by senior officials. While his broader objectives were to underscore the place of Africa in U.S. foreign policy, he also attempted to garner support for the African Crisis Response Force and participated in regional discussions on Burundi. Response to Christopher's initiatives was mixed. Organization of African Unity (OAU) Secretary-General Salim Ahmed Salim was positive. Ethiopia and Mali endorsed the plan almost immediately. South Africa's President Nelson Mandela was unenthusiastic, and French officials blasted the proposal as a potential encroachment on Paris's traditional sphere of influence. Nigeria also opposed the African peace force.

Zaire Erupts

Shortly after Christopher's departure from Africa, the situation in the region underwent a dramatic and catastrophic change. In mid-October, while Zaire's president, Mobutu Sese Seko, was in Switzerland for treatment of prostate cancer, fighting broke out between ethnic Tutsi rebels and Zairean troops in eastern Zaire. The rebels were members of a group called the Banyamulenge, descendants of Tutsi farmers who emigrated to Zaire in the 17th century and had systematically been repressed by the Mobutu government. As the rebel forces gained important objectives, Hutu refugees by the hundreds of thousands abandoned the camps in eastern Zaire and began moving into the countryside. Meeting in Nairobi, Kenya, African leaders called for the UN Security Council to deploy a military force to assist an estimated 1.1 million refugees facing famine and disease. Western and African diplomats traded assessments, but failed to come up with a concrete plan to aid the refugees and stabilize the situation. France proposed creation of a multinational force and was joined by Spain, but the United States and other countries were skeptical of the plan, provoking a French charge of "spinelessness."

Frustrated by the lack of action, Canada on November 12 announced its willingness to take the lead in organizing an international intervention force. Prime Minister Jean Chretien said, "To not act at all would be immoral. . . . We may not be a superpower, but we are a nation that speaks on the international scene with a great moral authority. Now is the time to use that authority to avert a disaster." [13] The United States quickly agreed to provide troops, and Zaire, facing continuing rebel gains, indicated openness to a U.S. intervention. Burundi refused to assist until the embargo was lifted. Some nongovernmental organizations (NGOs) also opposed the plan on the grounds that it did not do enough to confront the violent forces in the region. On November 15, the Security Council approved the establishment of a temporary multinational force. But Pentagon planners made it known that they would insist on a formal cease-fire before deploying U.S. troops in eastern Zaire—a condition unlikely to be accepted by the rebel forces.

Suddenly, the situation changed dramatically once more, as hundreds of thousands of Rwandan Hutu refugees changed direction and streamed back into Rwanda. The unanticipated movement threw the planning for an international intervention into a turmoil, as nations seized on the new situation as a rationale for scaling back their commitments. Disagreements broke out between aid officials and governments about the number and location of the refugees still in Zaire, but Canadian leaders and military commanders continued pressing for a variety of possible missions. At the end of November, Canadian General Baril, commander of the proposed force, indicated that a consensus had been reached to deploy a neutral force to facilitate delivery of supplies and to assist in the voluntary repatriation of refugees. The United States agreed to a plan to base an aid mission in Entebbe, Uganda, and indicated that the 400 troops deployed earlier probably could handle the mission. By December, the crisis in Zaire had disappeared from the front pages.

Back in Burundi

With the attention of the world focused on Zaire, the political situation in Burundi continued to stagnate while the violence continued, on a scale that was difficult to estimate. Neighboring states continued the sanctions, but they had no measurable effect on the government or the key rebel groups. In mid-October 1996, the prime minister indicated that the sanctions had cost Burundi about 1 percent of its Gross National Product. The foreign minister amplified the statement at the United Nations, reporting a 30 percent decline in food production and a similar drop in the industrial sector. Inflation, he said, was running at 40 percent.

Aid organizations expressed continuing concern about the impact of sanctions on humanitarian relief, but the figures they provided were not as dramatic as those of the Burundian government. According to UN officials, total food production fell about 3 percent in 1996, with significant shortages in the northern parts of the country. The World Food Program reported in December that the number of displaced people being fed in Burundi had doubled to about 80,000, and that food supplies were nearly exhausted.

One indirect effect of the sanctions was an increase in uncertainty about the scale of violence in Burundi. With most reporters filing their stories from Nairobi, and essentially no human rights observers on the ground, reports of violence became more sporadic. Moreover, many reports came from either the government or the rebels, making it difficult to ascertain their validity. Reports of clashes between government troops and rebels surfaced every few weeks during the fall of 1996. In late October, the Tutsi military governor of Cibitoke province was assassinated.

On October 31, Boutros-Ghali condemned the violence and asserted that there had been more than 10,000 casualties since the July coup. (A Burundi government spokesman said that the figure was greatly exaggerated.) In November, Amnesty International reported numerous massacres of Burundian refugees returning from Zaire. It condemned not only the government but also CNDD, PALIPEHUTU and other opposition groups. In December, security forces reportedly massacred more than 500 Hutu civilians. The CNDD and some religious sources claimed that over 3,000 civilians were killed by the Tutsi-dominated army in December alone. In January 1997, army forces allegedly killed 126 Hutu refugees fleeing a detention center.

The Situation in 1997

As 1997 began, political influence in Burundi remained in the hands of the extremists. Buyoya held political consultations in response to international pressure, but remained adamant in his refusal to talk with Nyangoma unless he renounced violence. International concern centered on Zaire, where army forces, reportedly augmented by foreign troops and mercenaries, began a major offensive against rebel forces. The new UN secretary-general, Kofi Annan, appointed another special envoy to the region and gave his endorsement to the U.S.-proposed African Crisis Response Force. In the United States, however, the prospects for leadership on humanitarian intervention became muddied as a new national security team took office. Secretary of State Madeleine Albright gave only passing attention to Africa in her first press conference, and Secretary of Defense William Cohen made clear that he favored humanitarian intervention only "from time to time" and preferred to focus U.S. forces on defending vital interests.[14] National Security Adviser Anthony Lake, a proponent of humanitarian operations, withdrew as a candidate for the position of director of Central Intelligence (DCI). His NSC post was taken by Sandy Berger, who had no track record of promoting intervention, and the DCI position went to George Tenet, a veteran of congressional staffs and a specialist in arms control.

The U.S.-sponsored African Crisis Response Force project was downgraded to an "initiative" as support remained lukewarm. Buyoya continued to press for an easing of sanctions, and Kenya responded by permitting more petroleum imports. In mid-1997, the international community learned that there had been secret negotiations in Rome between members of the military government and representatives of the principal guerrilla groups. The talks, sponsored by a Catholic lay organization, the Community of Saint Egidio, were controversial among governments and NGOs. Some supported the start of a dialogue, while others thought the talks gave legitimacy to the insurgents and would spark further violence.

The military government in Burundi continued its policy of "regrouping" rural Hutus into camps. An attempt to resume the formal peace talks at Arusha fizzled in September. Opposition politicians and extremist groups criticized the process, and Buyoya pulled out at the last minute, alleging that the meeting had not been adequately planned. International attention focused on Zaire (now renamed Congo), where rebel forces under Laurent Kabila overthrew Mobutu, who died shortly after his ouster. The government dragged its feet on collaboration with a UN human rights team sent to investigate reports of rebel massacres. At the end of the year, fighting between Burundian rebels and the army continued, and incidents of civilian casualties were reported with depressing frequency.

The Gordian Knot

What accounted for the confusion and delays in international action on Burundi? One explanation is the sheer complexity of the situation. The crisis in Burundi was devastating in its scope and harshness. Underlying the crisis was a complex knot of tensions and disagreements that prevented political leaders, both within and outside Burundi, from taking effective action:

- Within Burundi, relationships among Tutsi, Hutu and their subgroups exploded into violence in the postcolonial period, partly because of historic injustices but also because the colonial powers perpetuated these injustices and failed to prepare indigenous leaders for independence. The ensuing murders began a cycle of revenge and retribution that now pervades the society.

- As a result of a series of coups and countercoups, these internal tensions were being manipulated and exacerbated by political leaders and groups bent on promoting their own agendas. These efforts were abetted by intellectuals who promulgated competing ethnic myths that inflamed hatred and dehumanized members of opposing ethnic groups, the essential psychological basis for genocide.

- These traditional ethnic rivalries were compounded by tensions between and within the two principal parties, FRODEBU and UPRONA, and between the army and the members of the former civilian administration. Politicians from both sides contributed to the violence by supporting insurgent and militia groups, and by using ethnic ideologies to fuel hatred in hope of securing political gains.

- Burundi's problems are embedded in those of a complex and volatile region. Regional leaders, particularly Zaire's Mobutu, exploited the refugee crisis to promote their own political agendas; and those who, like former Tanzanian President Nyerere, sought an end to the violence were frustrated by the recalcitrance of the warring parties.

- Attempts by the United Nations secretary-general to develop a military force for humanitarian intervention were hampered by disagreements within the Security Council, U.S. reluctance to take a leadership role and French obstructionism.

- U.S. decision-making on the Burundi crisis was complicated by disagreements among executive agencies, concern about congressional opposition, the appointment of a new national security team and focus on domestic issues.

- The levels of aid provided by lending institutions and governments were wholly inadequate, reflecting a contradiction between their desire for security for their assets and the realities of the total lack of security in Burundi.

- Private aid was also inadequate, and limited by the tense relationship between humanitarian relief organizations and UN officials in the region, which undercut efforts to improve the support of refugees beyond a minimal level.

As these tensions were being played out, thousands of Burundi's people were murdered or fell victim to malnutrition or disease.

THE MORAL ARGUMENTS

There are two basic categories of moral argumentation that are relevant to the international community's responsibilities in the Burundi crisis. First, there is the argument, proposed by modern authorities in the just-war tradition, that external intervention in the affairs of sovereign nations is an exceptional act that must be justified. In the debates over Burundi, many nation-states, including Burundi itself, France and the United States (especially its military institutions), have focused on this argument. Second, there is the view that people have a positive obligation to relieve suffering unless there are countervailing ethical considerations. Humanitarian and international organizations, as well as UN Secretary-General Boutros-Ghali and Canadian Prime Minister Chretien, have used this argument.

The Justification of Intervention

In the modern version of the just-war tradition, Michael Walzer includes in his "legalist paradigm" a provision to use force "to rescue peoples threatened with massacre."[15] He also would permit "humanitarian intervention" as a response to acts "that shock the moral conscience of mankind."[16]

Walzer's paradigm is controversial. Some have argued that humanitarian intervention is an oxymoron, while others believe that Walzer sets the threshold too high.[17] Critics such as Gerald Doppelt, Charles Beitz and David Luban argue that waiting for massacres to begin is an inadequate approach to protecting basic human rights. [18]

James Turner Johnson notes that there are two developments that should be taken into account in considering humanitarian intervention: the emergence of the United Nations and other international organizations to which nations cede some of their sovereignty, and the growth of internationally accepted definitions of human rights. He argues that these factors allow intervention in case of egregious violations of accepted rights, when sanctioned by the international community, even when carried out by a single nation.[19]

Bryan Hehir has put forward a provocative revisionist argument on intervention. He indicates that, because of the factors cited by Johnson and other developments, the international system may be entering a period of profound transition, of a sort historically associated with major wars. This disturbance reinforces a longer process of evolutionary erosion of the principle of sovereignty. This erosion has accelerated over the past 25 years under assault from normative claims for universal rights, the strategic logic of deterrence, economic interdependence and regional integration. This new stage in the international system, Hehir argues, requires new norms for intervention. One is that not only genocide, but also "ethnic cleansing" and the total collapse of states like Somalia, constitute justifiable conditions for military intervention. Another is that multilateral authorization should be a requirement.[20]

Codifying Humanitarian Intervention

In the last decade, international courts, UN agencies and scholarly gatherings have attempted to spell out the conditions that justify humanitarian intervention. In 1986, the International Court of Justice held that "there can be no doubt that the provision of strictly humanitarian aid to persons or forces in another country, whatever their political affiliations or objectives, cannot be regarded as unlawful intervention, or as in any other way contrary to international law."[21] In 1991, the UN General Assembly asserted a right of humanitarian intervention even without the consent of the state concerned, and a year later authorized the use of force to protect civilians in Somalia.[22]

The prescriptions that have been offered vary, but most are a logical extension of the just-war tradition. They all proceed from the presumption that adherence to the tradition's criterion of just intention, specifically the mitigation of human suffering, is essential. Those that list specific conditions that warrant intervention include, at a minimum, genocide, either explicitly or implicitly. They support the criteria long associated with the just-war tradition—that intervention must be ordered by a proper authority, be a last resort and be proportional to the evil it seeks to remedy. The proposed codes for intervention would observe neutrality and honor the integrity of the affected state, except when that would result in further abuses of basic rights.[23]

Objections to this putative consensus come from several sources. The first is developing countries that fear humanitarian intervention could be simply a new rationale for interference by the developed nations in their internal affairs. The second is aid officials who regard humanitarian activities as fundamentally consensual, and fear that armed intervention simply makes reconciliation harder. Moreover, these practitioners argue that military intervention may undercut or profoundly delay the development of civilian institutions on which the preservation of fundamental rights depends.[24] Others echo the skepticism of the pacifists regarding the extent to which nations can actually carry out a disinterested humanitarian intervention.[25] Finally, experienced practitioners argue that it is extremely difficult for a humanitarian intervention to meet the stringent just-war criterion of having a reasonable probability of success. Indeed, some assert that humanitarian aid, whether accompanied by the use of force or not, can sometimes exacerbate conflict and make the achievement of lasting peace problematic.[26]

The Argument from Beneficence

The second type of moral argument proceeds from the premise that there is a universal obligation to relieve suffering. A succinct statement of this principle is utilitarian Peter Singer's.[27] His argument is simply that because suffering is evil, people must relieve suffering whenever they are in a position to do so. Singer uses a simple analogy. He imagines that he comes across a child who is drowning. Surely, he says, it would be wrong not to rescue the child if we can do so. From this, he deduces a general principle: "If it is in our power to prevent something very bad happening, without thereby sacrificing anything of comparable moral significance, we ought to do it."[28]

The objections to this proposal hinge on two key aspects of Singer's proposition: the idea that we may have an obligation for situations that we did not cause, and the question of what circumstances, if any, could mitigate or eliminate the obligation.[29] On the first point, as John Harriss notes, causal responsibility can be both positive and negative. That is, when one is aware of threats to other people's lives, the failure to take available steps to avert those threats is unkind and unjust, unless there are countervailing considerations.[30]

Countervailing considerations can, in theory, either annul or outweigh the obligation to aid. (Even Kant considered the duty to rescue to be an "imperfect" one, to be interpreted narrowly, based on particular circumstances.[31]) For example, if one was incapable, say because of physical disability, of coming to another's aid, then the obligation would be annulled. Moreover, if aiding would involve a risk of death to the potential rescuer or to others, then it is conceivable that the obligation could be removed or at least mitigated. On the other hand, the mere fact that one does not currently face the same dire circumstances as those to be aided is not an acceptable excuse for inaction.[32]

It is also possible that limitations on resources and the presence of competing priorities could influence the obligation to aid those in distress. Under these circumstances, there is a need for a system of priorities, and one common one is to aid those closest, in either a physical or a relational sense, first.[33] Henry Shue argues, however, that one must not fall into the trap of thinking of "concentric circles" of obligation that become weaker at a distance from the agent. While conceding the priority of duties to "intimates," Shue sees no practical distinction between those in the next county and those on the next continent: a stranger is a stranger, and there is no reason to believe that duties to strangers diminish with distance.[34]

Gerard Elfstrom has analyzed the analogy between the obligations of individuals and those of nations. He notes that considerable perplexity surrounds the notion of a duty by those outside a nation-state to intervene in its affairs when they have no explicit authority to do so and have not contributed to the state of affairs about which they are concerned.[35] He argues that individuals acquire moral responsibility when they have done something to bring about the situation at hand, when they have accepted or acknowledged a specific commitment or when they have entered into a relationship (friendship, marriage) that inherently entails such an obligation. He notes as well that morally sensitive individuals are aware of both their responsibilities and their limitations.[36]

None of the three conditions that apply to individual moral obligation are, according to Elfstrom, operative on the international level. Most of the things that occur within states are not caused by other states; there are no specific authorities granted to international bodies to regulate events within countries; and nation-states do not readily lend themselves to the kinds of relationships that would entail moral obligation within the boundaries of another state.[37] Thus, he concludes that moral intervention in states is normally not justified, and is warranted only "in exceptional cases when serious and lasting harm is apt to befall the citizenry of a nation-state unless immediate action is taken by some outside party."[38]

Elfstrom's argument is attractive, but there appear to be several types of situations in which it would not be compelling. Clearly, colonialism is an example of a situation in which the current conditions within a state are affected by the actions of others. Second, there are many instances now in which either tacit or actual international commitments regarding international moral obligations have been codified. (The Universal Declaration of Human Rights is an example of the former, and the Organization for Security and Cooperation in Europe is one of the latter.) Finally, nations have claimed a right of intervention under mutual defense agreements and the United Nations has authorized intervention in Somalia, Haiti and Bosnia.

These objections notwithstanding, Elfstrom's position can be taken as a kind of "floor" for the argument from beneficence. Even with all of the restrictions that he notes, the assertion that preventing "serious and lasting" harm triggers an obligation of international intervention is at the core of the argument.

JUSTIFICATION, DUTY AND THE BURUNDI CRISIS

Thus two cogent arguments can be made regarding international intervention in Burundi. The argument from the legalist paradigm and the just-war tradition indicates that humanitarian intervention can be justified when necessary to halt or forestall genocide, provided the other conditions (just intention, competent authority, last resort, probability of success, proportionality) can be met. And the argument from beneficence seeks not only to justify, but also to obligate, the international community to act, if it has the capability, to prevent the "serious and lasting" harm of ethnic annihilation, unless there are countervailing circumstances. The key, then, to determining the limits of humanitarian obligation is whether or not genocide is taking place in Burundi.

Is It Genocide?

As of June 1996, the United States Department of State had concluded that genocide had been committed by both sides in the Burundi dispute. In its 1996 Human Rights Report, the department avoided using the term, but referred to "ethnically motivated extrajudicial killings" numbering more than 100,000. If there has been genocide, as was argued above, there is both the justification and a moral obligation for the international community to act. And, according to international law, if the actions in Burundi violate the 1951 United Nations Convention Against Genocide, then any state that is party to the convention may call upon the United Nations to act to prevent or punish acts of genocide.

Much weight, then, hinges on how genocide is defined and whether the violence in Burundi meets the definition. The term was first used by the jurist Raphel Lemkin in 1944 and appears in the indictment of Nazi war criminals at Nuremberg in 1945.[39] Lemkin defined genocide as "the coordinated and planned annihilation of a national, religious or racial group by a variety of actions aimed at undermining the foundations essential to the survival of the group as a whole."[40] There have been a number of definitions of genocide in legal and academic writing, ranging from objective attempts to ethnocentric assertions on the fate of a particular group.[41] Sociologist Helen Fein, for example, referred to "sustained purposeful action" to physically destroy a collectivity, regardless of the surrender or lack of threat offered by the victims.[42] The simplest definition is that of Kurt Jonassohn: "a form of one-sided mass killing in which a state or other authority intends to destroy a group, as that group and membership in it are defined by the perpetrator."[43]

Most commentators have, as a practical matter, accepted the definition in the 1951 UN Convention. The UN Convention defines genocide as acts committed with the intent to destroy, in whole or in part, a national, ethnic, racial or religious group. Such acts include the killing of members of such groups because of their membership in that group, causing serious bodily or mental harm to members of the group and inflicting on members of the group conditions of life intended to destroy them as such. Genocide, and conspiracy or incitement to commit genocide, are deemed illegal under international law, and individuals committing such acts are held responsible whether they are acting in official capacities or as private individuals.

The key words in this definition are "intent" and "as such." These distinguish genocide from large-scale violence that is, for example, coincident to military operations and not directed specifically against the indicated types of groups. Moreover, it is noteworthy that violence directed against political groups or social classes is not included in the convention's definition.[44]

Burundi's Hutu and Tutsi have no doubt that genocide has occurred. But they blame one another for its origin and its continuation. In effect, each group has developed a complex mythological history that has fueled the perception of the other as evil incarnate. Not all outside observers share the certitude of the Hutu and Tutsi victims of the atrocities. While many are willing to acknowledge that "acts of genocide" have occurred, they are reluctant to apply the label to the violence as a whole. Some former senior officials asserted that a Rwanda-style genocide was impossible in Burundi, because the violence is more decentralized and spontaneous, rather than intentional and planned. But government officials claim to have knowledge of lists of potential victims on both sides of the Burundi conflict.

While conclusive evidence of intent to carry out genocide may be difficult to obtain, there is no doubt that the scale of killing (more than 150,000 in three years, according to Amnesty International) and the cyclical nature of the retribution create a presumptive case for the occurrence of genocide. According to State Department officials, it is their view that the very scale of the killing carries with it the presumption of intent. And the analogy with neighboring Rwanda is strong. It is now commonly assumed that what happened there in 1994 was genocide. It is difficult, then, to argue that violence of nearly the same order of magnitude in Burundi, involving essentially the same ethnic groups, is not.

Other Considerations of Justice and Obligation

If we assume that genocide is actually occurring in Burundi, the rights and obligations of the international community depend importantly on its ability to meet other standards of the just-war tradition, and on whether or not there are mitigating or countervailing considerations.

Just Intention: Questions of intention arise when there is reason to question the disinterestedness of the intervening parties.[45] Given Burundi's endemic poverty and geographic isolation, it would be difficult to find an economic or strategic rationale for intervention. While it is impossible completely to eliminate nonhumanitarian political motives from the calculations of any state, those with the greatest degree of self-interest would appear to be the neighboring African states (especially Congo and Rwanda, with their internal political turmoil) and those Western nations that left their colonial legacy to Burundi (Germany and Belgium). Therefore, a just intention on the part of most noncontiguous states, and especially the Western states that were not part of Burundi's colonial past, is a reasonable presumption. Thus, curiously, the criterion of just intention offsets to some extent the argument for an African intervention force, by balancing the presumed greater obligation of nearby states against the concern about self-interest. (Shue presumably would reject the argument about "concentric circles" of obligation and assert that there is actually no greater obligation to Burundi on the part of Africans than of others.)

Competent Authority: In traditional just-war formulations this criterion applied primarily to the internal decision procedures of the warring states. In the context of humanitarian intervention, however, it is best interpreted as requiring the explicit sanction of the international community, expressed by both the United Nations and the appropriate regional organizations. In the case of Burundi, both the United Nations and the OAU have sanctioned intervention. The authority of these bodies is bolstered by the fact that the government that held power in Burundi in June 1996 requested an intervention. The objections of the Buyoya government must be weighed against the fact that it came to power outside the constitutional process.

Last Resort: This principle normally dictates that other types of measures (diplomatic efforts, economic sanctions, etc.) be attempted before resorting to force. In the case of Burundi, neither diplomatic efforts nor economic sanctions have had a measurable effect. And economic sanctions themselves, because they typically cause more harm to innocent people than to decision makers, should be subject to stringent criteria as well. (See chapter 6.) Moreover, it is not clear that the criterion of last resort must be applied in a strictly chronological sense. If it can be reasonably determined that economic pressure will not lead to a cessation of mass killing, there would seem to be no need to test that determination in practice. Indeed, it seems logical to presume that a genocidal regime, facing economic deprivation, might actually accelerate the killing to reduce the number of claimants on resources. This would certainly be consistent both with the history of violence in Burundi and Rwanda, and with the competing ethnic ideologies.

Proportionality and Discrimination: If an intervention could be carried out by largely disinterested parties, with effective command structures, it should be possible to intervene with due regard to the principle of proportionality. This criterion actually has two aspects. With respect to the decision to intervene, it is necessary to conclude that the violence done in the course of the incursion will likely be less than that in its absence. This seems reasonable. With respect to the conduct of the intervention, it would be necessary to use no more force than required and, moreover, to take specific steps to protect the innocent. This could prove to be difficult in Burundi, as it has been in Rwanda, where generations of retribution have confused the concepts of guilt and innocence. In the initial stages, when stability and cessation of violence are the objectives, it may be necessary to use force on a significant scale to establish credibility and control. Thus, the 10,000 troops of the proposed African Crisis Response Force would probably not be sufficient; indeed, the 25,000 proposed by former Secretary-General Boutros-Ghali might not be enough. It might be necessary to deploy a force of up to 50,000 initially. Thereafter, the scale of force required would likely diminish.

Probability of Success: This is a key tenet of the just-war tradition and the most problematic of the criteria for intervening in Burundi. The violence there is so endemic to the society, so intertwined with political corruption and poverty and so personal to individuals, families and clans, that it is easy to despair of any possibility for long-term peace and stability. The experience in prior humanitarian interventions is not reassuring. Somalia, Iraqi Kurdistan and Bosnia continue to simmer with rivalries compounded by economic troubles. In a nation like Burundi that lacks even the rudiments of a democratic system of administration and justice, and is mired in deep poverty, the challenge is daunting. Thus, humanitarian intervention must be viewed as only a first step toward a long-term security, political and economic transformation not only of Burundi but also of the entire Great Lakes region of Africa. It may be that for Burundi, a long period of international trusteeship, and possible partition into separate ethnic enclaves, may be required stops on the route to independent political stability. And it would be essential to couple military intervention with large-scale economic aid and assistance in building durable political institutions.

International Attention Disorder

The fact that there is growing recognition of universal rights and an emerging consensus on intervention to prevent genocide does not automatically translate into international action. Nation-states remain mired in their own interests, as their slowness in responding to the events in Burundi indicates. International organizations are hemmed in by prevailing legal strictures, and major NGOs, such as the Red Cross, are reluctant to act without the consent of states. Though some smaller NGOs may be less reluctant to violate national law to assist the needy, they are powerless in the face of massive violence and displacement.[46]

Jack Donnelly argues that states will act to remedy humanitarian tragedies only when the costs are very low, there are considerable selfish national concerns and there is an unusually high degree of popular interest.[47] While the efforts put forward by the United States, Canada and others show at least some limited altruism, Donnelly's view seems to explain international inaction on Burundi all too well. Nevertheless, it is important to note that these considerations do not absolve the international community of responsibility. As Garrett Cullity notes, the absence of any direct experience of a hardship does not mitigate our obligation to relieve it in others.[48] Self-absorption, preoccupation with domestic problems and the vagaries of popular opinion may explain international inaction, but they do not justify it.

THE LIMITS OF HUMANITARIAN OBLIGATION

This survey of the literature on intervention and of the situation in Burundi leads to a significant conclusion. There are limits to what nations, international organizations and NGOs can and should do. The limits are not those of sovereignty; there is ample justification to override Burundi's sovereignty to save its people. And the limits are not those of duty; there is a clear international obligation to rescue the citizens of Burundi—Hutu, Tutsi or Twa—from genocide. Rather, the limits are those of vision, of the ability of the international community to understand the complexity and chaos of Burundi, and of the impact of its own actions on the volatile situation there and in the Great Lakes region as a whole.[49] It is for good reason that the situation in Burundi, and similar crises, are now labeled "complex humanitarian emergencies."[50]

Burundi and the surrounding region are a textbook example of chaos and complexity.[51] The political, economic, social and security prospects for Burundi are embedded in the more complex systems of neighboring states, so that seemingly minor events in one country reverberate through the region. And, just as physicists cannot observe subatomic activity without altering it, so the international community inevitably influences events in Burundi, whether through action or inaction. Any semblance of predictability is an illusion in Burundi. Thus the international community faces a Hobson's choice, and must be guided by both a sense of duty and by profound humility as it attempts to tackle the crisis.

Preparing for Uncertainty

In a chaotic environment, such as that in Central and East Africa, the first responsibility of the international community is to be prepared for the unexpected through better contingency planning and more resources for complex emergencies. A related obligation is to improve the information available to the parties to the conflict. This includes nation-states, international organizations and NGOs. Finally, there is an obligation to create a more inclusive decision-making process, one that accommodates the arguments on humanitarian obligation on an equal footing with those on sovereignty.

Within the three broad themes identified above—improved contingency planning, better gathering and coordination of information, and more open decision-making—there are some specific actions that the international community should take.

The U.S.-proposed African Crisis Intervention Initiative should be implemented as soon as possible. But this force alone will not be sufficient even for Burundi, let alone for the multiplicity of potential crises in Africa and elsewhere. It will be essential for the United Nations to acquire a significant, dedicated capability for intervention under Chapter VII of its charter. One essential step is to improve the size and capability of the UN military planning staff. In addition, steps should be taken to identify and earmark dedicated military forces that can be deployed under UN auspices at short notice. Initiatives by the Scandinavian countries are particularly promising, because these nations do not have a legacy of colonialism. But to be effective, any UN force must also draw on the airlift, sealift and support capabilities of the United States, the United Kingdom and France. In that respect, Secretary Cohen's views on humanitarian operations are distinctly unhelpful. It is essential that the United States exercise leadership if the obligation to prepare for urgent interventions is to be met.

Information on Burundi and the surrounding region is abundant, but there are significant gaps in the international community's ability to use it effectively. In part, this results from the fact that many organizations—from the CIA to Amnesty International—regard their information sources as proprietary and protect them by limiting the information that they disseminate. In other cases, information is reported vertically and not shared across organizations because their internal imperatives do not require collaboration. One official of an advocacy organization, for example, remarked that the group had all of the data necessary to carry out its mission, and thus there was no need for new mechanisms to exchange and coordinate information.

Recently, there have been some important strides in the collection and dissemination of information on complex emergencies. For example, ReliefWeb (http://www.reliefweb.int) is a major project of the United Nations Department of Humanitarian Affairs (UNDHA). The purpose of this effort is to strengthen the response capacity for prevention, preparedness and disaster response. It compiles information from both government and nongovernment sources, and provides links that users can follow to acquire the data. UNDHA also provides helpful, periodic situation reports on developing crises that are available through the African News Service (http://www.nando.net/ans).

In addition to the new electronic data sources, organizations have been formed to share information and insights. These have joined the older humanitarian organizations and advocacy groups such as Amnesty International as important centers of information and expertise. The International Crisis Group, based in London and composed of former senior officials from throughout the world, conducts research and on-site investigations. The Great Lakes Policy Forum, sponsored by the Center for Preventive Action of the Council on Foreign Relations, meets monthly in Washington. It has initiated a similar dialogue in Europe. There has been an initiative to identify key indicators of change in Burundi and the region, and to monitor them on a systematic basis. This is the establishment, on an experimental basis, of the Forum on Early Warning and Early Response, a promising joint project of the United Nations and International Alert, London.

It is also important to improve access to information about developments in Burundi and the surrounding region, and especially to improve the quality of reporting on incidents of violence. One significant step would be the deployment, under UN auspices and protection, of many more human rights observers. Steps should be taken to ensure that these observers receive adequate security, and reporting channels should be clearly identified to ensure the broadest possible dissemination while preserving the observers from harm.

Jessica Matthews argues that the influence of nation-states is declining and that of nonstate actors, including NGOs, is increasing.[52] Though the disproportion in power remains immense, the NGOs carry great moral weight, and are increasingly able to make their voices heard in the councils of government. There is also a need to open up decision-making to include these organizations that can make the argument from beneficence more frequently and more forcefully than in the past. Such changes would likely increase the influence of both international and substate actors, in order to better pool information and resources, and to limit competition.[53]

This is a complicated process, but there is a precedent in the significant roles that NGOs had at the Rio conference on the environment. There, they did not actually make decisions for nation-states but significantly influenced them, served as private channels for resolving disputes and brought perspectives and arguments that were not in the vocabulary of national leaders. Again, this is an area in which Secretary-General Annan can take the lead, but support from the Security Council members will be essential. If this can be done, there is some hope that the quality of dialogue on tragedies such as that in Burundi will improve.

There is a need for continued efforts at institution-building in Burundi and the neighboring states. These must focus primarily on the army, the police and the judicial system. Possible initiatives include structural reform of government institutions, introduction of temporary jurists and lawyers, and restoration of the historic custom of using designated "wise persons" to resolve disputes and enhance the credibility of the nation's justice system. Some efforts have been made at democracy-building in Burundi. The National Democratic Institute (NDI), for example, developed educational materials in Kirundi and French, the two official languages, under a program funded by the National Endowment for Democracy. NDI's efforts resulted in the distribution of pamphlets explaining basic concepts of democracy. T-shirts with democratic slogans were made available, and reports indicated that they were being worn by both Hutu and Tutsi. These efforts face an uphill struggle, however, in a nation whose indigenous language has no words for "equality" and "liberty."[54]

One specific initiative that could have far-reaching consequences would be the reform of the UN War Crimes Tribunal in neighboring Rwanda. The tribunal has been woefully inefficient in bringing perpetrators of genocide to justice, owing to complex procedures, poor communications and unqualified staff. There is an urgent need for the United Nations to repair the tribunal, not only to serve the cause of justice in Rwanda but also to signal to perpetrators of genocide in Burundi that they will pay the price for their crimes. Ending impunity for mass murders is a prerequisite to ending the murder itself.

Another key to reducing the violence is to stanch the flow of arms to the region. Both nation-states and international arms merchants have been guilty of abetting the distribution of sophisticated weaponry to both governments and rebel groups. There should be immediate investigations in the countries concerned, aimed at halting and punishing illegal arms traffickers. In addition, the United Nations should consider an arms embargo on the region, as well as measures to end the use of mercenaries from other parts of the world.

Finally, there can be no long-term solution to the problems of Burundi without attending to its utter poverty. In the near term, continued assistance to refugees is essential, and this should be expanded to include assistance to survivors of genocide and violence throughout the region. Long-term development assistance, already sizable, must be expanded. It is essential that the private sector take a role in this. While the economic potential of the region is currently limited, its mineral deposits and coffee exports provide a basis for improving competitiveness, and training programs and educational reform are a prerequisite to eventual self-sufficiency.

LOOKING AHEAD

Thus, the conclusion of this chapter is that there is a profound international obligation to be better prepared—through contingency planning, information sharing and other measures—to aid Burundi and its neighbors. This responsibility transcends the traditional nation-state system and even conventional international organizations.

Increasingly, the responsibility is falling on NGOs to act when nations and international bodies cannot and will not. And their most immediate obligation is to share information and plans, increase collaboration, continue to alleviate suffering as they can and pressure governments for more dramatic action when necessary.

NOTES

1. Basic information on Burundi is taken from *World Factbook* (Washington, DC: Central Intelligence Agency, 1996); *International Yearbook of Industrial Statistics* (Vienna: United Nations Industrial Development Organization, 1996); and *The Least Developed Countries: 1996 Report* (New York and Geneva: United Nations, 1996). Historical information on Burundi is derived principally from Rene Lemarchand, *Rwanda and Burundi* (London: Pall Mall Press, 1970) and *Burundi: Ethnocide as Discourse and Practice* (Cambridge, MA: Woodrow Wilson Center Press, 1994). Information on the developing situation in Burundi since 1996 comes primarily from news reporting *(Washington Post, New York Times, Christian Science Monitor*, Panafrican News Agency, Associated Press); from international and regional magazines *(Time, The Economist, Africa Report, Africa Confidential, Africa Research Bulletin)*; from regional media monitored by the Foreign Broadcast Information Service; from press briefings at the United Nations, the White House and the United States Department of State; and from reporting by the United Nations Department of Humanitarian Affairs. In addition, valuable information on the situation, as well as on the actions of nations, international organizations and NGOs, comes from meetings of the Great Lakes Policy Forum, a monthly gathering of interested parties that operates under a nonattribution rule. Thus, to protect the confidentiality of the Forum, some statements in this chapter have not been individually sourced.

2. United Nations, *Report of the Secretary General on the Situation in Burundi*, S/1996/335 (May 3, 1996), p. 4.

3. Catherine Watson, "Burundi: The Death of Democracy," *Africa Report* 39, no. 1 (January–February 1994): 28. This is in contrast to the massacres of 1972, which fell disproportionately on the Hutu.

4. See, for example, the press release dated December 20, 1995, "Burundi: How Many More Must Die before the International Community Takes Action?"

5. U.S. Department of State, *Burundi: Human Rights Practices, 1996* (Washington, DC: U.S. Government Printing Office, 1996).

6. United Nations, statement by United Nations High Commissioner for Refugees Mrs. Sadako Ogata, to the Regional Conference on Assistance to Refugees, Returnees and Displaced Persons in the Great Lakes Region, February 15,1995.

7. Amnesty International, "Rwanda/Burundi: Recent Research Visit Highlights Need for Human Rights Protection for Refugees Returning to Rwanda and Burundi," press release (October 25, 1995).

8. Amnesty International, "Rwanda/Burundi: Urgent Steps Needed to Resolve Refugee Crisis," press release (February 20, 1996).

9. United Nations, *Report of the Secretary General on the Situation in Burundi*, S/1996/335.

10. United Nations, *Report of the Secretary General on the Situation in Burundi*, S/1996/116 (February 15, 1996).

11. This prompted one experienced diplomat to quip, "Tanzania knows a lot about intervention," referring to Nyerere's 1978–79 incursion into Uganda.

12. James A. Barry, "President Who Feels Others' Pain Should Aid Burundi," *Christian Science Monitor,* September 27, 1996, p. 19; Salih Booker, "United States Should Do the Right Thing" (New York: Council on Foreign Relations, September 27, 1996), distributed by African News Service.

13. "Canada Volunteers Troops to Fill Void on Zaire Aid," *Washington Post,* Nov. 12, 1996, sec. A, p. 20.

14. "Cohen Issues Caution on Peacekeeping," *Washington Post,* January 25, 1997, sec. A, p. 8.

15. Michael Walzer, *Just and Unjust Wars,* 2nd ed. (New York: Basic Books, 1992), p. 108.

16. Ibid. P. 107.

17. Stanley Hoffman, *Duties Beyond Borders* (Syracuse, NY: Syracuse University Press, 1981), p. 64; Jack Donnelly, "Human Rights: The Impact of International Action," *International Journal* 43, no. 2 (Spring 1988): 252; Robert L. Phillips and Duane L. Cady, *Humanitarian Intervention: Just War vs Pacifism* (Boston: Rowman and Littlefield, 1996), p. 54.

18. Gerald Doppelt, "Statism Without Foundations," *Philosophy and Public Affairs* 9, no. 4 (Summer 1980): 402; Charles Beitz, "Nonintervention and Communal Integrity," *Philosophy and Public Affairs* 9, no. 4 (Summer 1980): 391; David Luban, "The Romance of the Nation-State," *Philosophy and Public Affairs* 9, no. 4 (Summer 1980): 397.

19. James Turner Johnson, "Just War Tradition and Low Intensity Conflict," paper presented at the Low Intensity Conflict Symposium, Naval War College, April 9–10, 1992, p. 29.

20. J. Bryan Hehir, "Intervention: From Theories to Cases," *Ethics and International Affairs* 9 (1995): 1–13.

21. John Harriss, *The Politics of Humanitarian Intervention* (New York: Pinter, 1995)., p. 42.

22. Jessica Matthews, "Power Shift," *Foreign Affairs* 76, no. 1 (January/February 1997): 59.

23. The criteria for humanitarian intervention are enumerated in, inter alia, Harriss, *The Politics of Humanitarian Intervention.*

24. Thomas G. Weiss, "UN Responses in the Former Yugoslavia: Moral and Operational Choices," *Ethics and International Affairs* 8 (1994): 4–5.

25. Charles W. Kegley, "International Peacemaking and Peacekeeping: The Morality of Multinational Measures," *Ethics and International Affairs* 10 (1996): 38.

26. John Prendergast, *Frontline Diplomacy: Humanitarian Aid and Conflict in Africa* (Washington, DC: Center of Concern, 1996).

27. Peter Singer, "Famine, Affluence and Morality," *Philosophy and Public Affairs* 1, no. 3 (Spring 1972): 229–43.

28. Garrett Cullity, "International Aid and the Scope of Kindness," *Ethics* 105, no. 1 (October 1994): 103.

29. These are well summarized in Susan James, "The Duty to Relieve Suffering," *Ethics* 93, no. 1 (October 1982): 4.

30. Cullity, "International Aid and the Scope of Kindness," p. 111.

31. Howard Caygill, *A Kant Dictionary* (Cambridge, MA: Blackwell, 1995), p. 167.

32. Ibid., p. 118.

33. Thomas Donaldson, *The Ethics of International Business,* (New York: Oxford University Press, 1989), p. 117.

34. Henry Shue, "Mediating Duties," *Ethics* 98, no. 4 (July 1988): 693.

35. Gerard Elfstrom, "On Dilemmas of Intervention," *Ethics,* 93, no. 4 (July 1983): 709.

36. Ibid., p. 711.

37. Ibid., p. 713.

38. Ibid., p. 725.

39.   Peter DuPreez, *Genocide: The Psychology of Mass Murder* (London: Boyars/ Bowerdean, 1994), p. 7.

40. Frank Chalk, "Redefining Genocide," in *Genocide: Conceptual and Historical Dimensions,* George Andreopoulos, ed. (Philadelphia: University of Pennsylvania Press, 1994), p. 48.

41. Leo Kuper, "Theoretical Issues Relating to Genocide: Uses and Abuses," in Andreopoulos, *Genocide: Conceptual and Historical Dimensions,* p. 31.

42. Chalk, "Redefining Genocide," p. 49.

43. "What Is Genocide," in *Genocide Watch*, Helen Fein, ed. (New Haven: Yale University Press, 1992), p. 19.

44. Ibid., p. 10.

45.   Kenneth R. Himes, "Just War, Pacifism and Humanitarian Intervention," *America* 169, no. 4 (August 14, 1993): 15.

46. Larry Minear and Thomas G. Weiss, *Mercy Under Fire: War and the Global Humanitarian Community* (Boulder, CO: Westview Press, 1995), p. 37.

47. Donnelly, "Human Rights: The Impact of International Action," p. 252.

48. Cullity, "International Aid and the Scope of Kindness," p. 120.

49. For an extensive treatment of this issue, see James. S. Fishkin, *The Limits of Obligation* (New Haven: Yale University Press, 1982). Fishkin ultimately fails to provide specific suggestions for balancing the obligation to provide aid against the inherent unreasonableness of unmitigated responsibility and the "overload of obligation."

50. Sissela Bok, *Common Values* (Columbia: University of Missouri Press, 1995), pp. 104–27.

51. Margaret Wheatly, *Leadership and the New Science* (San Francisco: Berrett-Koehler, 1992).

52. Matthews, "Power Shift," p. 59.

53. See Michael Marin, *The Road to Hell: The Ravaging Effects of Foreign Aid and International Charity* (New York: Free Press, 1997), for a stinging critique of the NGOs and national aid programs.

54. Lemarchand, *Burundi: Ethnocide as Discourse and Practice*, p. 16.

5

Can Covert Action Be Just?
Lessons from U.S. Intervention in Chile

COVERT ACTION IN THE COLD WAR ERA

In 1954, President Eisenhower appointed a panel to make recommendations regarding covert political action as an instrument of foreign policy. The panel, chaired by General Jimmy Doolittle, included the following statement in its report:

It is now clear that we are facing an implacable enemy whose avowed objective is world domination by whatever means and at whatever cost. There are no rules in such a game. Hitherto acceptable norms of human conduct do not apply. If the United States is to survive, long-standing American concepts of "fair play" must be reconsidered. We must develop effective espionage and counterespionage services and must learn to subvert, sabotage and destroy our enemies by more clever, more sophisticated means than those used against us. It may become necessary that the American people be made acquainted with, understand and support this fundamentally repugnant philosophy. [1]

The "more clever, more sophisticated means" that the committee had in mind referred principally to covert political action. Covert attempts to influence developments abroad have long been an important tool of statecraft. Benjamin Franklin is said to have carried out covert propaganda activities during the Revolutionary War. And during World War II, the Office of Strategic Services (OSS) conducted large-scale resistance, sabotage and propaganda programs.

In the United States, covert action, sometimes also called "special activities," is defined as follows:

[A]ctivities conducted in support of national foreign policy objectives abroad which are planned and executed so that the role of the United States Government is not apparent or acknowledged publicly, and functions in support of such activities, but which are not intended to influence United States political processes, public opinion, policies, or media, and do not include diplomatic activities and collection of intelligence or related support functions. [2]

This definition seeks to distinguish covert action from diplomacy and espionage, which may also involve secrecy, as well as to make clear that the United States intelligence agencies are not authorized to meddle in domestic affairs. In layman's terms, covert action can be described as "secret activity to influence the behavior of a foreign government or political, military, economic, or societal events and circumstances in a foreign country."[3] Covert action encompasses a variety of activities, and these fall principally into three categories: propaganda, political action and paramilitary operations.

Propaganda is the use of information to influence perceptions and actions abroad. This includes the use of the news media, as well as "agents of influence" who are recruited in the hope that they will influence a foreign country's decisions directly. Media operations can be characterized with respect to their apparent source. Overt, or "white," propaganda is openly attributed to its true source. Media activities of official organs such as the U.S. Information Agency fall into this category. Covert or "gray" propaganda operations are carried out so that the true source of the information is masked. For example, if the Central Intelligence Agency (CIA) recruits a foreign journalist and provides her with information that is published under her byline, that is a "gray propaganda" operation. "Black" propaganda is information that is falsely attributed to a target of covert action. An example would be the forgery and dissemination of a document that ostensibly is published by a foreign organization, and that is designed to discredit that organization among its supporters.[4]

Covert political action includes the provision of material or moral support to foreign governments, political parties, civic groups, labor unions or other politically active organizations. For example, the CIA covertly funded noncommunist political parties and candidates in the Italian elections of 1948. It also developed a network of political action groups and information sources to contest Soviet political influence in Europe and elsewhere, and subsidized youth movements, labor groups and other political organizations.[5]

The final type of covert action encompasses the use of violent force to influence events abroad. Such covert action is termed "lethal" to distinguish it from "nonlethal" propaganda and political action. Lethal covert action can include secret provision of arms and materiel, funds or intelligence support to foreign resistance movements or to governments fighting against such movements. The United States and other foreign countries, for example, covertly supported the Afghan resistance to Soviet occupation, and successive U.S. administrations assisted the government of El Salvador in counterinsurgency activities. Covert paramilitary action can also include the development of insurgent forces (usually centered around exile groups) that would not exist without outside support. The contras of Nicaragua, who were supported by the Reagan administration, are an example.

In addition to the support of such paramilitary forces, covert action may include operations by small groups to sabotage military or economic targets (as described in chapter 6 with respect to U.S. operations against Cuba), or even assassination of foreign leaders. During the Cold War, the CIA attempted, unsuccessfully, to assassinate Fidel Castro and was involved with foreign groups that were responsible for assassinating Patrice Lumumba of the Congo and Rafael Trujillo of the Dominican

Republic. Public outrage over revelation of these activities prompted President Ford to promulgate an executive order prohibiting U.S. officials from "engag[ing] in or conspir[ing] to engage in, political assassinations." This ban remains in effect.[6]

ORGANIZATION OF COVERT ACTION

Covert action initiatives were envisioned by the framers of the National Security Act of 1947. This legislation established the CIA and outlined its missions in general terms. Among those missions was a charge to "carry out other activities related to intelligence as the National Security Council may direct." This circumlocution provided, until the mid-1970s, the only legislative foundation for covert action. In 1948, National Security Council (NSC) directive 10/2 established the Office of Special Projects, later renamed the Office of Policy Coordination (OPC), to carry out covert operations. In setting up this organization, the NSC pointed to the "vicious covert activities of the USSR, its satellite countries and communist groups."[7]

OPC suffered from a congenital structural defect, however. Its funding and personnel came from the CIA, but its director was appointed by the secretary of state and reported jointly to him and to the secretary of defense. The State and Defense departments struggled continuously over control and priorities for OPC programs. In addition, OPC activities often duplicated or crossed paths with programs of the CIA's Office of Special Operations, which was charged with collection of intelligence in those countries where OPC was trying to influence policy.[8] As a result, in 1952 the two offices were merged into the CIA's Directorate of Plans (DP), headed by Allen Dulles, brother of Secretary of State John Foster Dulles and later a director of Central Intelligence (DCI).[9] The DP carried out its activities in coordination with the Department of State, and relied on the Department of Defense for help in lethal operations, but reported independently to the president and the NSC. There was no regular practice of reporting to the Congress on covert action.

As a function of the DP (later renamed the Directorate of Operations—DO), covert action had to compete for resources and attention with two other missions, the collection of foreign intelligence, and counterintelligence to defeat foreign intelligence operations. This was especially true at CIA overseas posts, called "stations," where teams of operations officers were responsible for all three types of activities, and often were stretched very thin. The priority given to covert action remained high through the 1950s, bolstered by successful overthrows of left-leaning heads of state in Iran and Guatemala, as well as the establishment of a worldwide propaganda and political action network jokingly called the "Mighty Wurlitzer."[10]

The humiliating rout of U.S.-supported Cuban exile forces at the Bay of Pigs discredited the CIA's covert action efforts and led to stricter supervision. Congressional questions became more frequent and penetrating, but there was no independent oversight body. Within the executive branch, a series of high-level committees, variously named the Special Group, 303 Committee and 40 Committee, coordinated policy on covert action. The CIA's covert action operations, however, remained responsive primarily to presidential direction through the early 1970s. The basic doctrine was that of "plausible deniability." Operations were to be organized and carried out so that United States officials, including the president himself, could plausibly assert that they had no knowledge of the activities.[11]

APPLYING JUST-WAR CRITERIA: THE CHILE CASE

Covert action presents a particularly challenging moral problem. On the one hand, secret activities are the very stuff of international relations, as countries seek to protect and promote their interests and to safeguard the methods they use to do so. On the other hand, targets of covert action rightly resent secret interference in their affairs. Such interference, and especially its aspect of secrecy, is particularly disturbing to Americans, who put such great stock in democratic accountability. It would appear that the just-war tradition could be useful for analyzing choices regarding covert actions, since they can cause suffering or moral damage, just as war causes physical destruction.[12] To explore this, this chapter considers covert U.S. intervention in Chile in 1964 and 1970.[13]

The 1964 Election Operation

As part of its worldwide buildup of covert action capabilities in the early 1950s, the CIA established a capacity to conduct covert propaganda and political influence operations in Chile. In 1961, President Kennedy established the Alliance for Progress to promote the growth of democratic institutions. He also became convinced that the Chilean Christian Democratic party shared his belief in democratic social reform and had the organizational competence to achieve their common goals, but lacked the resources to compete with extremist parties of the left and right.

During 1961, the CIA established relationships with key political parties in Chile, as well as propaganda and organizational mechanisms. In 1962, the Special Group (the interagency body charged with reviewing covert actions), approved two CIA proposals to provide support to the Christian Democrats. The program was intended to strengthen center democratic forces against the leftist challenge from Salvador Allende Gossens, who was supported by the Soviet Union and Cuba. When Lyndon Johnson succeeded Kennedy, he continued the covert subsidies, with the objectives of making Chile a model of democracy and preventing nationalization of Chilean components of American multinational corporations.

The Chilean presidential election of 1964 was a battle between Allende and Eduardo Frei Montalva, a liberal Christian Democrat. The election was viewed with great alarm in Washington. The *New York Times* compared it with the Italian election of 1948, when the Communists had threatened to take over by means of the ballot box and the United States had intervened covertly to support democratic parties. Similarly, in 1964 the Johnson administration intervened in Chile, according to congressional documents, to prevent or minimize the influence of Marxists in the government that would emerge from the election. Cord Meyer, a former CIA covert action manager, argued that the intervention was intended to preserve Chile's constitutional order.

In considering the 1964 election operation, the Johnson administration used the established mechanism, the interagency Special Group. By 1963, according to

Gregory Treverton, the Special Group had developed criteria for evaluating covert action proposals. All expenditures of covert funds for the 1964 operation (some $3 million in all) were approved by the group. (There is no indication that the Congress approved these expenditures, or was even informed in detail of the operation.) In addition, an interagency committee was set up in Washington to manage the operation, and was paralleled by a group in the U.S. embassy in Santiago. Meyer contends that covert intervention on behalf of Christian Democratic candidates had very wide support in the administration, and congressional documents confirm that the covert action was decided upon at the highest levels of government.

Covert action by the CIA was an important element, but not the only aspect of U.S. policy. Chile was chosen to become a showcase of economic development programs under the Alliance for Progress. Between 1964 and 1969, Chile received well over a billion dollars in direct, overt U.S. aid—more per capita than any other country in the hemisphere. Moreover, funding to support the Frei candidacy was funneled overtly through the Agency for International Development as well as secretly through the CIA. Frei also received covert aid from a group of American corporations known as the Business Group for Latin America.

In the 1964 election operation the CIA employed virtually its entire arsenal of non-lethal methods:

- The CIA spent some $3 million, or about $1 per Chilean voter. (U.S. candidates in the 1964 presidential election spent about 50 cents per voter.)[14] Funds were passed through intermediaries to the Christian Democrats, who received some $2.6 million, as well as to the Radical party.

- The CIA provided a consultant to assist the Christian Democrats in running an American-style campaign, which included polling, voter registration and get-out-the-vote drives.

- Political action operations, including polls and grassroots organizing, were conducted among important voting blocs, including slum dwellers, peasants, organized labor and dissident Socialists.

- CIA-controlled assets placed propaganda in major Chilean newspapers, and on radio and television; put up wall posters; passed out political leaflets; and organized demonstrations. Some of this propaganda employed "scare tactics" to link Allende to Soviet and Cuban atrocities.

- Other assets manufactured "black propaganda"—that is, material falsely attributed to Allende's supporters that was intended to discredit them.[15]

Other activities were carried out to complement the election operations. These, according to CIA documents, included projects to accomplish the following:

- Wrest control of the Chilean organization of university students from the Communists

- Support a women's group that was thought to be influential in Chilean political and intellectual life

- Exploit a civic action front group to counter Communist influence in cultural and intellectual circles

- Assist private-sector trade organizations, primarily for voter-registration and get-out-the-vote drives.[16]

Significant constraints were imposed, however. Paramilitary and other lethal methods were not employed. The CIA rejected a proposal from the Chilean Defense Council to carry out a coup if Allende won. The Department of State turned down a similar proposal from a Chilean Air Force officer. Moreover, the Special Group declined an offer from American businessmen to provide funds for covert disbursement. According to a congressional report, the Group considered this "neither a secure nor an honorable way of doing business."

The 1964 covert action succeeded; Frei won a clear majority (56 percent) of the vote. A CIA postmortem concluded that the covert campaign had had a decisive impact. It is not clear from available records whether a calculation of the likelihood of success was part of the decision-making process. According to Treverton, the CIA was required, under Special Group procedures to make such an estimate, and it is likely that its view would have been optimistic, since it had penetrated all significant elements of the Chilean political system.

The 1970 Elections and "Track II"

Under Chilean law, Frei could not serve two consecutive terms as president. As the 1970 elections approached, the United States faced a dilemma. The Christian Democrats had drifted to the left and were out of step with the Nixon administration's views. The conservative candidate, Jorge Alessandri, was not attractive, but there was even greater concern about an Allende victory.

Senior U.S. officials maintained that their preoccupation with Allende was defensive, and aimed at allaying fears of a Communist victory both abroad and at home. Henry Kissinger, Nixon's national security adviser, noted that what worried the United States was Allende's proclaimed hostility and his perceived intention to create "another Cuba." Nixon stated in a *New York Times* interview: "There was a great deal of concern expressed in 1964 and again in 1970 by neighboring South American countries that if Mr. Allende were elected president, Chile would quickly become a haven for Communist operatives who could infiltrate and undermine independent governments throughout South America."[17]

Kissinger reportedly told an interagency group, "I don't see why we need to stand by and watch a country go communist due to the irresponsibility of its own people."[18] This is the same Kissinger who once ridiculed Chile's strategic importance by calling it "a dagger pointed at the heart of Antarctica." Presumably his concern had been heightened by the discovery earlier in 1970 of a possible Soviet submarine base under construction in Cuba. Similar facilities in Chile could expand the requirement for U.S. naval forces into the South Pacific, and stretch the available resources very thin.

The intelligence community, however, held a more nuanced view of the potential impact of Allende's election on U.S. strategic interests. According to an assessment by the CIA's Directorate of Intelligence:

Regarding threats to U.S. interests, we conclude that:
1. The U.S. has no vital national interests in Chile. There would, however, be tangible economic losses.
2. The world balance of power would not be significantly altered by an Allende government.
3. An Allende victory would, however, create considerable political and psychological costs:
   a. Hemispheric cohesion would be threatened by the challenge that an Allende government would pose to the OAS [Organization of American States], and by the reactions that it would create in other countries. We do not see, however, any likely threat to the peace of the region.
   b. An Allende victory would represent a definite psychological setback to the U.S. and a definite psychological advance for the Marxist idea.[19]

The CIA began to warn policy makers early in 1969 that an Allende victory was likely. In Santiago, Ambassador Edward Korry and CIA Station Chief Henry Hecksher disagreed about how to respond to the Allende challenge. Korry was instinctively opposed to covert operations, but was concerned that he had a special responsibility to safeguard the sizable American investment in Chile under the Alliance for Progress. Hecksher, a veteran of covert operations in Guatemala and Southeast Asia, was concerned about Allende's Communist leanings and favored covert intervention to stop him from taking power. In one notable exchange, Hecksher reportedly asked Korry, "Do you want to be responsible for electing a Communist as president of Chile?"[20]

Given the stakes, and the history of U.S. intervention in the Chilean election process, Korry eventually agreed to support covert action. He and Hecksher forwarded a joint proposal under which the CIA would conduct propaganda and other operations but not directly fund Allende's opponents. Even the compromise proposal, however, was controversial in Washington. The State Department representative to the interagency committee, Undersecretary U. Alexis Johnson, opposed any intervention, while the CIA argued that it could stop Allende by providing both money and active help to his principal opponent, Alessandri.[21]

While the U.S. government deliberated, others acted. Several large multinational corporations had major investments in Chile. Fearful that Allende would nationalize industry, two of them, International Telephone and Telegraph (ITT) and Anaconda Copper, made plans to finance the opposition parties. John McCone, a former DCI, was a member of the board of directors of ITT.[22]

In March 1970, the 40 Committee (successor to the Special Group) decided that the United States would not support any particular candidate, but would conduct a "spoiling operation," aimed at discrediting Allende through propaganda. The effort failed when Allende won a slim plurality in the September 4 election. He garnered 36.3 percent of the vote, with Alessandri running a close second at 34.9 percent. Since no candidate won a clear majority, the election was referred to a joint session of Congress, which in the past had always endorsed the candidate who had received the highest popular vote. The joint session was set for October 24, 1970.

On September 8, the 40 Committee met and requested a "cold-blooded assessment" by the embassy of the pros and cons of a military coup organized with U.S. assistance. Korry was pessimistic. He told the committee that he, the CIA station chief and "Our own military people [are] unanimous in rejecting [the] possibility of successful military intervention."[23] The committee considered various options for political action and authorized an additional $250,000 to bribe Chilean congressmen, but the money was never spent.[24]

Until the middle of September, management of the covert action against Allende was entrusted to the 40 Committee. But shortly thereafter, President Nixon took a personal role. On September 15, Donald Kendall, chief executive officer of Pepsi Cola, and Augustine Edwards, an influential Chilean publisher who had supported Frei during the 1964 election, communicated their concern at the prospect of an Allende victory to the Nixon administration   According to Kissinger, Nixon was alarmed by their views and decided that more direct action was necessary. He called in DCI Richard Helms and ordered the CIA to play a direct role in organizing a military coup. In effect, Nixon ordered an escalation of the covert operation, to include potentially lethal activities. Further, Helms was told not to coordinate CIA activities with the departments of State and Defense and not to inform Ambassador Korry. The 40 Committee was not informed, nor was the Congress. This activity was called "Track II," to distinguish it from the 40 Committee program, "Track I."[25]

Helms testified to the Congress that there was no doubt in his mind that Nixon wanted to prevent Allende from taking office, using any means possible: "[I had] the impression . . . that the President came down very hard that he wanted something done and didn't much care how and that he was prepared to make money available. . . . This was a pretty much all-inclusive order. . . . If I ever carried a marshall's baton in my knapsack out of the Oval Office, it was that day."[26]

The notes that Helms took at the meeting conveyed the sense of urgency and the president's resolve:

One in 10 chance perhaps, but save Chile!
worth spending
not concerned risks involved
no involvement of Embassy
$10,000,000 available, more if necessary
full-time job—best men we have
game plan
make the economy scream
48 hours for plan of action[27]

Helms has adamantly denied, however, that his instructions included the assassination of Allende. When Senator Gary Hart asked if the mandate included Allende's physical elimination, Helms replied, "Well, not in my mind, because when I became Director, I had already made up my mind that we were not going to have any of that business."[28]

Track II was a carefully guarded secret, but U.S. displeasure with the prospect of an Allende victory was not. According to Kissinger, all agencies were working to prevent the election.   The Chilean government was threatened with economic reprisals, and steps were taken to inform the Chilean armed forces that military aid would be cut off.

Helms had no illusions about the difficulty of the task Nixon had assigned. "What I came away from the meeting with [was] the distinct impression that we were being asked to do almost the impossible, and trying to indicate this was going to be pretty tough[sic]."[29]   His pessimistic assessment was echoed by Ambassador Korry. According to his correspondence with congressional investigators, Korry consistently warned the Nixon administration that the Chilean military was no policy alternative. From Santiago, according to congressional documents, the CIA reported: "Military action is impossible; the military is incapable and unwilling to seize power. We have no capability to motivate or instigate a coup."

This view was shared by the managers of Track II. According to David Phillips, chief of the CIA's Chile Task Force, both he and his supervisor were convinced that Track II was unworkable. Deputy Director for Plans Thomas Karamessines was adamant that the CIA could not refuse the assignment, but briefed Nixon several times on the progress of the operation, always pessimistically.[30]

Although both Track I and Track II were intended to prevent Allende's taking power, they employed different methods. Track I included funding to bribe Chilean congressmen, propaganda and economic activities, and contacts with Frei and elements of the military to foster opposition to Allende. Track II was more direct, stressing active CIA involvement in and support for a coup without Frei's knowledge. The CIA specifically offered encouragement to dissident Chilean military officers who opposed Allende but recognized that General Rene Schneider, the Chilean chief of staff, would not support a coup. These dissidents developed a plan to kidnap Schneider and take over the government, and this became known to CIA officials. Two unsuccessful kidnap attempts were made, and on the third attempt, on October 22, 1970, General Schneider was shot; he subsequently died. Both U.S. and Chilean inquiries concluded that the weapons used were not supplied by the United States, and that American officials did not desire or encourage Schneider's death. Neither, however, did they prevent it.

Unlike the covert program of 1964, the 1970 covert operation did not involve extensive public opinion polling, grassroots organizing or direct funding of any candidate. Moreover, Helms made clear that assassination of Allende was not an option; and when a right-wing Chilean fanatic, General Arturo Marshall, offered to help prevent Allende's confirmation, the CIA declined because of his earlier involvement in bombings in Santiago.

In the event, Allende was inaugurated as president of Chile. But covert operations against him continued. According to Thomas Karamessines, "Track II was never really ended."[31] The CIA began to rebuild its network of agents. By the fall of 1971, the CIA station received reports of coup plotting almost daily. Although the agency had no formal authorization to promote a coup, senior intelligence officials directed the station to maintain contact with the plotters. They also authorized deception operations designed to convince Chilean military officials that the armed forces had been penetrated by Cuban intelligence. None of these activities were made known to the new U.S. ambassador, Nathaniel Davis.

There were other activities as well. In 1972 and 1973, strikes racked the Chilean economy. In September 1972, the 40 Committee authorized $24,000 in funding for a business organization that had been involved in the strikes. The next month it approved $100,000 in funding for other private-sector organizations, and in 1973 the CIA provided three-quarters of the funding for a conservative research organization.[32]

The CIA maintained relationships with coup plotters throughout 1972 and 1973. In July 1973 a truckers' strike paralyzed the country. The objective apparently was to provoke a military intervention. The United States rejected requests to support this effort, but in August did approve funding of $1 million for political parties and private-sector groups. Some of this money may have reached the truckers. Finally, in September 1973, Allende was ousted and killed, and a military junta took power, ushering in a period of repression in Chile that awakened worldwide protest.[33] The reign of the Chilean military became synonymous with the abuse of human rights; thousands were killed or "disappeared" on suspicion of leftist activities. It is a wound from which Chile has still not recovered.

In the wake of the coup, there were mass demonstrations in Europe against the CIA's alleged involvement, and in the United Nations, Cuba denounced the "many plots hatched by the United States Embassy." The U.S. representative denied "categorically that the United States was involved in any way in the events which have occurred in Chile."[34]

Treverton maintains that neither the CIA nor the U.S. military was directly involved in the coup or the assassination of Allende. He is uncertain how much the United States knew in advance about the military plans. He argues, however, that the United States still bears some moral responsibility. His view is corroborated by senior diplomats and intelligence officials. Ambassador Davis asserted that "The U.S. government wished success to opposition forces."[35] Karamessines noted, "I am sure that the seeds that were laid in that effort in 1970 had their impact in 1973."[36] And former DCI William Colby said, "Certainly in Track II in 1970 it [the CIA] sought a military coup. . . . Certainly, having launched such an attempt, CIA was responsible to some degree for the final outcome, no matter that it tried to 'distance' itself and turn away well before 1973."[37]

Exactly who within the United States government was responsible is a matter of continuing uncertainty. CIA officials have testified that higher authorities, presumably meaning Nixon and Kissinger, were aware of and authorized their ongoing activities. Henry Kissinger and General Alexander Haig asserted to the congressional committee investigating assassination plots that the White House ordered a stand-down in coup plotting after October 15, 1979, and that they were unaware of CIA coup activities after that date.[38]

COVERT ACTION AND THE NEW WORLD ORDER

The Chilean operations were typical examples of Cold War covert actions. They were conducted under a realist set of assumptions regarding ethics and international politics. Machiavelli probably would have admired the rhetoric of the Doolittle Report, and the hard-nosed actions of Nixon and Kissinger. He also would have applauded the bureaucratic arrangements that left Nixon, as head of state, relatively free of political constraints in using covert action. In short, the Cold War philosophy of covert action is a lineal descendent of Machiavelli's realpolitik.

This view of the ethics of covert action had its roots in the notion that the Soviet Union was a unique sort of enemy that engendered a particular need for an unbridled response to its aggression, both actual and potential. This argument made sense to many through the Cold War period. With the dismantling of the Berlin Wall, the abortive coup in the Soviet Union and the dissolution of the Soviet empire, however, this formerly compelling anticommunist rationale for covert action lost any validity it may have enjoyed. But it is clearly inappropriate that in a dangerous world the United States should eschew all covert methods. The Gulf War shows that aggression by hostile states remains a threat; and other challenges, such as terrorism, narcotics trafficking and the proliferation of weapons of mass destruction, are likely to motivate the United States to consider covert responses. What frame of reference, then, should replace the Cold War philosophy that has shaped covert action policy since the founding of the CIA?

Some would argue that covert action should be prohibited altogether. Taking a Kantian liberal approach, they would ban all covert political operations as inconsistent with a search for global order.[39] Others would like to subordinate covert action more strictly to international law and impose a strong bias against secret methods when overt approaches are possible, even if the risk of failure is higher.[40]

A middle-ground approach to assessing the justification for intervention overseas can be found in the natural law and just-war traditions. A number of commentators, including jurists, philosophers, theologians, government officials and military officers, have maintained that just-war concepts are useful in evaluating not only large-scale warfare but low-intensity conflict as well.[41] This clearly includes covert paramilitary action. This chapter argues that the just-war tradition can provide useful insights regarding propaganda and political action as well. In particular, the tradition's criteria of just cause, just intention, competent authority, last resort, probability of success, proportionality and discrimination can pose difficult and important questions for those advocating covert interference abroad.

JUST-WAR AND COVERT ACTION

The Doolittle Report's adamant espousal of covert action appears in hindsight to be extreme, and even its authors were uncomfortable with the "repugnant philosophy" that they deemed necessary. Indeed, although covert political action became an important tool of U.S. policy, America never abandoned its moral traditions. The threat of international communism, however, became so compelling a rationale that most covert action operations needed no more specific justification.

This Cold War facade began to crumble in the late 1960s with opposition to the Vietnam War and the revelation of abuses by the Central Intelligence Agency. As a result, greater attention has been paid to managing covert actions, but until the 1990s the Soviet threat was a dominant consideration in most covert action decisions.

For members of the Doolittle Committee, and for many intelligence practitioners, the justification for intelligence activities is to be found in the need to promote the U.S. national interest. In this regard, commentators distinguish between covert action and classic espionage or intelligence-gathering. Former DCI James Woolsey has put forward the following justification for espionage, drawing on work by ethicist John Langan.

First, the state has a responsibility to its citizens to protect their lives, welfare and property; so it must take steps to understand foreign threats, if any, to those citizens as well as to the nation as a whole. In order to accomplish this, particularly in a world in which many societies are themselves closed and secretive, the government must engage in clandestine information-gathering efforts. *Provided that the least intrusive means of doing so are used whenever possible* and that the resulting analysis is presented to policy makers without bias or political taint, we may assert an ethical foundation for our official involvement in espionage.[42]

Critics of intelligence activities would argue that the least intrusive means are not always used, and that intelligence services spy even when they could uncover the same information through using less morally questionable techniques. Moreover, even some who support secret intelligence-gathering have grave reservations about covert interference in the affairs of foreign countries. Some of these critics would allow such activities in wartime but oppose them in times of peace.[43]

One former intelligence practitioner, William Colby, has argued that "a standard for selection of covert actions that are just can be developed by analogy with the long-standing efforts to differentiate just from unjust wars."[44] And former DCI William Webster has noted that in its deliberations the CIA's Covert Action Review Group explores three key questions regarding a proposed covert action: Is it entirely consistent with U.S. laws? Is it consistent with American values? And will it make sense to the American people?[45] With respect to the latter two considerations, a reformulation of the just-war criteria in commonsense terms would probably appeal to the American people. It seems fair to conclude that the people would support covert actions under the following conditions:

- The action is approved by the president, after due deliberation within the executive branch, and with the full knowledge and concurrence of appropriate members of the Congress

- The intentions and objectives are clearly spelled out, reasonable and just

- Other means of achieving the objectives would not be effective

- There is a reasonable probability of success

- The methods envisioned are commensurate with the objectives.

Further, it is reasonable to presume that the American people would approve of methods that minimize injury (physical, economic or psychological) to innocent people, and are proportionate to the threat and are under firm U.S. control.

Secrecy As an Element of Covert Action

Those who advocate or approve such covert actions, however, bear the additional burden of demonstrating why they must be conducted secretly. As ethicist Sissela Bok has pointed out, secrecy, in itself, is morally neutral. "Secrecy differs in this respect from lying, promise-breaking, violence, and other practices for which the burden of proof rests on those who would defend them. Conversely, secrecy differs from truthfulness, friendship and other practices carrying a favorable presumption."[46]

Secrecy becomes a particular problem, however, when combined with political power. Secrecy may increase the temptation to act in one's selfish interest. In addition, secrecy eliminates the possibility of accountability.[47] Every state requires a measure of secrecy to defend itself, but when secrecy is invoked, citizens lose the ordinary democratic checks on those matters that can affect them most strongly.[48] In addition, as Charles Beitz has argued, a special problem of operational control can arise when secret agents are employed as intermediaries—because their aims may differ from ours, and because the chain of command may be ambiguous or unreliable.[49] Finally, most covert actions will necessarily lack the public legitimacy and legal status under international law of a declared, justifiable war. This makes it incumbent on those advocating such actions to take into account the consequences of possible public misunderstanding and international opprobrium.

There is another dimension to the moral problem of secret political activities abroad. Such activities inevitably involve not merely secrecy but deception as well. At a minimum, the details regarding individuals involved and methods of support are concealed to prevent compromise and counteraction. The agents who conduct covert action must have "cover stories" to explain their identities and actions. Funding channels must be kept secret by falsely attributing them to individuals or groups other than those in whose benefit they are operating.

More significantly, governments that conduct covert action must inevitably misrepresent their policies and activities to the rest of the world. It can be difficult to walk the fine line between maintaining the secrecy necessary to protect covert operations and deceiving the public on whose behalf the activities are ostensibly being carried out. It can be tempting for political leaders to believe that deceptive statements, or "noble lies," must be made in the public interest. Bok warns that such behavior is arrogant. "The powerful tell lies believing that they have greater than ordinary understanding of what is at stake; very often, they regard their dupes as having inadequate judgment, or as likely to respond in the wrong way to truthful information."[50]

This attitude, and the dilemma it poses for policy makers, can work to undermine democratic processes and create serious moral problems for covert action practitioners. This is well illustrated by the case of Richard Helms, former DCI and ambassador to Iran. During his confirmation hearings, he was asked if the CIA had tried to overthrow the government of Chile, to which he replied in the negative. The CIA did indeed intervene covertly and on a broad scale in the Chilean political process. Yet Helms felt bound by his oath to protect intelligence sources and methods, and thus dissembled in order not to reveal publicly what the CIA had done secretly. For his statement, Helms was convicted of giving false testimony to a congressional committee and was fined. Helms's two oaths, to the CIA and to the committee, and the differing weights given to them by him and by the court, illustrate the complexity of the moral dilemmas involved in using deception to protect covert action operations.[51]

Evaluating the 1964 and 1970 Chile Operations

A just-war proponent reviewing the two covert operations in Chile would likely reach two conclusions: first, the 1964 operation was more justifiable than the 1970 activity; second, both operations would have benefited from a more rigorous application of the *jus ad bellum* and *jus in bello* criteria.

U.S. authorities probably would have considered that their covert intervention in the 1964 election was generally consistent with the *jus ad bellum*. It had clear objectives (preservation of an important democratic force in Chile and defense against the establishment of another Communist stronghold in the western hemisphere). These were set by President Kennedy, based on his assessment of the commonality of U.S. and Chilean interests. While not a last resort, it was conducted in the context of, and was consistent with, an overall overt policy (the Alliance for Progress); was likely to be successful; and was limited in scope and generally proportionate to the perceived threat. It was approved in accordance with the established procedures, though in retrospect the process would have been strengthened if Congress had been consulted. There was a rationale for secret, as opposed to overt, funding of the elections: if U.S. support were revealed, it could discredit the candidate.

Some doubts can be raised regarding consistency with the *jus in bello*. The need for "scare tactics" and "black propaganda" is not obvious. (If indeed Allende's affinities to the USSR and Cuba were on the public record, promulgation of this truthful information should have been adequate.) As Bok notes, lying and deception carry a "negative weight," and require explanation and justification.[52] If not clearly necessary to respond to Cuban or Soviet activities, such deceptive actions would not meet the test of proportionality.

The 1970 "Track II" operation, in contrast, violated virtually all of the just-war guidelines. Its objective was clear (prevent Allende's confirmation), but little thought apparently was given to the consequences for the Chilean people or political system. As William Bundy noted, "In legal terms, a U.S. judicial proceeding would surely have concluded that U.S. agents (acting on presidential authority) had been at least accessories before the fact and co-conspirators in the kidnapping [of Schneider] and thus in the killing that resulted from it."[53]

There were also moral flaws in the decision-making process. The normal procedures were bypassed, and Nixon made the fateful Track II decision in a state of high emotion. According to Bundy, "Nixon and Kissinger never gave Chile the attention required under their own decision-making system, and acted impulsively, with inadequate reflection. Their acts were not only morally repugnant but ran grave risks of the eventual exposure that damaged the United States in Latin American eyes."[54]

No expert believed that in the 1970 operation success was likely. The methods chosen were initially inadequate (the "spoiling operation") and subsequently, when support for coup plotting took center stage, the intermediaries could not be controlled. Despite the fact that injury to innocent parties was a foreseeable outcome of the coup, no advance provision was made to prevent or minimize it. In light of the intelligence assessment that the United States lacked vital interests in Chile, it is hard to rationalize support for a potentially violent military coup as a proportionate response. The rationalization for the secrecy surrounding the operation is questionable. There was no specific candidate who needed protection, and the secrecy concealed the support of violent interference with Chile's constitutional process.

In sum, the Chile case shows that the just-war tradition can provide a useful framework for evaluating covert political action by asking penetrating questions: Is the operation directed at a just cause, properly authorized, necessary and proportionate? Is it likely to succeed, and how will it be controlled? Is it a last resort, a convenience or merely an action taken in frustration? In the case of the 1964 operation, the answers to most of these questions were satisfactory; in 1970 they were not.

Reforms Since the 1970s

In the more than two decades since Track II, significant improvements have been made in controlling covert action. The doctrine of "plausible deniability," which allowed senior officials to disclaim responsibility for their actions, has been replaced by one intended to secure direct presidential accountability. Since the Hughes–Ryan Amendment of 1974, a series of laws has been enacted requiring the president personally to "find" that proposed covert actions are important to the national security, and to report such operations to Congress in a timely manner. (Debate has continued over what constitutes timely notification.) In the wake of the Iran–contra scandal, more stringent procedures were implemented by the executive branch and then by Congress.

Under the current system, established by the Reagan administration in 1987 and refined by legislation in 1991, a written "finding" must be signed before a covert action operation commences; in extreme circumstances an oral finding may be made and then immediately documented in writing. A memorandum of notification (MON), also approved by the president, is required for a significant change in the means of implementation, level of resources, assets, operational conditions, cooperating foreign countries or risks associated with a covert action. Each finding or MON includes a statement of policy objectives; a description of the actions authorized, resources required and participating organizations; a statement that indicates whether private individuals or organizations or foreign governments will be involved; and an assessment of risk. A finding or MON is reviewed by a senior committee of the NSC, and by the NSC legal advisor and counsel to the president. Copies of findings and MONs are provided to the Congress at the time of notification, except in rare cases of extreme sensitivity.[55]

The Bush and Clinton administrations have followed essentially the same procedures, but the end of the Cold War has meant a redirection of covert action resources. As described in chapter 3, President Bush initiated covert attempts to weaken Iraqi dictator Saddam Hussein. This activity continued into the Clinton administration, generating considerable controversy but little in the way of results. According to press reports, the effort against Saddam included propaganda as well as military training of Kurdish guerrillas in northern Iraq. A former CIA official, whose comments to the press were investigated by the Department of Justice, has claimed that factionalism within the CIA, as well as disagreement among U.S. government agencies, undermined the covert program and led to the compromise of individuals and groups that had been recruited to oppose Saddam.[56]

In response to the changing challenge to U.S. interests, the Clinton administration has redirected its covert action efforts toward disrupting terrorist groups, drug traffickers and nations or groups engaged in proliferation of advanced weapons. According to press stories, intelligence agencies now use computer technology to interfere with money transfers, sabotage shipments of weapons or drugs and attempt to spoil relationships among adversary groups. While "traditional" operations are under way, including activities directed against Iran and Iraq, the emphasis has shifted to the new global threats. This change reflects not only a recognition of the new challenges but also an attitude that the arming of exile groups and guerillas requires sizable resources and management attention, and that such groups often cannot be controlled adequately to ensure the accountability that Congress and the American public require.[57]

AN APPROACH FOR THE TWENTY-FIRST CENTURY

The reforms carried out since the 1970s are positive, because they provide for broader consultation, a legal review, presidential accountability and congressional involvement in covert action decisions. And the Clinton administration's decision to deemphasize covert interference with foreign governments in favor of targeting terrorism, drugs and illicit weapons is also a move in the right direction. However, the content of findings and MONs, as described above, leaves much to be desired from the perspective of the just-war tradition. The Chile case suggests that explicit attention to the key questions raised by just-war guidelines can strengthen the ethical content of covert actions. Recent activities, including the abortive Iraq operation, indicate that continued sharp questioning of proposed covert activities is essential. In short, the current system addresses the legality, feasibility and political sensitivity of proposed covert actions. It does not, however, ensure that they are conducted according to a rigorous ethical standard.

The United States needs a new policy for managing covert action. While it is not necessary that political leaders become philosophers, they would be well served by establishing a policy process modeled after the just-war criteria. To do this, the current procedures should be revised so that at each stage in the covert action approval process, difficult questions are asked about the objectives, methods and management of a proposed operation. It is equally important that they be answered in detail, with rigor and in writing—even (perhaps especially) when time is of the essence. Covert operators are reluctant to commit sensitive details to paper, but this is essential if the United States is to meet high standards of accountability when the easy rationalization of fighting communism is no longer available.

A decision-making process structured explicitly around just-war guidelines is, in many ways, simply a restatement of Webster's criteria of consistency with law, American values and public mores. In that sense, just-war criteria merely reiterate the obvious, and make explicit the goals toward which the United States has strived in its reforms of the covert action process since the mid-1970s. But there is value to building a more systematic framework for substantive debate, even if many of these questions are already considered in the CIA's Covert Action Review Group, the senior NSC groups or the oversight committees. The questions of concern include the following:

Just Cause: Exactly what are the objectives of the operation? Is it defensive—to repel an identifiable threat—or is it intended to redress a wrong, to punish wrongdoing or to reform a foreign country? Against whom or what are we conducting the operation? Whom are we for? What specific changes in the behavior or policy of the target country, group or individual do we seek?

Just Intention: What will be the likely result in the target country and in other countries? How will we or the international community be better off? How will we know if we have succeeded? What will we do if we win? If we lose?

Competent Authority: Who has reviewed the proposal? Are there dissents? What is the view of intelligence analysts on the problem being considered? Have senior government officials discussed the proposal in detail? Has the Congress been advised of all significant aspects of the covert activity? If notification has been restricted, what is the justification?

Last Resort: What overt options are being considered? What are their strengths and weaknesses? Why is covert action necessary? Why must the proposed activity be secret? What steps will be taken to ensure that proposed secret activities are consistent with openly declared policies and that the appropriate oversight bodies are informed?

Probability of Success: What is the likelihood that the action will succeed? Are there differing views of the probability of success? Is the view of disinterested observers different from that of advocates or opponents? Why?

Proportionality: What specific methods are being considered? Does the proposal envision the use of lethal force, sabotage, economic disruption or false information? Why are these methods necessary? Are they the same as those being used by the adversary, or are they potentially more damaging or disruptive? If so, what is the justification?

Discrimination: What steps will be taken to safeguard the innocent against death, injury, economic hardship or psychological damage? What will be done to protect political institutions and processes against disproportionate damage? If some damage is inevitable, what steps are being taken to minimize it? What controls does the United States exercise over the agents to be employed? What steps will be taken if they disregard our directions? What steps will be taken to protect the agents, and what are our obligations to them? How will the operation be terminated if its objectives are achieved? How will it be terminated if it fails?

Each of these questions should be investigated in the initial approval process, and in periodic reviews by the NSC and the oversight committees.

The Casuistry of Covert Action: Just Cause and Proportionality

Critics of the just-war tradition note that in the hands of advocates, the criteria can deteriorate into mere rationalizations of intended actions. Scholars acknowledge that moral reasoning is especially complex and difficult in cases involving politics and international affairs.[58] Just-war criteria, then, can be exceedingly useful as an organizing principle, but—in themselves—do not necessarily provide clear answers.[59] How can this inherent uncertainty be minimized? William Colby has suggested giving special attention to the criteria of just cause and proportionality.[60] With respect to just cause, a report by a panel of distinguished scholars has recommended that covert action should be undertaken only in support of a publicly articulated policy.[61] Open, public debate would go a long way toward determining whether a proposed course of action could be construed as a just cause. The need for such debate is so fundamental that if it cannot be conducted, this in itself would seem to be grounds for rejection of any suggested operation.

Assessments of proportionality cannot have the same open scrutiny, because they involve secret methods. Nevertheless, proposed activities must meet strict tests of consistency with American values. Loch Johnson has attempted to rank-order various types of covert operations into a "ladder of escalation," and he introduces a useful concept of "thresholds" that involve different degrees of risk and interference in foreign countries.[62] Following Johnson, proposed covert activities could be arrayed for debate under thresholds of increasing ethical concern:

Limited Concern: Benign provision of truthful information or support to existing political forces; intervention to keep election processes honest

Significant Concern: Manipulative use of information; rigging of elections or other distortion of political processes; creating new political forces or strengthening existing ones out of proportion to their indigenous support

Serious Concern: Deceptive use of information, nonlethal sabotage and economic disruption

Grave Concern: Use of lethal force; forcible changes in government.

Policy Implications

The end of the Cold War means that U.S. policy on covert action can no longer be based on sweeping generalities. Covert interventions abroad should be less frequent; each proposed action must be justified on a case-by-case basis and on its own merits. Adopting a covert action management system that makes explicit use of the guidelines and thresholds above would move the process substantially in this direction.

Under these guidelines, the types of covert actions that involve the gravest moral risks—lethal force and forcible changes of government—would be exceedingly rare, reserved to be employed only for the clearest threats to U.S. security or redressing the most serious abuses of human rights. The bias would be toward the lower levels of intervention—primarily propaganda and political action programs that carry less risk of destruction and moral damage. This would mean that the United States would have less need for a standing capability for large-scale covert military action than during the Cold War, but it should retain a modest infrastructure of covert action programs to provide a base for mobilization if necessary.

Covert action programs of the "traditional" type, those aimed at overthrowing foreign governments or influencing political processes, would be subjected to particularly close scrutiny and would be undertaken very rarely. Instead, there would be a continuation of the Clinton administration's policy of shifting covert action resources to countering international terrorism, crime, drug trafficking and weapons proliferation. To the extent that the targets of these covert programs are in violation of laws or international norms, the secret operations become more analogous to undercover police activities than to interference with foreign governments.

Equally important, a covert action policy process derived from just-war guidelines would obligate the United States to keep faith with its foreign agents. Indeed, the criteria would strongly discourage any covert action in which the United States raises the hopes of its supporters overseas, only to abandon them when the political will to continue the operation is lost. U.S. officials would be required to level with their agents about the risks of an operation, the probability of success and the steps that would be taken to safeguard their interests.

The just-war guidelines set a higher ethical standard than a policy based solely on realpolitik. Although the recommended process would likely result in far fewer covert actions, there is no reason to believe that the United States would be prevented from responding to serious threats. Kissinger's high-handed, disproportionate manipulation of the Chilean political system would be prohibited. But other types of covert action, carefully crafted and keyed to the interests they are intended to support, would still be possible. Moreover, they would likely receive greater political support, and thus have a greater likelihood of success, than some of the poorly thought out, unfocused programs of the past. In sum, there is no necessary contradiction between a systematic, thoughtful process for managing covert action and a realistic appraisal of national interest.

It is important to note a limitation to this proposed policy. Reforms of congressional oversight and executive branch supervision, and even a rigorous set of guidelines based on the just-war tradition, would not prevent unwise decisions or close all barriers to ineffective or harmful programs. It is important that leaders implement the suggested reforms in good faith. In this, they must be guided by Aristotle and Aquinas's principles of normative prudence. They must deliberate, and not rush to judgment as Nixon did in 1970. They must consider the details of proposed programs, and all possible contingent outcomes, not just the ones they prefer. They must take the risk of seeking advice outside the closed circle of covert action advocates, and in particular consult with people who are likely to raise difficult questions and challenges.

Presidents must also abandon the practice of using covert action when they are frustrated by diplomatic failure but unwilling to use military force. Just as the just-war tradition has a strong bias against the use of military force, so the proposed approach to managing covert action would have a strong bias against secret intervention. While not necessarily a last resort, covert action should not be an easy step for policy makers to take. Above all, key leaders, especially the president, must be convinced that secret operations are essential, not merely a political convenience. They must consciously weigh the short-term benefit of secrecy and deception against the long-term impact on the credibility and efficacy of the democratic form of government.

CONCLUSION

Such an application of the just-war framework would not end controversy regarding covert action, nor would it prevent inappropriate or unethical actions. The claim for a conscious application of just-war guidelines is modest: it will help to make Webster's commonsense criteria more rigorous, and to improve the quality of decisions regarding one of the most controversial aspects of U.S. national security policy.

Reforming the process along the lines suggested would signal that the United States is concerned—even in secret activities—with issues of right and wrong, and not merely with power. It would promote openness and accountability, and underscore that the United States firmly rejects the "repugnant philosophy" of the Doolittle Report.

NOTES

An early version of this chapter appeared as "Managing Covert Political Action: Insights from Just War Theory," *Studies in Intelligence* (1992). A revised version was first published as "Covert Action Can Be Just," *Orbis* (Summer 1993), copyright by Foreign Policy Research Institute, Philadelphia, PA, 1993; used with permission.

1. "Report of the Special Study Group [Doolittle Committee] on the Covert Activities of the Central Intelligence Agency, September 30, 1954 [excerpts]," in *The Central Intelligence Agency, History and Documents,* William M. Leary, ed. (University: The University of Alabama Press, 1984), p. 144.

2. Excerpt from Executive Order 12333, December 4, 1981, quoted in Abram N. Shulsky, *Silent Warfare: Understanding the World of Intelligence* (Washington, DC: Brassey's, 1991), p. 74.

3. Shulsky, *Silent Warfare*, p. 73

4. Ibid., pp. 79–85.

5. Ibid., pp. 86–87.

6. Ibid., pp. 89–90.

7. John Ranelagh, *The Agency: The Rise and Decline of the CIA* (New York: Simon & Schuster, 1986), p. 133.

8. Ibid., p. 137.

9. Ibid.

10. Ibid., p. 216.

11. Gregory Treverton, *Covert Action: The Limits of Intervention in the Postwar World* (New York: Basic Books, 1987), p. 5.

12. Langan notes that just-war theory has both material and formal aspects, and that the formal aspects, such as just intention and proportionality, are applicable to a broad range of situations where one has to do harm to another, including punishment, surgery and—by extension—political or economic intervention. John P. Langan, letter to author dated May 28, 1992.

13. The following discussion is drawn primarily from documents of the United States Senate's Church Committee, which investigated CIA covert actions in the mid-1970s, as well as from memoirs of some of the participants and other government officials and commentators (including William Colby, Henry Kissinger, Cord Meyer, David Atlee Phillips and Arthur Schlesinger). A summary of the Church Committee's findings and recommendations for reform is found in Treverton, *Covert Action.* A case study based on Treverton's research was published by the Carnegie Council on Ethics and International Affairs in 1990 under the title, "Covert Intervention in Chile, 1970-1973."

14. Treverton, *Covert Action,* p. 18.

15. United States Senate, *Staff Report of the Select Committee to Study Government Operations with Respect to Intelligence Activities: Covert Action in Chile, 1963–73,* 94th Cong., 1st sess. (Washington, DC: U.S. Government Printing Office, 1975), pp. 15–17.

16. Treverton, *Covert Action,* p. 21.

17. *New York Times,* March 12, 1976, sec. 1, p. 14.

18. Ranelagh, *The Agency,* p. 515.

19. Assessment dated September 7, 1970, declassified and quoted in United States Senate, *Staff Report of the Select Committee.*

20. Treverton, *Covert Action,* p. 100.

21. Ibid., p. 102.

22. Ranelagh, The Agency, p. 515.

23. Treverton, *Covert Action,* p. 103.

24. Ibid., p. 104.

25. The U. S. decision process is described in detail in United States Senate Select Committee to Study Governmental Operations with Respect to Intelligence Activities, *Alleged Assassination Attempts Involving Foreign Leaders,* 94th Cong., 1st sess., Rept 94-465 (Washington, DC: U.S. Government Printing Office, 1975), as well as in Ranelagh, *The Agency,* pp. 514–520.

26. U.S. Senate Select Committee, *Alleged Assassination Attempts Involving Foreign Leaders,* pp. 227–28.

27. Ibid., p. 227.

28. Ibid., p. 228.

29. Ibid., p. 233.

30. David Atlee Phillips, *The Night Watch* (New York: Ballentine Books, 1977), pp. 283–87.

31. Treverton, *Covert Action,* p. 133.

32. Ibid., p. 141.

33. Ibid., p. 142.

34. W. Michael Reisman and James E. Baker, *Regulating Covert Action* (New Haven: Yale University Press, 1992), p. 60.

35. Treverton, *Covert Action.*, p. 143.

36. Quoted in ibid., p. 137.

37. Ibid.

38. U.S. Senate Select Committee, *Alleged Assassination Attempts Involving Foreign Leaders*, p. 246.

39. *Report of the Twentieth Century Fund Task Force on Covert Action and American Democracy* (New York,:Twentieth Century Press, 1992).

40. Riesman and Baker, *Regulating Covert Action*, pp. 140–41.

41. See chapter 4. A wide-ranging discussion of this topic was held at the Symposium on Moral and Legal Constraints on Low-Intensity Conflict, sponsored by the Office of the Assistant Secretary of Defense for Special Operations and Low Intensity Conflict, U.S. Naval War College, Newport, RI, April 9–10, 1992.

42. R. James Woolsey, Address to the 1994 Office of Government Ethics Conference, September 13, 1994. Emphasis added. Langan's seminal work appears in "National Interest, Morality and Intelligence," paper presented to CIA-sponsored Conference on Ethics and the Profession of Intelligence, held at a CIA facility, May 1983.

43. Arthur S. Hulnick and Daniel W. Mattausch, "Ethics and Morality in United States Secret Intelligence," *Harvard Journal of Law and Public Policy* 87, no. 1 (Spring 1989): 512.

44. William E. Colby, "Public Policy, Secret Action," *Ethics and International Affairs* 3 (1989): 63.

45. William H. Webster, "Ethics: A Respect for Truth," *Cornell International Law Journal* 23, no. 1 (Winter 1990): 51.

46. Sissela Bok, *Secrets: On the Ethics of Concealment and Revelation* (New York: Pantheon Books, 1982), p. 27.

47. Ibid., p. 107.

48. Ibid., p. 191.

49. Charles R. Beitz, "Covert Intervention as a Moral Problem," *Ethics and International Affairs* 3 (1989): 49–50.

50. Sissela Bok, *Lying: Moral Choice in Public and Private Life* (New York: Random House, 1978), p. 168.

51. Mark Lilla, *The Two Oaths of Richard Helms*, case study C14-83-525.0 (Cambridge, MA: John F. Kennedy School of Government, Harvard University, 1983).

52. Bok, *Lying*, p. 30.

53. William P. Bundy, *A Tangled Web: The Making of Foreign Policy in the Nixon Presidency* (New York: Hill and Wang, 1998), p. 203.

54. Ibid.

55. Executive Office of the President, National Security Council, National Security Decision Directive (NSDD) 286, partially declassified on December 15, 1987; Intelligence Authorization Act, Fiscal Year 1991, Title VI.

56. "How CIA's Secret War on Saddam Collapsed," *Washington Post*, June 26, 1997, sec. A, p. 21.

57. "CIA Turns to Boutique Operations, Covert Action Against Terrorism, Drugs, Arms," *Washington Post*, September 14, 1997, sec. A, p. 6.

58. Joseph Boyle, "Natural Law and International Ethics," in *Traditions of International Ethics*, Terry Nardin and David Mapel, eds., (Cambridge: Cambridge University Press, 1992) p. 115.

59. The author is indebted to Joel Rosenthal of the Carnegie Council on Ethics and International Affairs for this point. Letter to author, May 12, 1992.

60. Colby, "Public Policy, Secret Action."

61. *Report of the Twentieth Century Fund Task Force on Covert Action and American Democracy*, p. 8.

62. Loch K. Johnson, "On Drawing a Bright Line for Covert Operations," *American Journal of International Law* 86, no. 2 (April 1992): 286.

6

The Ethics of Economic Warfare:
The United States and Castro's Cuba

CASTRO'S CHALLENGE

When Fidel Castro proclaimed in December 1961 that he was, and always had been, a Marxist, his statement merely confirmed a judgment that had been reached nearly two years before in U.S. government and business circles. Since Castro had taken power in January 1959, the United States had watched warily as he progressively tightened his control over political and economic activity in Cuba. By the end of that year, he had promulgated a radical Agrarian Reform Act, delivered a biting anti-American speech at the United Nations and purged the anticommunist elements from his government. At the turn of the year, the Eisenhower administration had concluded that Castro was a threat to U.S. interests, and in the spring of 1960 the president approved a program of covert and overt actions intended to overthrow Castro and replace his government with one more malleable and acceptable to the United States. The program included both economic sanctions and clandestine sabotage of the Cuban economy, aimed at undercutting Castro's hold on power and inciting resistance among the Cuban people.[1]

This chapter explores the United States' response to Castro's challenge and, in particular, its use of economic coercion. The focus is on several key turning points in U.S. economic policy toward Cuba: Eisenhower's decisions to cut the Cuban sugar quota and to impose an embargo, Kennedy's expansion of the embargo following the failure of the Bay of Pigs invasion and the further strengthening and extension of sanctions under the Helms–Burton Act of 1996. Though not an exhaustive recounting of U.S. policy toward the Castro regime, these decisions help to clarify the intent of U.S. actions, as well as the arguments for and against economic coercion. Together, they provide insight into the ethical dimensions of economic measures as a tool of statecraft.

THE SETTING

Given Cuba's strategic location, it is no surprise that the island has been a focal point of U.S. concern since the early days of the republic. Located some 90 miles from Florida, Cuba commands the major sea routes from the eastern United States to the Gulf Coast and the approaches to the Panama Canal. It has been a major source of sugar for the U.S. market, a playground for tourists and a haven for gamblers and racketeers.

President Jefferson tried to buy Cuba from Spain in 1807, fearing that it would fall into British hands. In 1823, John Quincy Adams, then secretary of state, cited the following as among the factors that gave Cuba its strategic importance:

Its commanding position with reference to the Gulf of Mexico and the West India seas; the character of its population; its situation midway between our southern coast and the island of San Domingo; its safe and capacious harbor of . . . Havana . . . the nature of its productions and of its wants, furnishing the supplies and needing the returns of a commerce immensely profitable and mutually beneficial.[2]

From Adams's day until the end of the nineteenth century, Cuba remained a Spanish possession, but one with a special and complex relationship with the United States. The United States' motivation was both idealistic and pragmatic. While secretary of state in 1905, Elihu Root referred to American attitudes toward Cuba as "altruistic and sentimental;" President Cleveland had earlier observed that economic (as well as strategic) interests were dominant.[3]

In the period before the American Civil War, three presidents made offers to buy the island, primarily because of pressures from slaveholding interests that feared an "Africanization of Cuba."[4] There were also several unsuccessful armed expeditions. Following the Civil War, Cuban liberators, propagandizing and organizing forces on U.S. territory, fomented resistance to Spanish rule, leading to the unsuccessful Ten Years' War for independence from 1868 to 1878. Lobbying by Cuban exiles nearly provoked the United States into military intervention, and the United States unsuccessfully tried to negotiate a truce in 1875.[5] One result of the insurrection and the U.S. pressure was the abolition of slavery in Cuba in 1888.[6]

In the 1890s, several events finally pushed the United States to intervene militarily in Cuba. Sugar prices fell dramatically, and the United States' imposition of tariffs contributed to economic panic in Cuba. In 1895, Cuban rebels under José Martí, representing a junta based in New York, established a "republican government" in the eastern portion of the island and demanded the recall of the Spanish governor.[7] Reports of repression and unrest in Cuba reached Washington, and President McKinley dispatched the battleship *Maine* to Havana to protect American citizens. The destruction of the ship in a mysterious explosion inflamed U.S. opinion, and in April 1898 the Congress called on the president to use military force to liberate Cuba from Spain.

Following a bloody conflict that turned out not to be the "splendid little war" that had been expected, the United States set up a military government in Cuba. In 1899, General Leonard Wood, a proponent of annexation, became governor and imposed a series of administrative and political reforms, almost totally ignoring Cuban leaders in the process.[8]

From November 1900 to February 1901, a constitutional convention was held in Cuba. The United States pressured the delegates to enshrine America's special relationship to Cuba in the constitution, and Secretary of War Root threatened to extend the U.S. occupation until such a provision was enacted. Subsequently, Senator Orville Platt secured passage of a rider to an Army appropriation bill that limited Cuba's treaty-making power and gave the United States the right to intervene to preserve Cuba's independence or political stability.[9] The constitutional convention agreed, reluctantly, to these terms, and the Platt Amendment was incorporated into the Cuban constitution on June 2, 1901. By the middle of the next year, the U.S. occupation had ended and Cuba was formally independent. In fact, however, Cuba was to be "unoccupied but not fully sovereign" for more than 30 years.[10]

The United States not only reserved the right of military intervention, but it virtually ran the Cuban economy. Between 1913 and 1928, American investments in Cuba increased by more than 500 percent. American sugar interests, which had produced about 15 percent of the Cuban crop in 1906, controlled some 70–80 percent by the late 1920s.[11] The United States also dominated Cuban tobacco, ranching, mining, utilities, railroads and banking.[12] Political disputes arose over American sugar tariffs in the 1920s and 1930s, and a succession of Cuban political leaders exploited them in their attempts to secure power.

In 1933, a Cuban Army sergeant, Fulgencio Batista, overthrew President Machado and consolidated his control over the political system (although he did not formally assume the presidency until 1940). In 1934, the new regime was recognized by the United States and a new treaty was negotiated, eliminating the despised Platt Amendment. In addition, a new Reciprocal Trade Agreement provided tariff relief and a second law established a quota for sugar.[13] Batista was careful to protect U.S. business interests and, although he did not hold political office continuously, he dominated Cuban political life until his ouster in 1959. In the 1950s, Cubans gained a greater measure of control of their economy; by the middle of the decade most banks were Cuban-owned, and by 1958, the U.S.-controlled share of sugar production fell to 37 percent. The United States still dominated Cuba's economic destiny, continuing to be the dominant market for its exports.[14] And the influence of American organized crime on the Cuban economy grew as mobsters "collaborated with Batista to turn the island into a tourist playground of gambling, sex and booze."[15]

But while Cubans achieved some economic gains under Batista, they paid a heavy cost. Political repression was common. "Graft and corruption, inhuman cruelties, gross misuse of government power, and many other manifestations of tyranny became conspicuous."[16] Opposition arose both to Batista's rule and to the active role of the United States in supporting him. Guerrilla operations increased in frequency and intensity, and anti-Batista and anti-U.S. sentiment fused into an opposition ideology that stressed Cuban control over the island's resources and destiny.[17]

ACT ONE: EISENHOWER AND CASTRO

The principal proponent of this ideology was Fidel Castro. He first burst onto the scene on July 26, 1953, when he led an abortive attack on an army barracks in Santiago. Tried and imprisoned for his deeds, he was released by Batista in a general amnesty in 1955. Castro stayed briefly in Mexico, then returned to lead a small guerrilla army sequestered in the Sierra Maestra mountains. Castro and his followers espoused the ideology of Cuban nationalism, with vaguely socialistic overtones. He pledged the ouster of Batista, to be followed by free elections, constitutional reform and exclusion of foreign intervention.[18]

By mid-1957, opposition to Batista was growing in Cuba. First working-class Cubans, then the bourgeoisie, and finally business and civic leaders expressed their discontent and provided both moral and material support to Castro's 26 July Movement.[19] By early 1958, U.S. officials were aware that the Batista regime was weakening, and by midyear, Batista's army had essentially lost its effectiveness as a fighting force. At the urging of the U.S. ambassador, Batista called elections for November 3. Voter apathy and rebel threats combined to keep the turnout low, and Batista's hand-picked candidate won handily in a corrupt electoral process. In reaction, Washington withdrew its ambassador and sent a private citizen, William Pawley, to urge Batista to leave the country and turn the government over to a transitional military leadership. He refused.[20]

On New Years Day, 1959, Batista left Cuba, his power base shattered. Fidel Castro and his colleagues assumed power, and the United States recognized the new government on January 7.[21] The initial American reaction was mixed. The embassy in Havana characterized Castro's cabinet as "basically friendly toward the United States and oriented against communism."[22] In Congress, opinions ranged from approval of Batista's ouster to concerns that Castro would take a revolutionary course. A new American ambassador, Philip Bonsal, took up his post and pledged to pursue a policy of goodwill.

President Eisenhower and his closest advisers had already explored the implications of a Castro victory. At a meeting of the National Security Council (NSC) in December 1958, Allen Dulles, director of Central Intelligence (DCI), had proposed that the United States "ought to prevent a Castro victory." The rationale was that the Castro movement had been penetrated by Communists, "despite some efforts by Fidel to keep them out." Dulles was supported by Vice President Nixon, who cautioned that such an attempt should not involve support of Batista. Secretary of State Christian Herter proposed preparation of a contingency paper to explore creation of a "third force."[23]

The early months of Castro's regime found the United States embassy cautiously optimistic. A dispatch dated February 18, 1959, asserted that Castro's anti-U.S. attitude "is not deep-seated, and will give way in time to a general desire based largely on self interest, for good relations with the United States." U.S. policy, the embassy went on, should "hasten this process by showing patience, goodwill and cooperation toward Cuba."[24] Similarly, officials at the Department of State counseled that the United States should pursue "strengthening the mature, moderate group in Cuba

... [and] seeking to influence Fidel Castro and his more moderate supporters."[25] In pursuit of these objectives, the United States ambassador offered to discuss a new tariff structure, a formula permitting nationalization of some American property and short-term financial assistance.[26]

Events during 1959, however, were to shake this optimism and reinforce the anti-Castro sentiment at the highest levels of the Eisenhower administration. These included: "The regime's execution of *batistianos* after showy trials, agrarian reform progam [sic] that undercut North American economic interests, control of utilities industries, postponement of elections, tolerance of Communists, calls for revolution throughout Latin America, hints that Cuba would follow a neutralist course in the Cold War and vituperative anti-American rhetoric."[27]

Particularly troubling to the United States was the Cuban Agrarian Reform Law of May, 1959. The initial U.S. response was to acknowledge the right of Cuba to nationalize property, combined with "subtle threats of retaliation in the event of nationalization of U.S.-owned properties unaccompanied by appropriate compensation." In reaction to the law, members of Congress began to discuss a reduction in the Cuban sugar quota, but in June the Department of State was wary that this would "antagonize moderate forces in Cuba."[28] During the summer, some 400 U.S.-owned properties were seized, and State Department officials began to reexamine their position. One official predicted that "Castro, in order to survive," will take over the direction of all elements of the national economy, as did Peron." He went on to say that "With the signature of the Agrarian Reform Law, it seems clear that our original hope [of giving Castro a chance to succeed and strengthening the moderates around him] was a vain one; Castro's government is not the kind worth saving."[29]

In early November, important U.S. agricultural and mining properties were seized by the Castro regime. On November 5, Secretary Herter wrote to the president that a close observation of Castro's policies had led to three conclusions:

(a) that there is no reasonable basis to found our policy on a hope that Castro will voluntarily adopt policies and attitudes consistent with minimum United States security requirements and policy interests; (b) that the prolonged continuation of the Castro regime in Cuba in its present form would have serious adverse effects on the United States position in Latin America and corresponding advantages for international Communism; and (c) that only by the building up within Cuba of a coherent opposition consisting of elements desirous of achieving political and economic progress within a framework of good United States–Cuban relations can the Castro regime be checked or replaced.[30]

At this point in time, State Department and CIA officials began to discuss a program of covert action and economic sabotage to complement overt U.S. political and economic initiatives.[31] U.S.-based Cuban exiles had been harassing the Castro regime for some time—on October 21 the former head of the rebel air force had dropped anti-Castro propaganda over Havana—and now the U.S. intelligence agency swung its support behind these exile activities.[32] The extent to which the president was briefed on the details of these initiatives is not clear from the documents that have been made public, but according to subsequent records he approved a program authorizing the State Department and the CIA to "support elements opposed to the Castro Government while making Castro's downfall seem to be the result of his own mistakes."[33] There was an increase in CIA-supported exile air raids following the adoption of the new policy toward Cuba in the winter of 1959–60.[34] In addition, State Department officials carried out a detailed analysis of the Cuban economy, and examined the impact of a reduction in the Cuban sugar quota on economic prospects. The study concluded that even the unlikely action of a total cutoff of sugar imports from Cuba would result in a "significant but tolerable loss to Cuba of . . . between 4 and 5 percent of the national income."[35]

The National Security Council met to discuss Cuba on December 16, 1959, and DCI Dulles briefed the group on Castro's initiatives to "establish closer relations with the Afro-Asian Bloc."[36] On January 13, the 5412 Committee, which was responsible for planning covert actions, discussed Cuba, and Dulles reviewed contingency plans for ousting Castro.[37] Another NSC meeting took place on January 14, 1960, at which Assistant Secretary of State for Latin American Affairs Roy Rubottom outlined policy objectives. He noted that the State Department had been cooperating with the CIA to build up opposition to Castro. He also told the president and his advisers that the State and Agriculture departments had agreed on a plan to propose legislation that would extend the president's authority to alter sugar quotas, and that it might be possible that U.S. oil companies would take the initiative to cut off supplies to the Castro regime as well. At the end of the meeting, Vice President Nixon suggested—and the principals agreed—to keep the discussion in the utmost secrecy.[38]

On January 25, President Eisenhower met with key diplomatic and military advisers to refine his administration's policy toward Cuba. The following day, he issued a statement outlining that policy. It included a commitment to a course of nonintervention in the domestic affairs of other countries in accordance with long-standing treaty obligations, and the assertion that the United States was "doing all in its power to prevent the use of its territory for illegal acts against Cuba." The statement also noted that the U.S. government had confidence in the ability of the Cuban people to "recognize and defeat the intrigues of international communism."[39] This carefully worded policy statement masked the United States' secret policy of aiding Castro's overthrow and its growing interest in increasing the economic pressures on the Castro regime.

U.S. antagonism toward Castro accelerated in February 1960 with the visit of high-level Soviet officials to Cuba and the signing of a trade and aid pact by the two countries.[40] On March 10, the NSC met again to discuss the policy of unseating Castro. In regard to economic policy, Undersecretary of State C. Douglas Dillon said that "economic measures against Castro probably would not have much effect in a short time. Moreover Castro would probably be able to counteract economic sanctions by receiving what he needed from the Soviets." The president responded by suggesting that a blockade could prevent Soviet aid.[41]

On March 17, Eisenhower gave his approval to a 5412 committee plan to overthrow Castro, including the creation of a paramilitary force. The president agreed that there was "no better plan for dealing with this situation."[42] Although Eisenhower later insisted that this decision was only a "plan," and not a "program," to invade

Cuba, it is clear that the seeds of the abortive Bay of Pigs invasion were sown at the March 17 meeting.[43] In addition, at about this time the CIA undertook operations aimed at "discrediting Castro personally by influencing his behavior or altering his appearance," a reference to bizarre plots to use cigars impregnated with chemical agents to cause the Cuban leader to behave irrationally, and to put chemicals on his shoes that would cause his beard to fall out.[44] The NSC participants also discussed overt economic measures in the event of further Cuban nationalization of U.S. assets, including a cutoff of fuel supplies and suggestions to U.S. businesses that they leave Cuba.

In the months following inauguration of the covert invasion plan, U.S. officials gave increased attention to economic pressure against Cuba. One State Department official recommended that "every possible means should be undertaken promptly to weaken the economic life of Cuba [through] denying money and supplies to Cuba, to decrease monetary and real wages, to bring about hunger, desperation and overthrow of government."[45] Assistant Secretary Rubottom urged that the United States use "judiciously selected economic pressures . . . to engender public discomfort and discontent" by reducing Cuba's access to foreign exchange, most importantly through reduction of the sugar quota.[46]

The situation came to a head in mid-1960 when the Castro government demanded that U.S. oil companies process Soviet crude oil in their Cuban refineries. In a meeting with oil executives on June 2, Treasury Secretary Robert Anderson urged the companies to refuse the demand and to act in concert with U.S. policy.[47] On June 7 they did so. Also in early June, State Department officials met with representatives of the National Foreign Trade Council, a private business group, who urged import and export controls to cripple the Cuban economy.[48] At a special meeting of the NSC on June 22, Vice President Nixon, who chaired the meeting, expressed his concern about the burgeoning Cuban–Soviet relationship and his frustration that the Cuban economic situation was not deteriorating more rapidly. In response, Secretary Anderson counseled that "a basic question had to be answered before any economic warfare action should be taken; i.e., it had to be agreed that we are prepared to go the whole way [including] tariffs, sugar quotas and oil [and] discreet cooperation with U.S. interests." Secretary Herter noted that such actions are "difficult" under the Charter of the Organization of American States (OAS), and that the United States would have to "properly disguise" them. Nixon asserted that the time had come to take strong, positive action to avoid being labeled "Uncle Sucker."[49]

A week later the Castro government took over the three U.S.-owned oil refineries in Cuba. On July 7, Eisenhower suspended the Cuban sugar quota for the balance of 1960. Although the timing suggested that the decision was related to the seizure of the refineries, the documentary record indicates that such a measure had been under consideration for months.[50] Moreover, the record of the July 7 NSC meeting makes it clear that the suspension was part of a broader program to unseat Castro. Undersecretary Dillon, for example, mentioned suspension of trade under the Trading with the Enemy Act, freezing of Cuban assets in the United States and the cutting off of all economic transactions as possible future initiatives. Military officials indicated that they had prepared plans for a blockade, a U.S. seaborne invasion and a joint

military operation with South American countries. The CIA briefed on plans for a
clandestine radio station to broadcast anti-Castro propaganda.[51] Apparently also in
July, the CIA's Havana station was given instructions to assassinate Raul Castro,
Fidel's brother; the authorization was withdrawn a few hours later.[52]

Even while invoking the sanctions, however, Eisenhower had reservations about
their efficacy. Meeting with his national security adviser the following week, the
president said that "he was not at all sure that economic sanctions would have any real
effect on the Castro regime."[53] His reservations notwithstanding, the president and his
advisers pressed ahead, discussing how to enlist other nations in the economic
pressures against Cuba.

In August, Eisenhower was briefed on the CIA's covert action program, and
indicated a willingness to increase its funding.[54] Subsequent testimony and
documentation have made clear that about this time, the CIA began to work with
underworld figures in a plot to assassinate Castro.[55] (The evidence is unclear
regarding Eisenhower's role in or knowledge of the assassination plots.[56]) Through
the summer and early fall, Castro increased the socialization of the Cuban economy,
enacting new nationalization laws and formally taking over U.S.-owned utility assets
in addition to the oil companies.[57] In September, Dulles briefed the NSC that "under
the Castro regime, Cuba was now virtually a member of the Communist Bloc."[58] In
October, the United States imposed a near-total trade embargo on Cuba, limiting
exports to food and medicines. It did this, in the words of one official, not to "bring
the Cuban economy to a grinding halt" but to "exert a serious pressure on the Cuban
economy and contribute to the growing dissatisfaction and unrest in the country [and
to] bolster the morale of the opposition groups now active in Cuba and elsewhere."[59]

Thus, at the end of the Eisenhower presidency, the economic sanctions had become
an explicit complement to the CIA-sponsored program to stimulate opposition to
Castro and his eventual overthrow. But the intelligence community's analysts had
serious reservations about such a course. In a National Intelligence Estimate
published in December 1960, they stated:

We believe that during the period of this estimate Castro's control of Cuba will be further
consolidated. Organized opposition appears to lack the strength and coherence to pose a major
threat to the regime, and we foresee no development in the internal economic or political
situation which would be likely to bring about a critical shift of popular opinion away from
Castro. ... [T]he Communist Bloc will almost certainly take whatever steps are necessary to
sustain the Cuban economy. Economic dislocations will occur but will not lead to the collapse
or significant weakening of the Castro regime. . . . The prospects for effective international
action against Cuba remain poor.[60]

As it prepared to leave office, the Eisenhower administration formally broke
diplomatic relations with Cuba. As a legacy, Eisenhower left his successor a covert
plan to murder or overthrow Castro, to which economic warfare was an important
complement. Many in the administration, including the president himself, had serious
reservations about the effectiveness of the policy. And, as President Kennedy was to
discover to his sorrow, the intelligence analysts were correct in judging that neither
covert paramilitary action nor economic sanctions would suffice to remove Castro.

ACT TWO: KENNEDY AND CASTRO

Cuba was a central preoccupation of the new president, and gave him both his greatest failure and his most enduring success. A significant part of the Kennedy legend is the story of how the president, naive and inexperienced in his first months in office, approved the continuation of covert operations against Cuba that culminated in what history has come to call the "abortive Bay of Pigs invasion." Subsequently, the legend continues, Kennedy learned from his mistakes so that he was able to act resolutely and effectively during the 1962 Cuban missile crisis.[61] The focus of this analysis is on the period between the failure of the CIA-organized invasion of April 1961 and the missile crisis of October 1962. During these 18 months the Kennedy administration crafted its own Cuba policy, ratcheting up the pressure to include a carefully orchestrated, but ultimately unsuccessful, program of overt and covert political and economic warfare.

The saga begins on April 20, the day after the collapse of the invasion effort. According to Chester Bowles, who attended in place of Secretary of State Dean Rusk, the cabinet meeting called to assess the situation was "about as grim as any meeting I can remember in all my experience." President Kennedy appeared to Bowles to be shattered, and at one point simply got up and walked toward his office. Bowles was concerned that, as a newcomer to foreign affairs, Kennedy would be "an easy target for the military-CIA-paramilitary type answers which are often in specific logistical terms and which can be added, subtracted, multiplied or divided." He also worried about the influence that Bobby Kennedy and Vice President Lyndon Johnson would have; they "have no experience in foreign affairs, and they both realize that this is the central question of this period and are determined to be experts at it."[62] As Bowles had feared, the president that day asked the Defense Department to develop a plan for the overthrow of the Castro government using U.S. military forces.[63] The plan, however, was never put into operation.

Two days later, the NSC met to discuss Cuba. Bowles's notes reflect a continuing concern about the substance and process of policy-making:

I left the meeting with a feeling of intense alarm, tempered somewhat with the hope that this represented largely an emotional reaction of a group of people who were not used to setbacks or defeats and whose pride and confidence had been deeply wounded. However, I felt again the great lack of moral integrity which I believe is the central guide in dealing with tense and difficult questions, particularly when the individuals involved are tired, frustrated, and personally humiliated. If every question in the world becomes an intellectual exercise on a totally pragmatic basis, with no reference to moral considerations, it may be that we can escape disaster, but it will certainly be putting the minds of the White House group to a test when it becomes necessary to add up the components, large and small on the plus or minus side of a ledger, and when the minds that are attempting to do this are tired, uneasy, and unsure, the values and the arithmetic are unlikely to reflect wise courses.[64]

On April 27 the NSC met again, and Bowles reported that the atmosphere was somewhat more businesslike. He noted that "plans continue for all kinds of harassment to punish Castro. . . . However, the general feeling is that all this should be handled carefully, that there should not be too much publicity, that the attitudes of others should be taken into account."[65] The president and his advisers discussed a proposal, prepared by the Department of State, "to remove the threat to the United States and to the hemisphere posed by the Soviet-dominated Castro regime in a manner that will advance rather than injure our other hemispheric and world-wide interests." The proposal recommended "Development of a realistic, sound and honest moral posture," then went on to suggest specific measures, including the following:

- An active overt and covert psychological campaign designed to weaken Castro

- Gradual reduction of the export of foods and medicines to Cuba

- Training Cuban freedom fighters

- Supporting Cuban underground capabilities for intensified sabotage of the Cuban economy

- Seeking OAS agreement to isolate Cuba diplomatically and economically.[66]

This plan became, in broad outline, the policy of the Kennedy administration during 1961.

Like Bowles, the president had been concerned about the policy-making process. Consequently, he charged a committee led by General Maxwell Taylor to investigate the Bay of Pigs operation and recommend changes in policy and process. The Taylor Committee reported in June. It called for a continuing emphasis on covert operations and recommended that a special interdepartmental committee be set up. The committee's stress on covert action against Castro found a receptive audience in the administration. The CIA tried, through the summer of 1961, to infiltrate agents and to force Castro to divert scarce resources through sabotage operations such as burning sugarcane.[67] In August, a new program of selected sabotage was developed.[68]

In November, Kennedy authorized a new, wide-ranging program of covert actions called Operation Mongoose, to be managed by a high-level policy group, called the Special Group (Augmented), that would include the president's brother, Attorney General Robert Kennedy. Among the tasks that ultimately became part of Mongoose were the penetration of the black market by using "gangster elements," and other measures to create economic chaos in Cuba.[69] Kennedy approved this effort despite an intelligence assessment that concluded, "The Castro regime has sufficient popular support and repressive capabilities to cope with any internal threat likely to develop within the foreseeable future. The regime faces serious, but not insurmountable, economic difficulties . . . [T]he regime's capabilities for repression are increasing more rapidly than are the potentialities for active resistance."[70]

In addition to the psychological and economic warfare elements, the assassination plots—which had been suspended after the Bay of Pigs—were rekindled late in 1961. They were to continue until after the missile crisis of October 1962.[71] CIA officials have stated that Attorney General Robert Kennedy was aware of previous plots involving underworld figures to kill Castro.[72] Whether the president (or the attorney general acting on his behalf) actually ordered the resumption of assassination activities against Castro remains a topic of controversy. Richard Helms, CIA's deputy director for plans at the time of Mongoose, testified that he "never received a direct order to assassinate Castro, [but] he fully believed that the CIA was at all times acting within the scope of its authority and that Castro's assassination came within the bounds of the Kennedy administration's effort to overthrow Castro and his regime."[73] Lawrence Houston, former inspector general of the CIA, is quoted as saying that Attorney General Kennedy was angry about the agency's use of underworld figures in the assassination plots. According to Houston, "Kennedy was mad. He was mad as hell. But what he objected to was the possibility it would impede prosecution against [Mafia figures] Giancana and Rosselli. He was not angry about the assassination plot, but about our involvement with the Mafia."[74]

Mongoose continued up until the missile crisis. Indeed, the week before Soviet missiles were discovered in Cuba, the attorney general met with CIA officials and expressed his dissatisfaction with "lack of action in the sabotage field." He directed the agency to prepare plans for specific sabotage operations and for mining Cuban harbors.[75]

The Kennedy administration also vigorously pursued the expansion of overt economic pressures against Cuba. According to a senior administration official, the covert sabotage activities were specifically designed to complement economic sanctions by "keeping the Castro regime so off stride and unsettled that it couldn't concentrate its activities in harmful ends elsewhere."[76] A major part of the economic program was to enlist the support of the OAS and the United States' European allies. Finally, it was Castro himself who provided the key with his "I am a Marxist" speech in December 1961. The following month, the United States convinced the Latin American countries to agree to "exclusion of the present government of Cuba from participation in the inter-American system."[77] The United States then moved progressively to tighten the noose. In February 1962, Kennedy banned virtually all imports from Cuba. In July, at U.S. behest, the OAS voted to suspend military sales to Cuba. In October, Kennedy received authority to withhold foreign aid from countries that allowed ships carrying their flag to transport goods to or from Cuba.[78]

Following the missile crisis, Kennedy took additional steps. He encouraged maritime unions to boycott ships that traded with Cuba. In July 1963, the United States, under the Trading with the Enemy Act, froze all Cuban assets, amounting to some $33 million. That same month, NATO agreed to a U.S. proposal to embargo military goods.[79]

Thus Kennedy, like his predecessor, embedded economic sanctions in a broader policy that included political pressure and, more important, a secret program of propaganda, sabotage and murder. And he did this despite a public stance that stressed America's moral leadership and responsibility. Kennedy said, according to biographer Ted Sorensen, "We cannot, as a free nation, compete with our adversaries in tactics of terror, assassination, false promises, counterfeit mobs and crises."[80] Kennedy knew, moreover, based on his experience as well as on intelligence assessments, that these methods were unlikely to be effective against Castro. But he certainly tried.

ENTR'ACTE: SUBMARINES, TROOPS AND REFUGEES

Following the assassination of President Kennedy, the emphasis in U.S. policy toward Cuba shifted from attempts to murder Castro or overthrow him by force to reliance on economic pressures to discredit his regime and moderate his behavior. President Johnson ordered a review of public and covert actions against Cuba and concluded that the United States should retain its anti-Castro policy, but downplay violent means in favor of strengthening the embargo.[81] By the time Nixon succeeded Johnson, however, the economic sanctions were losing their effectiveness as more of Washington's allies found trade with Cuba to be profitable and the political arguments against it to be uncompelling. Moreover, the drift to the left in Latin American politics in the late 1960s and early 1970s eroded Cuba's political isolation in the inter-American system.[82]

The Nixon administration reportedly ordered an increase in CIA activities against Cuba, excluding paramilitary operations. These presumably would have violated the U.S.-Soviet agreement reached during the 1962 missile crisis, in which the Soviets promised to remove their offensive missiles in exchange for a U.S. pledge not to invade Cuba. In 1970, however, that understanding was endangered by the discovery of a possible Soviet submarine base under construction at the Cuban port of Cienfuegos. National Security Adviser Henry Kissinger persuaded Nixon that he should take a hard line and the president authorized Kissinger to confront the Soviet ambassador. Soviet submarines were never stationed at Cienfuegos, although several, including some older submarines carrying small numbers of offensive missiles, did visit the port.[83]

In the late 1970s, Cuba posed a new challenge for the United States by sending troops to support leftist movements in Angola and Ethiopia. Some moderation in this Cuban "adventurism" in 1977 led to the opening of diplomatic interest sections in Washington and Havana, and to some broad-ranging political discussions. In 1979, however, intelligence analysts reported the existence of a Soviet "combat brigade" in Cuba, prompting congressional pressure on President Carter to take forceful action and derailing the dialogue. The fear of a Soviet presence turned into a fiasco for Carter, however, when further research showed that the brigade was a training unit that had been in Cuba since the early 1960s.[84]

In the 1980s another dimension of the Cuban problem emerged when Castro released large numbers of political prisoners, ordinary criminals and other "undesirables" from custody and they fled Cuba in frail boats headed for the United States. The Reagan administration condemned Castro's action, as well as his support for revolutionary movements in El Salvador, Grenada and Nicaragua. In 1981, Reagan further tightened the embargo and set up a new anti-Castro broadcasting station. In 1982, the United States banned business and tourist travel to Cuba.[85] Reagan's successor, George Bush, made the sanctions even more stringent by signing the Cuban Democracy (Torcelli) Act in 1992. The act, justified as a response to Castro's abuses of human rights, prohibited trade by all subsidiaries of U.S. corporations, including trade in food and medicines. It also prohibited foreign ships from docking at U.S. ports for six months after visiting Cuba, even if they had been carrying humanitarian goods.[86]

ACT THREE: CLINTON, HELMS AND CASTRO

As a candidate, President Bill Clinton initially favored moderating the sanctions against Cuba. In April 1992, however, he came out in favor of the Torcelli bill, a move that some commentators attributed to political and financial support from the Cuban-American community.[87] Clinton's Cuba policy has been marked by an attempt to placate conflicting constituencies within his party and within the American body politic. Thus, although the embargo was extended during the Clinton administration, the president suspended some of the more controversial aspects of the new provisions.

The major innovation in Cuba policy under Clinton was the 1996 Cuban Liberty and Democratic Solidarity *(Libertad)* Act, more commonly called the Helms–Burton Act, after its Senate and House sponsors. The act was passed shortly after Cuban military aircraft attacked two U.S.-registered aircraft, flown by members of a Cuban exile group, in international waters off Cuba. The act had initially faced a presidential veto, but the public clamor that followed the attack made it impossible for Clinton to reject the legislation.

The Helms–Burton Act contains a controversial new provision that extends the reach of the U.S. embargo to foreign companies "trafficking" in the property of U.S. nationals that had been "confiscated" by the Castro government. This provision aims at providing a mechanism for Cuban exiles in the United States to sue third-country companies that make use of assets that the exiles owned before leaving Cuba. Suits can be brought in U.S. courts, and persons found liable under that act may be required to pay damages up to the fair market value of the property, plus interest from the date of confiscation.[88]

The law, however, gives the president the authority to suspend enforcement of this provision for successive periods of six months, based on a finding that each suspension "is necessary to the national interest and will expedite a transition to democracy in Cuba." President Clinton has done so three times.

The Helms–Burton Act was criticized as politically unwise and as inconsistent with both international law and U.S. foreign trade goals. Foreign governments protested the extraterritorial application of U.S. law by attempting to regulate the business activities of third-country persons outside U.S. territory. This constituted, in the view of critics, a "secondary boycott" that is inconsistent with trade agreements administered by the World Trade Organization.[89] The Libertarian Cato Institute claimed that the act, in seeking to promote human rights in Cuba, fails to recognize that "free trade is itself a human right."[90] Some international legal specialists argued that Helms–Burton is flawed because it "hampers the discretion of the executive branch; it places too much emphasis on property issues almost two generations old; it perverts our immigration and travel laws; and it seeks to impose American policy judgments on nationals of friendly foreign states in a manner that is both unlawful and unwise."[91] Others contended that the United States has a legitimate interest in countering Castro's suppression of democracy and that "discouraging foreign investment in tainted Cuban property is an appropriate and proportionate means toward that goal."[92]

Another criticism of Helms–Burton was that the legislation has had perverse and unintended consequences. According to a study by the United Nations Economic Commission on Latin America and the Caribbean, after the Helms–Burton legislation was introduced, there was a sharp increase in the amount of U.S. currency sent by Cuban Americans to friends and relatives in Cuba. These remittances were estimated to have reached $800 million in 1996, an amount equal to Cuba's dollar earnings from tourism and sugar combined. Thus, the underlying intent of Helms–Burton was being undermined by the actions of the very political community that pressed for its passage.[93]

In the late 1990s, the United States continues its use of economic sanctions to force a change in Cuban external behavior and internal practices. Powerful constituencies and political figures argue for this policy. But the United States stands virtually alone. Opposition by major allies and trading partners has grown since the passage of Helms–Burton. And the broader community of nations has disassociated itself from the U.S. policy. The United Nations General Assembly has for a number of years passed an annual resolution calling for an end to the sanctions; in 1997, the vote was 144 countries in favor of their cessation, 7 countries abstaining and only 3 (including the United States) voting for continuation.[94]

JUST WAR AND ECONOMIC SANCTIONS

Economic sanctions cause harm. The formal aspects of the just-war tradition—those dealing with when harm may be done and how it should be limited—are applicable to any human activity involving deliberate or inadvertent injury to people. Albert Pierce, drawing on Michael Walzer's work, suggests an analogy between economic sanctions and siege warfare. Both are appropriate subjects for moral scrutiny because they "are intended to inflict great human suffering, pain, harm and even death."[95] Pierce argues that just-war principles, with some modifications, shed useful light on the use of sanctions as an instrument of foreign policy. In particular, he stresses the criteria of proportionality and discrimination as posing critical tests for any sanctions policy.[96]

How does the United States' Cuba policy measure up to the just-war criteria? With respect to the *jus ad bellum* standards, there are serious questions. Just cause and just intention are critical moral elements in any decision to do injury. The United States has, at various times, sought to overthrow the Castro government, to change its international behavior or to modify its internal policies, especially with respect to human rights. The first of these is not consistent with the just-war tradition. The responsibility for determining the form and composition of the Cuban government rests with the Cuban people. This is not to say that the United States, or any other power, could not aid a legitimate opposition movement, but that movement must first demonstrate that it is representative and capable of exercising political influence on its own merits. To create an opposition movement is different from aiding an existing one, and morally open to greater question. It risks violating the basic principle, formulated by John Stuart Mill and developed in a deontological formulation by Walzer, to "always act so as to recognize and uphold communal autonomy."[97] In this regard, the November 1959 revision of U.S. policy toward Cuba was explicit that one objective was to "build up" a credible opposition to Castro, not to aid an already credible opposition movement.

The justification of U.S. policy in terms of Cuban external behavior increased in importance over time. When Castro first took power, the threat to U.S. interests was nascent. It was not until the missile crisis of October 1962 that a serious military threat to U.S. sovereignty emerged, but the embargo, as well as the other elements of the anti-Castro policy, was well in place by that time. Subsequent tightenings of the embargo were rationalized, in part, as a response to Cuban "adventurism" in Angola, Ethiopia, Grenada, El Salvador and Nicaragua. Other things being equal, the use of force can be an appropriate response to aggression, but it is not at all clear that Cuban actions in these countries can be construed as aggressive. Rather, they were part of the Cold War gamesmanship by which the Soviet Union and its surrogates (as well as the United States and its supporters) maneuvered for influence in the developing world. Thus, the sanctions can be seen as a more limited response than the actual use of military force. In fact, however, U.S. actions were not limited to economic sanctions but included support (overt and covert) for the forces fighting against those supported by Cuba, as well as an actual invasion in the case of Grenada. The moral case for economic sanctions, then, was significantly weakened by the use of other, more questionable, measures.

Finally, the objective of improving human rights conditions in Cuba through economic sanctions fails the test. This is certainly a laudable goal, and the collapse of Communist systems in the former Soviet Union and Eastern Europe demonstrates that a sustained policy of promoting basic rights can be productive. But it is simply perverse to seek to enhance basic political rights by denying basic economic rights. It should have been obvious to U.S. policy makers that Castro was highly unlikely to respond to economic pressure by providing greater freedom; rather, his response was predictable: tightening political restrictions and requiring the population at large to bear the burden of the sanctions. Thus, in addition to undermining the principle of just cause, the way in which the sanctions were implemented violated the principle of discrimination by being directed at, rather than protecting, the innocent.

There certainly are conditions under which the cutoff of economic relations with violators of human rights is appropriate and justifiable. The most obvious of these is when trade provides the perpetrators with the means of repression, such as arms. One example is the decision by Polaroid Corporation to cease selling its cameras to South African authorities, who were using them to take the photographs for the infamous "passbooks" that were used to enforce racial restrictions in the apartheid era.[98] More broadly, Thomas Donaldson has proposed a "condition-of-business principle" based on the concept that there are some people (or regimes) with whom one simply shouldn't do business. His principle states that "ceteris paribus, business transactions by B with A are impermissible when A is a systematic violator of fundamental rights, unless those transactions serve to discourage the violation of rights and either harm or, at a minimum, fail to benefit A in consequence of A's rights-violating activity."[99]

Donaldson's principle stands the sanctions argument on its head. He argues that doing business with rights violators is simply wrong, even when ceasing to do business causes harm to innocents, unless the result is "extraordinary moral horrors."[100] Thus it is the continuance, not the cessation, of economic relations that must be justified.

Donaldson develops this argument in the context of the debate over disinvestment by companies doing business in South Africa. Thus, his focus is on individual corporations rather than governments. Government decisions, however, are more far-reaching and thus more weighty. Because a government policy of ceasing or restricting trade has such a far-reaching effect, it must be justified rigorously. It does not appear that either the Eisenhower or the Kennedy administration did this. Certainly human rights abuses under Castro are legion, and his imprisonment and execution of opponents in the early days of his regime were particularly heinous. But U.S. officials never used the Donaldson principle to justify their sanctions policy. They did not cut ties with Cuba because they did not want to do business with Castro; rather, the objective was to cause such economic hardship that Castro would be overthrown. In pursuit of a nominally just cause, then, U.S. officials' unjust intentions contaminated the moral quality of their actions.

Further, U.S. intentions in imposing sanctions are called further into question by the context in which they were applied. They were not part of a program of escalating pressure, beginning with diplomatic initiatives and ending with the overt use of force. Thus, the trade restrictions were not a last resort or a policy reluctantly undertaken after less harmful policies had failed or could be presumed to be ineffective. Nor were they conceived of as a proportionate response to specific actions by the Castro regime. The sanctions were, from the Eisenhower era on, seen as but one element in a multifaceted program intended to bring about Castro's ouster or demise. The program included actions ranging from diplomatic overtures to the OAS to sabotage, invasion and assassination. Indeed, the sanctions policy and the sabotage program were seen as complementary, intended to exacerbate Cuban economic hardship and induce a popular rebellion. By tying the sanctions so closely to even more violent and questionable activities, U.S. officials revealed their true intentions and their lack of consideration for the moral consequences of their actions.

In imposing sanctions and taking other actions against Castro, the United States was furthering its interests regarding a nation that had traditionally been considered part of the American sphere of influence. This is a common practice of nation-states, and states obviously have the legal authority to make their own policies regarding international trade. Recently, however, scholars and officials have argued that such unilateral actions to promote policy objectives should be replaced by collective enforcement to promote internationally accepted norms of behavior. The idea is that the just-war concept of competent authority should be modified to emphasize the moral authority of universal norms as embodied in collective decisions, rather than the legal authority of the nation-state. This concept has been used in the case of UN-sponsored sanctions against Iraq and Serbia, and arguably those against Haiti.[101] While the United States received support from its key allies, and from the appropriate regional alliance, the OAS, for elements of its Cuba policy, U.S. officials realized that other elements were inconsistent with the norms of that organization. This seriously weakens their moral standing. Moreover, the growing opposition to the sanctions, as evidenced by opposition to the Helms–Burton Act and the overwhelming vote in the UN General Assembly for ending the U.S. embargo, leaves the United States politically and morally isolated.

Even if the U.S. policies had met the tests of just cause, intention, last resort, proportionality and authority—which they did not—they are clearly inconsistent with one of the basic moral principles that underlies the just-war tradition. As a part of the natural law tradition, the notion of just-war embodies a profound respect for humanity. It has a strong bias against doing harm and restricts the doing of injury to situations in which it is unavoidable or subject to strict justification. A basic principle of the natural law tradition is that of Saint Paul in Romans 3: 7–8 that evil is not to be done so that good should come of it.[102] In other words, an evil means cannot be justified by the good ends that it achieves. Thus, even if the ouster of Castro were to be accepted as a just cause, the means that the United States used could still be questioned.

The exception to this principle is that known as "double effect." It may be permissible to use harmful means if only the good outcome is intended, and if both the good and the evil outcomes arise simultaneously from the means used. It is not acceptable, under this exception, for the good end to result directly from the evil action.

U.S. officials, however, were very explicit about the relationship between means and ends. They clearly understood that the sanctions would not impact simultaneously on Castro and on the Cuban people. Indeed, they were aware that Castro could cushion the impact on him and his supporters while the populace bore the brunt of the sanctions. The United States hope was that by exacerbating popular hardship, it could stimulate a popular rebellion. It could not, then, use the principle of double effect to justify its actions.

The questionable moral standing of the initial embargo has been further undermined by its extension to cover trade in food and medicine. With the tightening of the embargo under the Torcelli Act in 1992, many drugs manufactured exclusively in the United States became unobtainable in Cuba. Helms–Burton had a similar effect on products of non-U.S. medical companies.[103] A 1997 report by public health specialists concluded that the tightened restrictions were burdening the Cuban health care system, contributing to a rise in morbidity and mortality, especially among adult men and the elderly.[104]

The Question of Effectiveness

There is another key element in the moral evaluation of sanctions: their potential and actual effectiveness. The most comprehensive studies of economic sanctions as policy instruments suggest that their effectiveness is limited, and that the intended results are achieved only under restrictive circumstances. Hufbauer and Schott, for example, have concluded that "Sanctions often do not succeed in changing the behavior of foreign countries."[105] They cite four reasons for this: the sanctions may be inadequate to the objectives, they may create their own antidotes when target countries seek other sources of commerce, they may prompt responses by the target country's allies that undercut the sanctions' effectiveness, and they may result in a backlash both within the country that implements them and abroad. In a study of 103 cases, Hufbauer and Schott found that sanctions were effective in achieving their goals only 36 percent of the time. The authors were surprised that sanctions aimed at overthrowing governments succeeded 50 percent of the time, largely because they were usually accompanied by other overt or covert military or political measures. In contrast, "attempts to disrupt military adventures, to impair a foreign adversary's military potential, or otherwise to change its policies in a major way, generally fail."[106]

Hufbauer and Schott count the U.S. sanctions policy against Cuba as a failure.[107] While noting that it resulted in considerable economic damage, they point out that much of the cost was borne by the Soviet Union in the form of subsidies and aid to Cuba. Moreover, a predictable backlash among America's allies occurred, and has become more significant since the passage of Helms–Burton.

U.S. officials were aware from the beginning that the sanctions probably would not be effective, yet they persisted. A series of intelligence studies predicted that the impact of the sanctions would be minimal and that Castro would use whatever means were necessary to retain power. They also accurately foresaw that the Soviet Union would come to Cuba's aid. Senior State Department officials, including Undersecretary Dillon, agreed. Eisenhower himself expressed grave reservations about the potential effectiveness of sanctions. And the intelligence warnings continued into the Kennedy administration.

The Decision Process

Why, if U.S. officials knew the sanctions were unlikely to succeed, did they not only implement them but progressively tighten them at the cost of eventual political isolation? There are psychological, structural and moral explanations.

Daoudi and Dajani identify seven psychological and political factors that may be used by decision makers to rationalize the use of sanctions:

- Maintaining the perception that sanctions are inflicting damage on the target

- Expressing morality and justice

- Signifying disapproval or displeasure

- Satisfying the emotional needs of the sanctioner

- Maintaining the sanctioner's positive image and reputation

- Relieving domestic pressure on the sanctioner

- Inflicting symbolic vengeance.[108]

Almost all of these factors were present in U.S. decision-making on Cuba. The sanctions were consistently explained in terms of morality and justice. U.S. officials sought to contrast Castro's evils with the positive image of the United States. They expressed disapproval of Castro's foreign and domestic policies, and linked the sanctions to changes in his behavior. In effect, the sanctions became a symbol of American moral outrage, whether about the executions of Batista supporters or the shooting down of a Cuban Brotherhood aircraft.

Psychologically, U.S. officials in the late 1950s and 1960s believed they were in a life-and-death struggle with communism. They projected onto Castro the evil attributes of their adversaries, and he came to symbolize the threat in a particularly challenging way, because of both his extremist rhetoric and Cuba's geographic proximity. U.S. officials may have felt they had no choice but to act against this evil, even while knowing that their efforts might not be effective.

The structure and procedures of the decision makers, especially in the Eisenhower and Kennedy administrations, also help to explain the paradox of economic sanctions. The Eisenhower administration was based on the principle of orderly staff work, which the president had brought with him from his highly successful military career. Under Chief of Staff Sherman Adams, Eisenhower commissioned groups to deal with various policy fields, usually in isolation from one another. Because Eisenhower was not much of a reader and was impatient with paperwork, he was reliant on the bureaucracy to keep him informed of emerging issues and to provide him with options. In a sense, then, Eisenhower may have been constrained in his ability to draw the connections among various aspects of Cuba policy by the institutional setting in which decisions were made.[109]

Kennedy's style was in sharp contrast to Eisenhower's. He tended to ignore the formal procedures and organizations in favor of direct consultations with key individuals and informal groups.[110] Thus he was potentially open to a wider range of advice, but by ignoring the strengths of bureaucracy, procedure and record-keeping, Kennedy risked inconsistency and error. Bowles's descriptions of the meetings that followed the Bay of Pigs debacle convey an image not only of informality but also of chaos, confusion and mutual recrimination. It is not surprising, then, that Kennedy's response was to project the blame onto Castro, and then to use whatever methods were available, from economic sanctions to murder plots, to punish him.

At the heart of the matter, however, is the moral inconsistency of American policy makers. From Eisenhower to Clinton they have used high-sounding rhetoric to mask their reservations about the sanctions policy. The key may be that they did not heed Aristotle's caution that the prudent decision maker avoids "passionate attachments." By demonizing Castro, and by giving disproportionate influence to small but vocal anti-Castro forces in key states with large numbers of electoral votes, American political leaders have promoted their bankrupt policy with a zeal out of proportion to either the importance of the Cuba issue or the impact of the U.S. actions.

THE WAY FORWARD

The United States' economic embargo against Cuba is politically ineffective and morally unjustified. It is time that U.S. leaders exhibit the moral courage to seek a new dialogue with the Castro regime and to prepare more systematically for lifting of sanctions and an orderly transition to a post-Castro government. Castro himself has provided some openings, despite the regime's recurring ineptitude, demonstrated by the shooting down of U.S.-registered aircraft just before a key vote on sanctions. Since 1993, he has implemented a program of limited economic reforms, first authorizing Cubans to own and spend dollars, then establishing free farmers' markets and markets in handicrafts and light manufactures. In mid-1995, Cuba enacted a new foreign investment law that opens nearly the entire economy to outside investors. The result has been an economic rebound that provides the potential for greater foreign investment and influence.[111]

Members of the United States business community, aware of the potential of Cuba, have been lobbying for an end to the sanctions. While they are cognizant of the concerns of the Cuban exile community, business leaders see themselves as a potential force for democratic change in Cuba, as they have been in post-communist countries elsewhere.[112]

President Clinton's decision to suspend the most controversial provisions of the Helms-Burton Act shows that he understands the complexity of the Cuba issue, and that he is willing to risk the ire of congressional conservatives and outspoken Cuban Americans in order to reduce the political penalties abroad arising from the embargo. He should now heed Aristotle's counsel that true courage is to be found in the mean between cowardice and foolhardiness, by reopening a dialogue with the Castro regime and offering a phased removal of sanctions as an incentive. The visit of Pope John Paul II to Cuba in early 1998, and his call for an end to the embargo and for human rights in Cuba, provide an opportunity for a policy change.

The administration has rejected the pope's plea. But it recently announced a very limited easing of sanctions against Cuba and underscored by its increasing discomfort with sanctions as a policy tool. In January 1998, the administration announced a review of sanctions policy and the establishment of a "sanctions team" in the State Department to improve decision-making. According to Undersecretary of State Stuart Eizenstat, the new approach will be guided by several principles:

• The United States should resort to sanctions only after other diplomatic options have been tried and have failed.

• International support and participation should be sought.

• Unnecessary hardships to the innocent should be prevented.

• The views of Congress, business groups and others should be taken into account.[113]

If Clinton is really serious about altering U.S. sanctions policy, there is one more action that he should take, and this will not be easy. Because the economic sanctions imposed on Cuba were morally suspect, Clinton should acknowledge that fact and prepare to make amends. This would involve positive measures to stimulate economic growth in Cuba and thus to atone, in some small measure, for the damage done to the Cuban people.[114] This is what justice demands.

NOTES

1. The outline of U.S.–Cuban relations and of the significant decision points draws on a number of primary and secondary sources. Among the historical studies and political analyses consulted are Lynn Darrell Bender, *The Politics of Hostility: Castro's Revolution and United States Policy* (Hato Rey, Puerto Rico: Inter American University Press, 1975); David B. Capitanchik, *The Eisenhower Presidency and American Foreign Policy* (London: Routledge and Kegan Paul, 1969); Louise FitzSimmons, *The Kennedy Doctrine* (New York: Random House, 1972); Roger W. Fontaine, *On Negotiating with Cuba* (Washington, DC: American Enterprise Institute, 1965); Morris H. Morley, *Imperial State and Revolution: The United States and Cuba, 1953–1986* (Cambridge: Cambridge University Press, 1987); Thomas G. Paterson, *Contesting Castro: The United States and the Triumph of the Cuban Revolution* (Oxford: Oxford University Press, 1994); John Plank, ed., *Cuba and the United States: Long Range Perspectives* (Washington, DC: The Brookings Institution, 1967); Stephen G. Rabe, *Eisenhower and Latin America: The Foreign Policy of Anticommunism* (Chapel Hill: University of North Carolina Press, 1988); John Ranelagh, *The Agency: The Rise and Decline of the CIA* (New York: Simon & Schuster, 1986); Robert F. Smith, *The United States and Cuba: Business and Diplomacy, 1917–1960* (New York: Bookman Associates, 1960); and Richard E. Welch, Jr., *Response to Revolution: The United States and the Cuban Revolution, 1959–61* (Chapel Hill: University of North Carolina Press, 1985). Also useful are biographies, speeches and memoirs of key participants in the policy process, including: Philip W. Bonsal, *Cuba, Castro and the United States* (Pittsburgh: University of Pittsburgh Press, 1971); Dwight D. Eisenhower, *Peace with Justice* (New York: Columbia University Press, 1961) and *The White House Years: Waging Peace, 1956–1961* (New York: New American Library, 1965); Frederick W. Marks, *Power and Peace: The Diplomacy of John Foster Dulles* (Westport, CT: Praeger, 1993); Dean Rusk, *The Winds of Freedom* (Boston: Beacon Press, 1963); Earl T. Smith, *The Fourth Floor: An Account of the Castro Communist Revolution* (New York: Random House, 1962); and Theodore C. Sorensen, *Kennedy* (New York: Harper & Row, 1965). Many of these sources are well documented, but some exhibit evident biases in favor of or against U.S. policy, or provide only a restricted or self-serving view of the policy process. Fortunately, many original government documents have now been released to the public. While these have their flaws and gaps, they are a valuable counterweight to the biases of some of the secondary sources. A collection of primary source documents is in U.S. Department of State, *Foreign Relations of the United States, 1958– 1960,* Volume 6: *Cuba* (Washington, DC: U.S. Government Printing Office, 1961) and Volume 10: *Cuba: 1961–1963* <http://www.state.gov/www/ about_state/ history/ frusX /index. html>, hereafter cited as *FRUS, 1958-60,* Volume 6 and *FRUS, 1961-63,* Volume 10. This collection is supplemented by additional documents acquired under the Freedom of Information Act by the National Security Archive, Washington, DC, and maintained in its microfiche collection on Cuba, hereafter cited as *NSA Cuba Collection.* Also important to understanding U.S. policy toward the Castro regime is United States Senate Select Committee to Study Governmental Operations with Respect to Intelligence Activities, *Alleged Assassination Attempts Involving Foreign Leaders,* 94th Cong., 1st sess., Rept 94-465 (Washington, DC: U.S. Government Printing Office, 1975), hereafter cited as *Senate Report on Alleged Assassination Plots.*

2. Quoted in Fontaine, *On Negotiating with Cuba*, p. 12.

3. Ibid., pp. 14–15.

4. Henry Wriston, "A Historical Perspective," in Plank, *Cuba and the United States*, p. 9.

5. Fontaine, *On Negotiating with Cuba*, p. 16.

6. Wriston, "A Historical Perspective," pp. 9–10.

7. Ibid., p. 10.

8. Fontaine, *On Negotiating with Cuba*, p. 19.

9. Wriston, "A Historical Perspective," p. 12.

10. Fontaine, *On Negotiating with Cuba*, p. 20.

11. R.F. Smith, *The United States and Cuba*, p. 29.

12. Ibid., p. 31; Fontaine, *On Negotiating with Cuba*, p. 22.

13. Wriston, "A Historical Perspective," p. 19.

14. Ibid., p. 29.

15. Patterson, *Contesting Castro*, p. 7.

16. Wriston, "A Historical Perspective," p. 24.

17. Paterson, *Contesting Castro*, p. 8.

18. Welch, *Response to Revolution*, p. 4.

19. Morley, *Imperial State and Revolution*, p. 74.

20. Bonsal, *Cuba, Castro and the United States*, p. 75.

21. Ibid., p. 25.

22. Morley, *Imperial State and Revolution*, p. 75.

23. Memorandum of discussion at the 392nd meeting of the National Security Council, Washington, December 23, 1958, in *FRUS, 1958–60*, Volume 6.

24. Dispatch from the embassy in Cuba to the Department of State, no. 923, Havana, February 18, 1959, in *FRUS, 1958–60*, Volume 6.

25. Memorandum from the director of the Office of Mexican and Caribbean Affairs (Wieland) to the assistant secretary of state for inter-american affairs (Rubottom), February 19, 1959. Subject: short-range position toward government of Cuba, in *FRUS, 1958–60*, Volume 6.

26. Fontaine, *On Negotiating with Cuba*, p. 35.

27. Bonsal, *Cuba, Castro and the United States*, p. 255.

28. Memorandum of a conversation, Washington, June 1, 1959. Subject: sugar legislation, in *FRUS, 1958–60*, Volume 6.

29. Memorandum by the director of the Office of Inter-american Regional Economic Affairs (Turkel), July 1, 1959, Subject: Cuban economic prospects, 1959, and proposed U.S. action, in *FRUS, 1958–60*, Volume 6.

30. Memorandum from the secretary of state to the president, November 5, 1959. Subject: current basic United States policy toward Cuba, in *FRUS, 1958–60*, Volume 6.

31. Morley, *Imperial State and Revolution*, p. 85.

32. Bonsal, *Cuba, Castro and the United States*, p. 104.

33. Memorandum of discussion at the 432nd meeting of the National Security Council, Washington, January 14, 1960, in *FRUS, 1958–60*, Volume 6.

34. Morley, *Imperial State and Revolution*, p. 95.

35. Memorandum from the chairman of the Working Group on the Cuban Economic Situation (Young) to the assistant secretary of state for economic affairs (Mann), December 14 1959. Subject: estimate of economic outlook for Cuba, *FRUS, 1958–60*, Volume 6.

36. Memorandum of discussion at the 429th meeting of the National Security Council, Washington, December 16, 1959, in *FRUS, 1958–60*, Volume 6.

37. Rabe, *Eisenhower and Latin America*, p. 128.

38. Memorandum of discussion at the 432nd meeting of the National Security Council, Washington, January 14, 1960, in *FRUS, 1958–60*, Volume 6.

39. Welch, *Response to Revolution*, pp. 43–44.

40. Rabe, *Eisenhower and Latin America*, p. 128.

41. Memorandum of discussion at the 436th meeting of the National Security Council, Washington, March 10, 1960, in *FRUS, 1958–60*, Volume 6.

42. Memorandum of a conference with the president, White House, Washington, March 17, 1960, in *FRUS, 1958–60*, Volume 6.

43. Rabe, *Eisenhower and Latin America*, p. 129.

44. Memorandum for the record by CIA inspector general, May 23, 1975. Subject: report on plots to assassinate Fidel Castro, in *NSA Cuba Collection*.

45. Memorandum from the deputy assistant secretary of state for inter-American affairs (Mallory) to the assistant secretary of state for inter-American affairs (Rubottom), April 6, 1960. Subject: the decline and fall of Castro, in *FRUS, 1958–60*, Volume 6.

46. Memorandum from the assistant secretary of state for inter-American affairs (Rubottom) to the acting secretary of state, May 11, 1960, in *FRUS, 1958–60*, Volume 6.

47. Memorandum from the assistant secretary of state for inter-American Affairs to the secretary of state, June 2, 1960. Subject: action of U.S. oil companies and Shell in response to Cuban demand to process Russian oil, in *FRUS, 1958–60*, Volume 6.

48. Memorandum of a conference, Department of State, Washington, June 7, 1960. Subject: Cuban situation: meeting with representatives of the National Foreign Trade Council, in *FRUS, 1958–60*, Volume 6.

49. Notes on the discussion at the special meeting of the National Security Council, White House, Washington, June 22, 1960, in *FRUS, 1958–60*, Volume 6.

50. Bonsal, *Cuba, Castro and the United States*, p. 151.

51. Memorandum of discussion at the 450th meeting of the National Security Council, Washington, July 7, 1960, in *FRUS, 1958–60*, Volume 6.

52. Ranelagh, *The Agency*, p. 356.

53. Memorandum of a meeting between the president and his special assistant for national security affairs (Gray), Newport, Rhode Island, July 12, 1960, in *FRUS, 1958–60*, Volume 6.

54. Memorandum of a meeting with the president, White House, Washington, August 18, 1960, in *FRUS, 1958–60*, Volume 6.

55. Senate Select Committee to Study Governmental Operations with Respect to Intelligence Activities, *Alleged Assassination Attempts Involving Foreign Leaders*, pp 74–82.

56. Ibid., p. 109.

57. Morley, *Imperial State and Revolution*, p. 112.

58. Memorandum of discussion at the 461st meeting of the National Security Council, Washington, September 29, 1960. in *FRUS, 1958–60*, Volume 6.

59. Memorandum from the assistant secretary of state for inter-American Affairs (Mann) to the secretary of state, October 19, 1960, in *FRUS, 1958–60*, Volume 6.

60. Special National Intelligence Estimate, SNIE 85-3-60, "Prospects for the Castro Regime," December 8, 1960, in *FRUS, 1958–60*, Volume 6.

61. This contrast is portrayed effectively in Ernest May and Richard Neustadt, *Thinking in Time: The Uses of History for Decision Makers* (New York: Free Press, 1986), chapters 1 and 8.

62. Notes on cabinet meeting, Washington, April 20, 1961, in *FRUS, 1961–63*, Volume 10.

63. Memorandum from Secretary of Defense McNamara to the chairman of the Joint Chiefs of Staff (Lemnitzer), April 20, 1961, in *FRUS, 1961–63*, Volume 10.

64. Notes on Cuban crisis: NSC meeting, Saturday, April 22, in *FRUS, 1961–63*, Volume 10.

65. Notes on 479th meeting of the National Security Council, April 27, 1961, in *FRUS, 1961–63,* Volume 10.

66. Paper prepared for the National Security Council by the director of the Department of State Operations Center (Achiles), April 27, 1961. Subject: plan for Cuba, in *FRUS, 1961–63,* Volume 10.

67. Morley, *Imperial State and Revolution,* p. 148.

68. Welch, *Response to Revolution,* p. 98.

69. Operation Mongoose priority operations schedule, May 21–June 30, 1962, in *FRUS, 1961–63,* Volume 10.

70. Memorandum from the chairman of the Board of National Estimates (Kent) to director of Central Intelligence Dulles, November 3, 1961, in *FRUS, 1961–63,* Volume 10.

71. Memorandum for the record by CIA inspector general, May 23, 1975. Subject: report on plots to assassinate Fidel Castro, in *NSA Cuba Collection.*

72. Senate Select Committee to Study Governmental Operations with Respect to Intelligence Activities, *Alleged Assassination Attempts Involving Foreign Leaders,* p. 132.

73. Ibid., p. 135.

74. Ranelagh, *The Agency,* p. 384.

75. Memorandum of Mongoose meeting held on Thursday, October 4, 1962, chaired by the attorney general, *NSA Cuba Collection.*

76. Roswell Gilpatric, quoted in Morley, *Imperial State and Revolution,* p. 148.

77. Welch, *Response to Revolution,* p. 97.

78. Gary C. Hufbauer and Jeffrey J. Schott, assisted by Kimberly Ann Elliott, *Economic Sanctions Reconsidered: History and Current Policy* (Washington, DC: Institute for International Economics, 1985), p. 316.

79. Ibid.

80. Sorenson, *Kennedy,* p. 631.

81. Morley, *Imperial State and Revolution,* p. 205.

82. Ibid., p. 297.

83. Seymour M. Hersch, *The Price of Power: Kissinger in the Nixon White House* (New York: Simon & Schuster, 1983), pp. 250–57.

84. May and Neustadt, *Thinking in Time,* pp. 92–96.

85. Hufbauer and Schott, *Economic Sanctions Reconsidered,* pp. 316–17.

86. Richard Garfield and Sarah Santana, "The Impact of the Economic Crisis and the U.S. Embargo on Health in Cuba," *American Journal of Public Health* 87, no. 1 (January 1997): 15–16.

87. James M. Wall, "U.S. Cuba Policy Is Obsolete," *Christian Century* 111, no. 25 (September 7–14, 1994): 803.

88. Evan R. Berlack and Carl A. Valenstein, "The Cuban Liberty and Democratic Solidarity Act of 1996 (*Libertad*): Introduction and Executive Summary," *Arent Fox Legal Brief* (1997) <http://www.arentfox.com/features/international/cuba.htm> (October 10, 1997).

89. Peter Morici, "The United States, World Trade and the Helms–Burton Act," *Current History* 96 (February 1997): 87.

90. The Cato Institute, "Issue 50: Cuba," in *Cato Handbook for Congress* (1997), <http/www.cato.org/ pubs/handbook/hb105-50.htm> (October 10, 1997).

91. Andreas Lowenfeld, "Congress and Cuba: The Helms–Burton Act," *American Journal of International Law* 90, no. 3 (July 1996): 433–34.

92. Bruce M. Clagett, "Title III of the Helms–Burton Act Is Consistent with International Law," *American Journal of International Law* 90, no. 3 (July 1996): 436.

93. Ernest H. Preeg, "U.S. Embargo: The Illusion of Compliance," *Washington Post*, November 2, 1997, sec. C, p.3.

94. National Public Radio News, November 5, 1997.

95. Albert C. Pierce, "Just War Principles and Economic Sanctions," *Ethics and International Affairs* 10 (1996): 99.

96. Ibid., p. 110.

97. Michael Walzer, *Just and Unjust Wars*, 2nd ed. (New York: Basic Books, 1992), p. 90.

98. John M. Kline, *Doing Business in South Africa: Seeking Ethical Parameters for Business and Government Responsibilities*, Case Study in Ethics and International Affairs, no. 11 (New York: Carnegie Council on Ethics and International Affairs, 1995).

99. Thomas Donaldson, *The Ethics of International Business* (New York: Oxford University Press, 1989), p. 133.

100. Ibid., p. 144.

101. Lori Fisler Damrosch, "The Collective Enforcement of International Norms Through Economic Sanctions," *Ethics and International Affairs* 8 (1994): 64–65.

102. Terry Nardin, "Ethical Traditions in International Affairs," in Nardin and David Mapel, eds., *Traditions of International Ethics* (Cambridge: Cambridge University Press, 1992), p. 11.

103. Anthony F. Kirkpatrick, "Role of the United States in Shortage of Food and Medicine in Cuba," *Lancet* 348 (November 30, 1996): 1489.

104. Garfield and Santana, "The Impact of the Economic Crisis and the U.S. Embargo on Health in Cuba," p. 19.

105. Hufbauer and Schott, *Economic Sanctions Reconsidered*, p. 11.

106. Ibid., p. 80.

107. Ibid., p. 321.

108. M.S. Daoudi and M.S. Dajani, *Economic Sanctions: Ideals and Experience* (London: Routledge and Kegan Paul, 1983), p. 161.

109. Capitanchik, The *Eisenhower Presidency and American Foreign Policy*, pp. 25–26.

110. Ibid., p. 31.

111. Wayne S. Smith, "Cuba's Long Reform," *Foreign Affairs* 75, no. 2 (March/April 1996): 101–3.

112. Pamela S. Falk, "Eyes on Cuba: U.S. Business and the Embargo," *Foreign Affairs* 75, no. 2 (March/April 1996): 18.

113. "Sanctions Policy Review," *Washington Post*, January 8, 1998, sec. A, p. 11.

114. For a description of the general principle involved, see Myers S. McDougal and Florentine P. Feliciano, *Law and Minimum World Public Order: The Legal Regulation of International Coercion* (New Haven: Yale University Press, 1961), p. 329.

7

Coercion and Conciliation: The United States and the North Korean Nuclear Program

THE HERMIT KINGDOM

The Korean peninsula is home to an ancient and distinctive national tradition. The area has been inhabited for at least 20,000 years, and for nearly 13 centuries it functioned as a single nation-state. But this tradition has been maintained at great cost; there have been numerous invasions and occupations by Korea's more powerful neighbors, Russia, China and Japan. Nevertheless, for most of Korea's history, its rulers have pursued a policy of excluding foreigners and maintaining a strict social system based on Confucian principles.

At the end of World War II, this "Hermit Kingdom" was divided into Soviet and American spheres of influence. Although the partition was originally envisioned as temporary, the objective of reunification soon fell victim to Cold War politics, culminating in the Korean War of 1950–53. The North Korean war effort was led by Kim Il Sung, known to his people as the Great Leader. A man of limited education but great revolutionary zeal, Kim was apparently selected by Stalin to lead the Soviet-dominated region of Korea when he was in his mid-thirties. He was a despotic ruler who fostered a "cult of personality" among the North Korean people and installed a strict economic and political system that stressed indoctrination and loyalty to his particular brand of socialist thought.

Kim Il Sung's ideology reinforced Soviet-style communism with a distinctive Korean concept, *juche* (self-reliance). According to this philosophy, Korea is the center of world civilization and other nations are inferior. *Juche* rests on the decisions of the Great Leader, and the instruments of government and the people are regarded as organs that are responsive to his direction. Through Kim's leadership, the North Korean people are taught, they will be able to overcome all obstacles and fulfill their destiny of self-sufficiency and freedom from foreign influence.

Under Kim, North Korean society has been completely militarized. It has the fourth largest army in the world, with about 1.2 million troops, twice the number in South

Korea. U.S. estimates indicate that North Korean military spending is some 20–25 percent of the country's gross national product.[1] The military forces are organized for a protracted war of liberation against South Korea. In addition to maintaining a large conventional force in being, North Korea routinely engages in small-scale military penetrations of the South and in provocations along the border between the two countries. According to military analysts, this is part of a strategy of causing panic in South Korea, undermining public confidence in its government and eventually isolating the South in the world community. The concept is that this will provoke political instability, which in turn will facilitate a North Korean takeover and reunification of the peninsula under a socialist system based on *juche*.[2]

These were the country and the leader who challenged the United States and the international community over the issue of nuclear weapons. They were a system and a leader whose decisions were so opaque that outsiders had little ability to discern or predict policies or actions. Yet, in the mid-1990s, there was a real threat that this tiny, mysterious nation would develop a capability for mass destruction or begin a ruinous conventional war in the attempt. The question for outsiders, then, was how to balance coercion and conciliation in order to reduce the likelihood of widespread violence or of a major shift in the balance of power in the Northwest Pacific region.

NUCLEAR WEAPONS AND THE KOREAS

Korea's involvement with nuclear weapons dates from the latter years of World War II. Endowed with natural deposits of uranium ore, the northern part of the country was home to Japanese nuclear research projects.[3]   After the division of Korea, the USSR exploited the deposits for its own nuclear programs. During the Korean War, the United States made both explicit and implicit threats to attack the North with nuclear weapons. In July 1950, President Truman ordered 10 B-29 bombers, capable of carrying nuclear weapons, deployed to the Western Pacific. In November, he threatened to take "whatever steps are necessary" to stop Chinese intervention in the war, and sent a special envoy to convey this message to the Chinese.[4] General Douglas MacArthur and his successor as commander of United Nations forces, General Matthew Ridgway, both requested authority to use nuclear weapons.[5] Although the authority was never granted, the Eisenhower administration did use nuclear threats in an attempt to break the deadlocked peace negotiations in 1953.[6] The ploy apparently worked; an armistice was reached in July 1953, though no peace treaty ending the conflict has ever been concluded.

Following the war, the United States maintained a powerful military presence in South Korea. By the 1970s, U.S. forces there numbered some 37,000 troops, equipped with some 700 nuclear weapons in the country; there were also thousands of nuclear weapons available to other U.S. military units that would assist the deployed forces.[7] (The nuclear weapons in Korea included short-range artillery shells that had to be deployed near to the Demilitarized Zone or DMZ, separating the Koreas, where they could be vulnerable to being overrun by attacking North Korean forces.)

Not satisfied with the protection afforded by the United States' nuclear "umbrella," South Korean president Park Chung Hee in 1970 decided to develop the technology to manufacture nuclear weapons if required. Four years later, the program was in full swing, based on cooperative efforts between South Korea and France. U.S. officials became aware of the South Korean program in late 1974, and after a concerted effort to pressure the Park government, the contract with France was canceled in 1976. Some observers suspect, however, that the South Korean government acquired sufficient knowledge and technology that it could restart the program and produce nuclear weapons within several years.[8]

North Korea's nuclear efforts began in the late 1950s as cooperative projects with Soviet scientists working in the USSR. In 1964, North Korea and the Soviet Union established a joint nuclear research facility at Yongbyon, about 60 miles north of the capital of Pyongyang. The following year, the USSR delivered a small research reactor and a nuclear research laboratory. The reactor, with a power rating of 2–4 megawatts, became operational in 1967.[9]

Concerned about the nuclear program in the South and about the continued presence of U.S. nuclear weapons in the region, North Korea accelerated its own efforts in the 1970s. At the time, Kim was publicly deprecating the usefulness of nuclear weapons. In 1975 he asked, "How can they use nuclear weapons here in Korea where friend and foe will grapple [with] each other?"[10] Shortly thereafter, however, he arranged to purchase additional reactors from the USSR, including a larger graphite reactor to be constructed at Yongbyon.

Through the 1970s, North Korea pursued development of nuclear weapons for a variety of reasons. It sought to counterbalance U.S. nuclear forces, to provide a hedge against the qualitative strengths of South Korean forces, to gain independence from China and the USSR and to acquire a greater measure of international power at a time of potential transition from Kim's leadership to a successor. By the 1980s, there may have been another motive. The Hermit Kingdom was in increasingly dire economic straits, and it may have sought to use its nascent nuclear program as a source of potential leverage in negotiations with the outside world. This was a two-edged sword, however, since the growing need for external resources gave the world community its own leverage.[11]

THE CRISIS BEGINS

In April 1982, U.S. satellite photographs disclosed the nuclear reactor under construction at Yongbyon. Over the next several years, U.S. concern heightened as photographs showed that the layout of the reactor was very similar to models that the French and British had used to produce materials for weapons. In 1986, analysts detected possible evidence of high-explosive tests that could be associated with nuclear weapons designs, as well as the outlines of a new building that appeared similar to those used to separate weapons-grade plutonium from reactor fuel. Finally, in June 1988 a new reactor, 10 times more powerful than the existing Yongbyon reactor, was identified under construction.[12]

In addition to its own secret program, Kim Il Sung's regime had continued its nuclear cooperation with the Soviet Union. In 1985, the USSR promised to construct four light-waterreactors, contingent on North Korea joining the Nuclear Nonproliferation Treaty (NPT).[13] Under the treaty, North Korea would have to allow inspection of the reactors by the International Atomic Energy Agency (IAEA), the international body charged with monitoring compliance with the treaty's safeguards against the unauthorized spread of weapons-related materials and technology. In December 1985, North Korea signed the treaty, but in a comic-opera development with potentially tragic consequences, the IAEA sent the wrong technical documents, and discussions on inspections became mired in complex and frustrating negotiations. When the Bush administration took office in January 1989, it faced growing evidence of a North Korean nuclear program with no effective program of safeguards and inspections in place.

Reactions of the Reagan and Bush Administrations

Wary and contemptuous of North Korea, the Reagan administration had not responded directly to the evidence of nuclear activity. It did, according to one former official, "try to coax the North Koreans out of their shell through [a] modest initiative that allowed for first ever limited contact between . . . officials."[14] The Bush administration was also slow and indirect in its approach. American officials first briefed South Korean leaders in May 1989, and the information about North Korean nuclear activities, including an estimate that the Kim regime could produce bombs by 1990, promptly leaked to the press. North Korea denied the charges, but argued that it would never agree to IAEA inspections while threatened by U.S. nuclear weapons.

In the meantime, the Bush administration and its key military advisers had become increasingly skeptical of the efficacy of the nuclear weapons stationed in South Korea and concerned about their vulnerability in wartime. Secretly, the administration decided to remove all nuclear weapons from the peninsula. By the end of 1991, all American nuclear weapons had been removed, and South Korean president Roh Tae Woo was permitted to announce their withdrawal.[15]

The administration initiated discreet, high-level contacts with North Korea, and in December an agreement was reached that "specified that North and South Korea would possess no nuclear weapons, no uranium enrichment or plutonium reprocessing facilities, and provided for North–South mutual inspections."[16] For its part, the Bush administration offered a high-level meeting with North Korean officials, which took place on January 21, 1991, at the United Nations. Though formally staged and devoid of negotiation, the meeting was a major milestone in relations between the two countries and a coup for Kim Il Sung.[17]

In February 1992, North Korea finally agreed to IAEA inspections, and three months later Hans Blix, head of the agency, arrived in Yongbyon. He quickly discovered that the suspected reprocessing plant under construction was exactly what it appeared to be. His hosts insisted that while they were interested in principle in reprocessing, they had so far acquired only "tiny" amounts of weapons-grade plutonium, far short of the amount needed to produce bombs. Moreover, while permitting limited IAEA access, North Korean officials were stalling on the promised North–South inspection agreement, which included unscheduled "challenge" inspections of suspect facilities.

Then in the fall of 1992, the North–South dialogue was derailed by the discovery of a large North Korean spy ring. Also, a U.S.–South Korean decision to go ahead with planning of the annual Team Spirit military exercise, which had been suspended in 1992 as a gesture to the North, further complicated the environment for talks. Finally, at the end of 1992, IAEA inspectors concluded that North Korea had reprocessed plutonium not once, as it had claimed, but at least three times.[18]

When the Bush administration left office in January 1993, it had failed to stop the North Korean nuclear program. While the nuclear balance in the region still overwhelmingly favored the United States and its South Korean ally, and while a limited dialogue with the Kim Il Sung regime had begun, the overall situation on the peninsula was one of concern and confusion. For the incoming president, the situation would soon turn to one of crisis.

NORTH KOREA THREATENS AND CLINTON RESPONDS

For the Clinton administration, as for its predecessor, the North Korean nuclear problem was initially perceived as a legal one. Under the NPT, North Korea had the obligation to permit inspections of its nuclear facilities. The U.S. policy objective was to force North Korea to comply with its obligation, thus revealing the truth about its nuclear programs. The international community would either be reassured that the threat of a nuclear capability was remote, or it would take steps to force North Korea to dismantle its facilities if the inspections proved a violation of the treaty. Given North Korean sensibilities, not to mention the fact that it had something to hide, this approach was unlikely to yield a ready solution.[19]

Some administration officials, however, argued for a broader approach. Secretary of Defense Les Aspin proposed direct negotiations with North Korea that focused on reducing the future nuclear threat rather than calling Kim to account for past activities. Aspin and his aides favored a mix of pressure and concessions in a package that one U.S. official described as a "sugar-coated ultimatum."[20]

Challenge to the NPT

Before the administration could act, North Korea upped the ante. On March 12, 1993, North Korea announced that it was giving a 90-day notice that it intended to withdraw from the NPT.[21] The effect was dramatic. No country had ever withdrawn from the treaty; U.S. and other concerned officials feared a precedent that could spread to other threshold nuclear states. The IAEA was livid at the challenge to its role.

Within two weeks of the announcement, the South Korean foreign minister, Han Sung Joo, visited Washington and offered his own package proposal. He argued that pressure alone would not induce North Korea to reverse its withdrawal decision. He suggested a "carrot and stick" approach. The sticks would be UN-sponsored sanctions ranging from diplomatic to economic or even military actions. The carrots would include suspension of the provocative Team Spirit exercise, as well as trade inducements and offers of high-level talks.[22]

Han's proposal was similar in concept to Aspin's, and also resonated with State Department officials. It was opposed, however, by some U.S. military officers and conservative elements in South Korea, who argued that it would simply reward North Korea for illicit behavior. At this point in the administration's history, decision-making was further complicated by turf battles within the Department of State. There were so many different organizations involved that press releases reportedly had to be cleared by 12 offices![23]

The disagreements made it difficult for the Clinton administration to develop a policy line, but in early May it was given a reprieve when a junior North Korean official at the United Nations called the State Department desk officer to request a meeting. The administration agreed, and selected Ambassador Robert L. Gallucci, director of the Bureau of Politico-Military Affairs at State, to be its point man. Gallucci was instructed to insist that North Korea remain in the NPT, but he also was authorized to offer incentives, including a pledge of nuclear nonaggression, an end to Team Spirit and an offer of further dialogue. A series of meetings involving Gallucci, the desk officer and a deputy foreign minister from North Korea took place. Notably, the North Korean side raised the possibility that it might moderate its nuclear activities in return for assistance in obtaining light water reactors (LWRs), a design that raised far fewer proliferation concerns. The United States, however, did not take the bait. Finally, the sides succeeded in hammering out an agreement on June 11, the day before the threatened withdrawal was to take place.[24]

The six-paragraph joint statement committed the sides to a continuing dialogue, and the United States pledged not to used armed forces, including nuclear weapons, against North Korea, nor to threaten such use. In return, North Korea offered to "suspend" its withdrawal. Conspicuous by its absence was any mention of Team Spirit, IAEA inspections or North–South agreement.[25] U.S. officials contended that they would pursue the inspection issue in follow-on talks, but there was no commitment by North Korea to do so.

This proved to be unfortunate, since differing interpretations of the joint statement soon confounded progress. The United States and other signatories interpreted North Korea's suspension of withdrawal from the NPT as implying a continuing obligation to fulfill its provisions, including IAEA inspections. Evidently, North Korea took the position that it had simply deferred a decision, and thus had no legal requirements whatsoever with respect to the IAEA. The IAEA continued to press for a literal interpretation of its mandate; in a September 1993 meeting in Pyongyang, IAEA officials continued to insist on inspections while their North Korean counterparts continued to reject them.[26]

Continuing Tensions

Tensions rose throughout the fall, and U.S. and South Korean officials pondered the need for sanctions. Intelligence sources reported a North Korean military buildup along the DMZ. While U.S.–North Korean discussions continued at the desk level, the IAEA pressed its demands, and in October it threatened to declare that the "continuity of safeguards" on the North Korean reactors had been broken. Translated into common language, this meant that the inspectors could not guarantee that nuclear materials had not been removed for reprocessing. U.S. press reports linked the loss of continuity to a threat of economic sanctions.[27] U.S. and South Korean officials explored the possible pressure points while concern about the possibility of war on the peninsula rose dramatically

At about the same time, North Korea informally floated a package of proposals that might help to defuse the crisis. In talks with the State Department desk officer, a North Korean official put forward a handwritten paper proposing a series of trade-offs. North Korea would remain in the NPT, allow regular inspections and discuss the "special inspections" that the IAEA wanted to confirm safeguards. In return, the United States and South Korea would cancel Team Spirit, long-standing U.S. economic sanctions would be lifted and the U.S.–North Korean negotiations on broader issues would continue. U.S. officials were skeptical.[28]

In November, war fears continued to rise. North Korea leaked its proposed package solution, and in response the Clinton administration put forward a proposal of its own. In return for resumption of regular inspections and the North–South dialogue, the United States would cancel Team Spirit for 1994 and convene a third round of formal negotiations with North Korea. Unfortunately, the proposal had not been cleared with South Korean president Kim Young Sam, who exploded when he was informed it had leaked to the U.S. media.[29]

In a November 1993 meeting with President Clinton, the South Korean president demanded changes in the package. Most important, he insisted that an exchange of special envoys between North and South must take place before the next round of U.S.–North Korean talks. The demand angered the North Koreans and nearly derailed the negotiating process. In Washington, officials began to understand the complexity of the Korean situation. In the words of one veteran observer:

In fact, the parties were arrayed in a series of overlapping circles: between North Korea and the International Atomic Energy Agency, between North Korea and South Korea, and between North Korea and the United States. As in a combination lock, all three had to be in alignment simultaneously for the talks to succeed. Now a fourth circle of problems had been added: between Washington and Seoul.[30]

Complications for the administration continued at home as well. The day after Christmas, the CIA reached a conclusion, promptly leaked to the *New York Times*, that North Korea probably had at least one nuclear weapon. This judgment contradicted administration policy, most recently articulated by Defense Secretary Aspin, that North Korean possession of the bomb would be unacceptable. As it turned out, the CIA conclusion was a worst-case assessment put forward among several possibilities, but it fueled hard-line opposition to any deal with Kim Il Sung and reduced the Clinton administration's flexibility for maneuvering in the complex environment on the peninsula.[31]

In January 1994, evangelist Billy Graham carried a private message from President Clinton to Kim Il Sung. While Graham and his aides attempted to moderate the tone of the message, its content was clear and blunt: further progress in U.S.–North Korean relations depended on resolution of the nuclear issue. Kim's reaction was one of anger. He charged that the United States itself was responsible for the nuclear issue and said, "Pressure and threat cannot work on us."[32] But pressure from the United States and South Korea was increasing. The day before Graham arrived in Pyongyang, the *New York Times* reported that U.S. forces in Korea would soon receive the Patriot antimissile system. Shortly thereafter, South Korea announced that the 1994 Team Spirit exercise would go ahead unless the North agreed to resume nuclear inspections.[33]

War Fever

North Korean officials blasted the U.S. and South Korean actions. On February 9, a North Korean diplomat declared that the country was prepared for war. A few days later, the regime announced that it would consider the imposition of UN sanctions to be a "declaration of war."[34]

The IAEA declared that inspections must resume by February 21, or it would turn the issue over to the UN Security Council. While U.S. officials consulted about possible sanctions, the United States ambassador to South Korea, James Laney, became increasingly concerned about the bellicose rhetoric emanating from Washington, Seoul and Pyongyang. In meetings with key U.S. officials, including Vice President Gore, he warned of the possibility of accidental war. In a dramatic illustration of the scale of potential casualties, he told White House officials, "You could have 50,000 body bags coming home."[35] One result of the ambassador's briefings was the designation of Gallucci as overall coordinator of U.S. policy toward North Korea, but he was unable to forge a consensus among the competing government agencies.

In mid-February, North Korea defused the latest crisis by announcing that it would accept resumption of IAEA inspections, but then delayed the issuance of visa to the inspectors. In a series of intensive talks, U.S. and North Korean negotiators agreed to a package of measures to be implemented on March 1: inspections were to resume, the Team Spirit exercise was to be canceled, North–South talks were to resume and the long-awaited third round of U.S.–North Korean talks was to be announced. Patriot deployments were suspended.

It appeared that United States officials had reached a consensus on their goals for resolving the North Korean nuclear issue. According to a variety of sources, the U.S. objective was to focus on North Korea's future nuclear capability and to defer decisions related to past activities. One State Department official, for example, reportedly said, "As soon as the bombs' existence is confirmed unambiguously, you have to do something about it. . . . Better to let what is be and move on to cap it at the present low-level threat."[36] William Perry, who had recently replaced Aspin as secretary of defense, told reporters, "Our policy right along has been oriented to try to keep North Korea from getting a significant nuclear weapons capability."[37] This was not actually a continuation of previous policy, but a new tack that put the United States at odds with the IAEA and others who wanted North Korea to live up to the letter of its NPT responsibilities. In effect, U.S. officials opted to focus on the security balance on the peninsula first, and to defer dealing with the legal issues until later. This caused them to agree to a continuation of regular IAEA inspections, but not to insist on North Korea's immediate agreement to the "special inspections" that would establish the nature of its previous reprocessing activities.

No sooner had the March 1 agreement been reached, however, than it began to fall apart. The North–South talks deadlocked, and the IAEA inspectors were barred from taking critical measurements at the plutonium reprocessing plant in Yongbyon. The IAEA withdrew its inspectors, and the agency's governing board decided to refer the matter to the Security Council. Consultations about rescheduling of Team Spirit were resumed, and the U.S.–North Korean negotiations were once again put on hold.[38]

On March 19, in an environment of increasing tension, the North Korean representative to the North–South talks asserted to his counterpart, "Seoul is not far from here. If a war breaks out, it will be a sea of fire. Mr. Song, it will probably be difficult for you to survive."[39] The talks had been televised for officials in the two capitals, and South Korean President Kim Young Sam released a videotape of the incident to the press. He then summoned his cabinet to approve resumption of the Patriot deployments. The North Koreans were outraged. Another downward spiral had begun.

THE SPRING 1994 CRISIS AND CARTER'S MEDIATION

The crisis deepened in April 1994, when North Korea notified the IAEA that it planned to defuel the 5-megawatt reactor at Yongbyon. This caused two concerns. If the fuel rods that powered the reactor were removed, IAEA inspectors would be unable to examine them to determine the extent to which they had previously been processed into weapons-grade plutonium. More important, the United States estimated that the fuel from the reactor could be converted into four or five nuclear weapons. In May, without waiting for international permission, the North Koreans began to remove the fuel rods.[40]

The crisis escalated rapidly. North Korea rebuffed an IAEA suggestion to permit segregation and inspection of the reactor fuel.[41] At the same time, the United States began to consider military options. Defense Secretary Perry met with key military commanders to assess war plans for Korea. They considered, and rejected, a proposal to bomb the North Korean reactors. They did, however, propose both a program of economic sanctions and a further augmentation of military forces. On May 19, Perry and his aides briefed President Clinton in stark terms. They estimated that a war on the Korean peninsula could lead to more than 50,000 U.S. casualties and nearly 500,000 among South Koreans. The cost of a 90-day conflict would exceed $60 billion, wreak havoc on the peninsula, and lead to massive civilian casualties.[42]

This sobering information convinced the president to redouble diplomatic efforts, both bilateral and multilateral, and to downplay the military option. The United States again suggested direct talks on May 20, and proposed that Senators Sam Nunn and

Richard Lugar fly to Pyongyang, but was rebuffed . On June 2, IAEA head Hans Blix reported to the UN Security Council that the agency had no confidence in its ability to determine if nuclear materials had been diverted to a weapons program. The same day, the United States asked the Security Council to impose economic sanctions on North Korea.[43]

The sanctions policy was risky and complex. On June 5, North Korea reiterated its position that "Sanctions mean war, and there is no mercy in war."[44] Any UN-sponsored sanctions would have to be approved by all of the permanent members of the Security Council, including China, which had opposed sanctions in the past. In addition, the European nations had been lukewarm in their support, Russia complained about not being consulted and Japan was waffling in the face of North Korean threats. Under these constraints, Madeleine Albright, the US ambassador to the United Nations, proposed a relatively mild sanctions package, including a halt to scientific and cultural exchanges, UN technical assistance and arms sales. If this did not do the trick, the United States envisioned a more severe sanctions program, including a cutoff of remittances from Koreans living in Japan and an oil embargo. Such an effort, however, would require active Japanese and Chinese support.[45]

As the tension mounted, and as the military and economic levers appeared to be limited in their potential, assistance was offered by an unlikely source, former President Jimmy Carter. Carter had had his problems with Korea. An initiative to withdraw American troops was derailed when intelligence estimates showed the North Korean military to be larger than previously assumed. The policy reversal contributed to an image that Carter was a weak and inconsistent leader.[46] As an elder statesman, however, Carter had been more effective, serving as a special emissary to such hot spots as the Middle East, Somalia and the former Yugoslavia. In early June, with Clinton's blessing, Carter decided to take up a long-standing invitation to visit Kim Il Sung.[47]

Although he had cleared his proposed approach with Gallucci, Carter certainly did not follow the administration line. After consulting with Kim, he announced that the North would freeze its nuclear weapons program in exchange for a package of benefits. This was essentially the same proposal floated by the North Koreans to Selig Harrison of the Carnegie Endowment for International Peace a few days earlier. Carter disparaged the use of pressure, saying, "In my opinion, the pursuit of sanctions is counterproductive in this particular and unique society."[48]

The package that Kim proposed, and that Carter relayed to Washington, called for a freeze on the North Korean nuclear program and the continued presence of international inspectors and monitoring equipment. In exchange, the U.S. government would support North Korea's acquisition of light-water reactors and offer to reconvene the bilateral negotiations. Carter reassured Kim that there were no U.S. nuclear weapons in South Korea and the vicinity.[49]

Shortly after his meeting with Kim, Carter telephoned the White House, where Clinton and his top advisers had gathered to discuss Korea. His announcement of a breakthrough shocked the group, which had been reviewing a plan to increase U.S. troop strength in South Korea. They were more concerned that Carter was about to go public with his announcement, and gathered around a television set to watch his statement on CNN. As they watched, Carter characterized his discussions as "a very important and positive step." Administration officials immediately began drafting a formal proposal to present to North Korea.[50]

What Carter had accomplished, among other things, was effectively to end the drive for sanctions. Former government officials are divided about whether this was a positive development. Gallucci maintains that the threat of sanctions helped pressure the North into negotiating with Carter, but others contend that sanctions would simply have accelerated North Korea's nuclear efforts. Other officials cite the embarrassment that the administration suffered when a former president was able to accomplish a breakthrough that its own officials could not. But Gallucci and some of his colleagues praise Clinton for agreeing to the Carter visit, saying that it "provided an opportunity for the North Koreans to back away in a face-saving way."[51]

The KEDO Solution

U.S. and North Korean negotiators quickly prepared to meet. On July 8, however, the negotiations were once again disrupted when Kim Il Sung died suddenly, apparently of a heart attack. The depth of the North Korean interest in settling the issue was demonstrated when, despite the leadership crisis, consensus on an "agreed statement" of principles was reached on August 12. The statement provided that

The DPRK [North Korea] is prepared to replace its graphite-moderated reactors and related facilities with light water reactor (LWR) power plants, and the U.S. is prepared to make arrangements for the provision of LWRs of approximately 2,000 MW(e) [megawatts electric] to the DPRK as soon as possible. . . . Upon receipt of U.S. assurances for the provision of LWRs and for arrangements for interim energy alternatives, the DPRK will freeze construction of the 50 MW(e) and 200 MW(e) reactors, forgo reprocessing, and seal the Radiochemical Laboratory [reprocessing facility], to be monitored by the IAEA.[52]

The agreement established general goals, but the details proved tricky to negotiate. Particularly problematic were the issues of access to North Korea's nuclear waste sites and the timing of U.S. and North Korean actions. Finally, in mid-October 1994, these issues were resolved when the United States conceded that North Korea need not open its waste sites to inspection until the LWR project was well under way. Gallucci defended this concession on the grounds that "Our eyes were wide open when we were negotiating this. Our objectives were all plutonium, plutonium, plutonium, plutonium."[53]

Finally, on October 21, the consensus was formalized in an "agreed framework." The key provisions were as follows. The United States would organize an international consortium (subsequently designated the Korean Energy Development Organization—KEDO) to finance and supply an LWR, with a goal of concluding a supply contract within six months. In the period before the LWR became operational, the United States would arrange for delivery of up to 500,000 tons of heavy oil annually, to replace the output of North Koreas's graphite-moderated reactors. Work on those reactors was to be frozen within a month of the agreement, with monitoring by the IAEA. The graphite-moderated reactors would be fully dismantled when the LWR project was completed.[54]

In addition, the two sides committed to move toward full normalization of political and economic relations and to take steps to "work for peace and security on a nuclear-free Korean peninsula," including a resumption of North–South talks.[55]

Subsequent Developments

Implementing the agreed framework has not been entirely a smooth process. On December 17, 1994, North Korea downed a U.S. helicopter that had strayed into its airspace, killing one U.S. serviceman and detaining another. Critics charged that some of the heavy fuel oil delivered under the agreement had been diverted to military forces. In April 1995, talks broke down when North Korea refused to accept South Korea as a source for the LWR.[56] The North finally agreed to South Korean participation in June, but U.S. officials remained cautious. "We're dealing with North Korea," Gallucci said. "If at any point we forget that, we deserve to be perceived as massively naive without any sense of history. We're not going to make that mistake."[57] In April 1996, during preparations for a visit by President Clinton to South Korea, the North again demonstrated its unpredictability by conducting large-scale military exercises and denouncing the armistice that ended the Korean War.[58] Nevertheless, North Korea did move expeditiously to fulfill its obligations regarding its nuclear reactors.

As the agreements were being implemented, a new and tragic dimension was added to the North Korean drama. Torrential rains began in the summer of 1995. The ensuing damage to crops stimulated the regime, for the first time in its history, to appeal to the United Nations for relief.[59] The dimensions of the tragedy slowly became evident. The grain shortfall reached 2 million tons by 1997, of which only 5 percent was met by UN World Food Program contributions. The United States had contributed some $18 million in food aid by early 1997, but the prospect of widespread hunger, and possible famine, remained. To outside observers, this raised the possibility of unrest and instability in the Hermit Kingdom.[60]

By April 1997, site preparation for the LWR was begun by a KEDO expert delegation.[61] In July, the United States extended additional food aid valued at $27 million.[62] Despite this response, the executive director of UNICEF said in August that 80,000 North Korean children could die of starvation and that 800,000 more were seriously malnourished.[63] A few days after this statement was made, ground was broken on the KEDO light-water reactor.[64] At the same time, preparatory talks for four-party negotiations among the United States, North and South Korea and China convened in New York. The talks stalled when North Korea insisted on a linkage between the negotiations and increased food aid. U.S. officials were adamant that there would be no linkage, but also underscored their continued commitment to humanitarian relief.[65]

In October, Kim Jong Il, the son of Kim Il Sung, was formally designated as North Korea's new leader. U.S. and international famine relief continued, despite controversy. Most observers, noting the severity of the North Korean situation, supported the U.S. policy of decoupling food aid and negotiations, but some argued for using the famine as a political weapon.[66] The administration rejected this notion, and in late November, North Korea agreed to four-party peace talks the following month. The first round convened in December, with a promise of further discussions in March 1998.[67] In the meantime, South Korea was rocked by a financial crisis, necessitating a massive international bailout. The economic problems facing the South made it even more unlikely that unification, with its estimated $1 trillion price tag, would come any time soon.[68] Thus, while implementation of the nuclear agreement proceeded, and political dialogue progressed, the prospects for peace and eventual reunification seemed remote as the two Koreas contemplated the economic consequences of the peninsula's division.

CRITICISMS OF THE AGREED FRAMEWORK

Given the checkered history of U.S.–North Korean relations, it is not surprising that the agreed framework was highly controversial. The administration had to face grilling from seven separate congressional committees, as well as a barrage of press and academic criticism, before the agreement could be implemented. One major line of criticism was that the North Koreans could not be trusted to keep their word. Opening hearings for the Committee on Foreign Relations, Senator Charles Robb noted that he had "serious reservations about giving North Korea the benefit of the doubt, given its track record of noncompliance and deceit."[69] Other members of Congress questioned whether the presumed benefits of the agreement justified the political and financial costs.[70] Former government officials expressed concern about the agreement's impact on the NPT and the IAEA. Some Europeans contended that the agreement dealt a "body blow" to the nonproliferation regime.[71] Kathleen Bailey, who had served in the Arms Control and Disarmament Agency in the Reagan administration, contended that the agreed framework "damaged the Nuclear Nonproliferation Treaty (NPT), as well as the system of international safeguards that help assure peaceful uses of nuclear energy."[72] She also argued that the North Korean nuclear program could trigger proliferation by Japan and South Korea, that North Korea could—given its unpredictable nature—choose to use any nuclear weapons currently in its arsenal and thus involve the United States in a nuclear conflict and, finally, that North Korea could sell its nuclear capabilities on the world market, as it had its missile systems.[73]

Other criticisms focused on the negotiating process. Robb expressed concern that the agreed framework "suggests a fundamental shift away from a long-standing U.S. policy of insuring nuclear deterrence by sanction and penalty. Rather than using pressure tactics against countries attempting to build an indigenous nuclear weapons program, it seems . . . that the administration leaves itself vulnerable to being forced to buy them off one by one."[74] Former National Security Adviser Brent Scowcroft complained that the United States had "promised North Korea everything we could conceivably promise them. . . . The one tiny stick we had [economic sanctions] Jimmy Carter gave away."[75] Robert Manning, a former Bush administration official, claimed that "The North Koreans had a very weak hand, and they played it brilliantly. We had a strong hand and didn't know how to play it."[76]

Supporters of the agreed framework claimed that the administration's hand was not really that strong, and that the outcome was about the best that could be expected. According to Mazarr, the agreement is "as near to a complete resolution of the nuclear issue as could be imagined in the real world. To argue otherwise presumes a flexibility in North Korean policy and a U.S. and allied willingness to risk conflict that simply did not exist at the time."[77] Oberdorfer praised U.S. flexibility and its dexterity in crafting a multilateral approach:

It is clear . . . that the United States responded to North Korea's nuclear challenge with a combination of force and diplomacy which, although often improvised and lacking coherence, was equal to the seriousness of the issue. While seeking a negotiated settlement, the United States demonstrated that it was prepared to sponsor UN sanctions and was ready to counter the North Korean threat of a violent response by adding powerfully to its military forces in the area. The American undertaking was backed by South Korea . . . and by China. . . . Japan . . . was preparing to join the informal coalition.[78]

Some critics faulted the negotiating process precisely because it used sticks as well as carrots. Leon Sigal of the Social Science Research Council argued that distorted images of nuclear diplomacy, as well as the domination of nonproliferation experts, resulted in an undue emphasis on coercion and a delay in recognizing that conciliatory gestures could defuse the crisis and lead toward resolving the nuclear issue. He noted that North Korea was categorized as an aggressive "rogue state" and that it is a common assumption of nonproliferation policy that such states will not abandon their nuclear ambitions unless demonized and forced to disarm. He traced this image to the influence of liberalism, with its espousal of democratic, market-oriented forms of government, as well as to realism, with its assumptions of international anarchy and antagonism among states. The liberal realists who managed U.S. policy, Sigal says, took an overly legalistic approach, largely ignored outside counsel and did not seriously entertain a compromise until Carter forced them to do so. In his view, an earlier effort to understand and meet North Korea's concerns would have avoided needless threats and the resultant atmosphere of crisis.[79]

The Clinton administration's top negotiator perhaps best summed up the inherent ambivalence about both the agreement and the process:

We went into the negotiations and we got 98 percent of what we wanted and 100 percent of the security issues, and we got a deal that allows us to verify it and allows us at no point to be disadvantaged if they walk away from the deal. And we have no body bags yet. We have no war yet. Good outcome. But in the end, how does your viscera feel? Those North Koreans are getting a $4 billion reactor project. Damn![80]

THE INTERNATIONALIST DILEMMA

In approaching the North Korean nuclear issue, the Clinton administration had to find a middle ground between coercion and conciliation. It had to uphold international norms of behavior while taking account of the unique circumstances of the Korean peninsula. Schooled in international relations, President Clinton acted as an internationalist, eschewing a narrow realist perspective that would have emphasized the use of force in pursuit of national self-interest. In so doing, he faced what Kjell Goldmann has called the internationalist dilemma. Internationalists, according to Goldmann, must be prepared both to ostracize and to empathize. When faced with a government that violates international norms, internationalists must take a stand in favor of preserving international law and organizations. But they also must attempt to see the point of view of other party and seek to prevent conflict from escalating in order to continue the long-term building of international society.[81]

In the most fundamental sense, this dilemma illustrates the basic tension embodied in the just-war tradition. The tradition is cosmopolitan and internationalist, in that it recognizes the universal sanctity of human life and seeks constraints on actions that endanger it. Thus, the tradition would support the development and implementation of international norms that reduce the possibility of violent conflict. The just-war tradition recognizes that violation of such norms can occasion a forceful response. But it also contains a strong presumption against the use of force and requires a rigorous justification for violent actions. Thus the tradition would also counsel understanding and accommodation where they can be successful, and prior to use of damaging force.

Coercive Diplomacy

One way to approach the internationalist dilemma is through a concept that has come to be known as "coercive diplomacy." Popularized by political scientist Alexander George, coercive diplomacy refers to a "defensive strategy that attempts to persuade an opponent to stop or undo an aggressive action . . . by the threat of force or a limited exemplary use of force."[82] George emphasizes that the concept is restricted to defensive uses and does not include offensive coercion and blackmail. It is also different from deterrence in that it seeks to reverse an adversary's actions that are under way rather than to dissuade him from a future action. As an alternative to military action it seeks to persuade rather than force an opponent into changing his actions.[83]

George's model of coercive diplomacy involves four policy "tasks." The first is to design a strategy. This includes determining what to demand of the opponent; whether and how to create a sense of urgency; what punishment ("sticks") to threaten for noncompliance; and what positive inducements ("carrots"), if any, to offer for compliance. The second task is to select a type of coercive action. George identifies four variants: the classic (explicit) ultimatum, the tacit ultimatum, the "gradual turning of the screw" and the "try and see approach." The third task for a policy maker is to set aside the concept that he is facing a "rational" opponent and attempt to derive an empirically based understanding of the adversary's motivations and goals. The final task is to look carefully at the context of the crisis, paying close attention to how that context will influence the effectiveness of the coercive strategy.[84]

George has examined a number of historical examples of coercive diplomacy, including the prelude to Pearl Harbor, the Cuban missile crisis, crises in Southeast Asia in the 1960s, the Reagan administration's coercive actions against Nicaragua and Libya, and the Gulf War. In some of these cases, coercive diplomacy was successful, but in others it did not achieve the objective, or force was ultimately used. George concludes that there are some conditions that favor success in coercive diplomacy, though he cautions that there is no single one that can be considered sufficient to ensure a favorable outcome. These conditions include the following:

- Clarity of objectives, and in particular clarity in what is demanded of the adversary

- Strength of motivation on the part of the coercing power—coercive diplomacy is likely to be more successful if the motivation of the coercing power is stronger than that of the adversary

- A sense of urgency and an effective means of communicating that urgency to the opponent

- Adequate domestic and international support for the coercing power

- A fear on the part of the opponent that escalation of the crisis would be unacceptable

- Clarity concerning the precise terms of settlement.

Of these factors, George considers three to be particularly important, because they have a decisive impact on the opponent's perception. These are the asymmetry of motivation in favor of the coercing power, the sense of time urgency and the fear of unacceptable escalation.[85]

George is cautious about advocating coercive diplomacy, even if all of these conditions are present. He notes that "there will be few crises in which coercive diplomacy will constitute a high-confidence strategy."[86] While it is a flexible strategy, coercive diplomacy is highly context-dependent. It also requires an uncommon degree of skill on the part of the policy maker.[87] It is, nevertheless, a useful alternative to military force, and thus there is value in looking at it in the context of moral assessment.

Morality and Coercive Diplomacy

The concept of coercive diplomacy, as George defines it, has much in common with the just-war tradition. Both have a strong bias against the actual use of violence. Both are defensive in nature, seeking to redress wrongs rather than to impose the will of the coercing party. Both are also firmly grounded in reality, recognizing the complexity of international life and the potential need to use force to prevent injustice. Coercive diplomacy is also consistent with the just-war precept that actual force should be used only as a last resort, after less harmful means have been exhausted. It also provides states with options that may better meet the criterion of proportionality than would other measures, such as military action or economic sanctions.

George notes that effective use of coercive diplomacy requires broad domestic and international support, a standard that is consistent with the just-war tradition's requirement that force be used only by competent authority. With regard to the just-war criterion of probability of success, however, George is more pessimistic. He notes that from his study of historical cases, coercive diplomacy is a high-risk strategy, unlikely to be successful in all instances. He puts great stress on the need for policy makers to understand the international context of the issues they face, as well as the psychology of the adversary. If these needs can be met, the probability of successful use of coercive diplomacy is enhanced.

There are two potential moral problems with coercive diplomacy. The first is analogous to the central problem of nuclear deterrence. To deter nuclear war requires a threat of nuclear retaliation against potential aggression. But if the use of nuclear weapons is morally unacceptable because of their devastating destructiveness, then it can be argued that the threat of use is similarly unacceptable. For this reason, many authorities in the just-war tradition reluctantly accept deterrence as a necessary step on the road to eventual nuclear disarmament.

Similarly, it can be argued that the threat to use force that is inherent in coercive diplomacy carries the same moral weight that actual use would entail. If that is so, then the threat would be morally permissible only if the circumstances would also justify the actual use. In the just-war tradition, only the repelling of aggression, the retaking of something wrongfully taken, the punishment of wrongdoing or the redressing of severe violations of human rights would justify military force. Are these, then, the only circumstances that can justify the threat of force?

George's analysis suggests that coercive diplomacy is most effective, and most appropriate, before the circumstances that would occasion the use of force have actually occurred. Coercive diplomacy is intended to forestall violations of sovereignty, law or rights, rather than to respond to them. It is analogous, then, to the preemptive use of force, in that it is attempted prior to actual aggression or attack by an adversary. Michael Walzer, in his analysis of just and unjust wars, refers to the use of force in circumstances of "legitimate anticipation." He notes that aggression can be recognized before an aggressor actually uses force, and that in such circumstances "states may use military force in the face of threats of war, whenever the failure to do so would seriously risk their territorial integrity or political independence."[88] If this is so, then it would seem that the threat of force or sanctions can be used by the international community (or by individual states or groups of states acting on its behalf) when there is reasonable evidence of an aggressor's preparations. These may include the acquisition of weapons or forces that exceed legitimate defensive needs, as well as offensive military doctrines and aggressive statements.

The second moral issue regarding coercive diplomacy relates to the outcome of negotiations. The objective of coercive diplomacy is to achieve some political settlement in which the parties agree to carry out (or refrain from) certain actions. In other words, the goal is to persuade the adversary to recognize certain obligations and to honor them. The problem is that most moral philosophers claim that coerced agreements do not impose binding obligations.[89] The argument is that one is obligated only to those agreements that one enters freely. Coercion constrains freedom, and thus reduces obligation. If a party is literally "forced" to enter into an agreement, then there is no freedom to choose, and thus no obligation. What this means is that while agreements reached through coercive diplomacy may be codified in treaties, and thus be legally binding, they may not actually be morally binding on the coerced party.

This concept of agreement and obligation relies on the notion that agreements are in a sense a pair of promises. The coerced party is like a child who promises, under duress, to do something but has her fingers crossed. She does not accept the obligation, and considers herself free to act as she would have before the promises were exchanged. This freedom, it is important to note, comes from the presence of duress that has limited her ability to exercise free will in the act of promising, and not from the deceptive act of crossing her fingers.

There is another concept, however, that leaves open the possibility that at least some coerced agreements may be binding. This concept sees an agreement not as an exchange of promises but as a joint decision to accept certain conditions. This joint acceptance results in a joint commitment.[90] If this concept is valid, then individual parties are committed to an obligation only to the extent that the other parties are. Mutual consent is required to rescind such an agreement. It follows, then, that if parties have agreed jointly to certain measures (rather than simply exchanged promises), then each is obligated to conform to the agreement, regardless of the circumstances under which it was reached.

This concept sees negotiation as a process whereby two parties combine their conflicting interests into a single decision.[91] This does not mean that a coercer is necessarily morally justified in making threats. Nor does it mean that coerced agreements may never be broken—for example, when to conform to them would entail doing evil.[92] It does, however, leave open the possibility that coerced agreements can be binding when the parties explicitly agree to agree.

It may also be morally appropriate to use coercion to force agreement with widely shared norms of international behavior.[93] If the international community has broadly agreed to certain standards, it may be acceptable to coerce a state into conforming to them, even if that state has not explicitly accepted them. Such standards might include the prohibition against aggression, or other agreements embodied in the United Nations Charter and similar documents, as well as treaties that are widely (though not universally) adhered to by the international community. This principle would entail a recognition that while nations may differ in interests, culture and specific interpretations of ethical principles, there is a shared interest in enforcing a norm of reciprocity that provides predictability and stability to international relations.[94]

Coercion and the Art of Negotiation

The idea that coercion is inherent in international negotiations certainly corresponds to the actual practices of states. The ancient Greeks were aware of this; the Athenian generals in Thucydides' Melian Conference attempted (unsuccessfully) to use coercive diplomacy against their adversaries. But there are alternatives. One, of course, is the direct use of force. The others include conflict resolution, an attempt to restructure perceived conflicts so as to reduce the apparent incompatibility of interests; and negotiation, a voluntary commitment of parties to enter into an agreement that does not fully meet the interests or objectives of any party.[95] Typically, the negotiating process is one in which "explicit proposals are put forward ostensibly for the purpose of reaching agreement on an exchange or on the realization of common interest where conflicting interests are present."[96]

Given the presence of both shared and conflicting interests, negotiating parties, including nation-states, typically use a mix of rewards and punishments, carrots and sticks, in the bargaining process. This stems from a perception that such a mixed strategy will be more effective than one that relies on coercion or conciliation alone. Studies of bargaining behavior have shown that the threat of punishment is often effective in discouraging unwanted behavior, but that the effectiveness may be limited to the short term. Often, studies indicate, the threat of coercive measures may lead to defiance, and thus to an escalating spiral of punishment and retaliation.[97] This may be because each side views the other as susceptible to coercion, yet resents the opponent's attempts to use coercion itself.[98] Statesmen, historical research has demonstrated, repeatedly overestimate the efficacy of coercion.[99]

On the other hand, the possibility of consensus is enhanced over the long term when both parties perceive inherent value in the agreement being pursued as well as in the concept of agreement per se.[100] The task for the negotiator is to uncover the areas of common interest and to make them central to both parties' perceptions. Thus, the negotiating process is as much about learning as about bargaining. It is an attempt to overcome the different conceptualizations of the issue that the parties bring to the table, and that mask the commonality of their concerns.[101] As summarized by Martin Patchen, a successful policy in international negotiation

combines both a measure of firmness and a measure of flexibility, both a willingness to vigorously resist coercion by an adversary and a willingness to reciprocate and sometimes to initiate concessions. By words, and especially by deeds, it is important to show the adversary that one will not be exploited but also that one is ready to cooperate. The adversary should be convinced that he has little to gain by coercion and much to gain by cooperation.[102]

EVALUATING THE NORTH KOREAN NUCLEAR AGREEMENT

The criteria enumerated above—those for effectiveness in negotiation and coercive diplomacy, as well as those of the just-war tradition—provide an interlocking framework of standards for evaluating the Clinton administration's performance in the North Korean nuclear crisis. The assessment is mixed, with respect both to the agreement itself and to the process by which it was achieved.

With respect to the standards of negotiation, the administration performed reasonably well. It used a mix of carrots and sticks, though the carrots were offered late in the process and reluctantly. In fact, despite the fact that a "package deal" had been discussed for some time, it took the intervention of an outside mediator, former President Carter, to stimulate the administration to make a concrete offer of assistance to North Korea. In making this concession, however, the administration demonstrated that it could learn from the process and identify areas of common interest. Robb was correct in suggesting that the United States had changed its nonproliferation stance in this instance from one centered on deterrence and coercion to one that admitted the possibility of concessions. This was not an inadvertent decision by the administration, however, but a deliberate choice that flowed from its additional insights about North Korean perceptions, as well as about the potential cost of military conflict and the limited efficacy of economic sanctions. Thus the administration chose a "market" approach. "Instead of using symbolic and moral incentives, along with the threat of coercion in event of noncompliance, the KEDO project extracts compliance with material incentives."[103]

Although the outcome was reasonably successful, the Clinton administration fell short of meeting George's standards for a subtle and flexible use of coercive diplomacy. The administration's objectives were not clear at the outset. Only after the Carter intervention did the United States decide to focus on North Korea's future nuclear potential rather than the legalistic goal of exacting an admission of past NPT violations. It is not clear to what extent there was an asymmetry of motivation in this case. Certainly the United States, the IAEA and most members of the Security Council felt strongly about preventing North Korea from obtaining a usable nuclear arsenal. But North Korea also was strongly motivated to pursue its nuclear program for a powerful set of political and security reasons. In the event, neither party had such an overwhelming motivation as to coerce the other successfully. Similarly, the United States had difficulty convincing North Korea of the time urgency of the crisis. This was because time was on the side of Kim Il Sung, and he demonstrated this in a series of delaying tactics that frustrated the international community.

Clinton also had difficulty in garnering the domestic and international support for effective coercion. There was no significant domestic opposition to the goal of countering the North Korean nuclear program. But there certainly was no appetite, even on the part of the military services, for a large-scale war to achieve this objective. In addition, international support for economic sanctions was lukewarm at best. UN Ambassador Albright had difficulty in selling even modest restrictions to the Europeans, Russians, Japanese and Chinese. It seems unlikely that economic sanctions on the scale and of a duration necessary to stimulate a change in North Korean policy would have been possible.

With respect to clarity of the resulting agreement, the administration can also be faulted. Many of the details were contained in a confidential protocol and a letter from President Clinton, and thus hidden from public scrutiny. Moreover, subsequent developments, especially North Korea's initial reluctance to accept a South Korean light-water reactor, indicate that there were important details were left unsettled when the agreement was signed in October 1994. On the other hand, ambiguity can often be useful in international agreements, especially when it gives the parties an opportunity to save face with domestic constituencies. And by using an agreed framework rather than a treaty, the administration gained flexibility in implementing the agreement without the requirement for congressional approval.

From the perspective of the just-war tradition, the administration comes off rather well, primarily for what it did not do. Specifically, the United States did not actually use military force, and was rather circumspect in the coercive measures that it chose. Thus, its mix of coercive and conciliatory tools seems morally appropriate to the circumstances.

The cause that occasioned the U.S. actions was a just one, enhancing international stability by preventing an unpredictable state, with a record of violence and terrorism, from acquiring nuclear weapons. Thus, it is analogous to the just-war standard of preventing aggression. President Clinton's intentions were also appropriate: seeking a continuation of an agreed international regime and limiting the risk of violent conflict. He acted under appropriate authority, upholding the NPT and the rights of the IAEA with the support of the UN Security Council.

Even with these justifications, however, it would not have been morally acceptable for the United States to use military force. Even on the small scale envisioned (an attack on the North Korean reactors), the potential for escalation to a large-scale conflict would have been great. Initiating military action would have risked violating the just-war principle of proportionality. It is also unclear whether it would have met the standard of a reasonable probability of success. In addition, any escalation to peninsula wide conflict would have entailed massive civilian casualties, in violation of the principle of discrimination. These problems were recognized by Clinton's military advisers, who counseled against such an attack.

Instead, Clinton chose (or was goaded into) a more discriminating and appropriate mix of policy tools. The modest augmentation of forces in Korea underscored U.S. resolve but was not provocative. UN discussions of sanctions also demonstrated the international community's concerns and effectively communicated to North Korea the seriousness of its actions. In the final analysis, however, coercive measures proved to be inadequate and had to be augmented by conciliatory steps. That the administration recognized this is to its credit. But its actions raise one final moral question.

Confronting Evil: Reward Versus Punishment

Some have argued that the agreed framework simply rewards North Korea for its misdeeds. A few critics have gone so far as to characterize North Korea as a "rogue" and a regime that is inherently evil.[104] It follows, then, according to these critics, that the administration's actions have the effect of aiding and promoting evil in the long term. This is a concern not only in the case of North Korea but also of states, such as Libya and Iraq, that the critics place in the same category.

This is indeed an important dilemma. Aquinas counseled that statesmen must always be cognizant of the presence of evil in the world. But at the same time he came from a religious tradition that counseled forgiveness. Similarly, Aristotle advised those seeking practical wisdom to cultivate a sympathetic understanding of the plight of others. This is a particular challenge in the case of North Korea. Certainly the regime has been guilty of horrendous acts of terrorism, and its rhetoric continually proclaims unending hostility to the South and to democratic values. On the other hand, it is a beleaguered nation wallowing in poverty and famine. Is it not, then, deserving of some measure of compassion? This is the internationalist dilemma translated to the moral dimension.

There is no simple answer to this dilemma, but the Clinton administration showed considerable courage in deciding to take a conciliatory stance. If North Korea is ever to join the community of nations, it must be convinced that its legitimate needs will be respected. Most important, these include a stable economy and an adequate supply of basic necessities, including energy. At the same time, Ambassador Gallucci is correct to point out that the United States was not dealing with just any country, but with one that has a history of deceit and manipulation as well as violence. In such a circumstance, courage, as Aristotle pointed out, means following a middle course between rashness and cowardice. In this case, the United States, albeit inadvertently, found its way onto this middle path.
104.

NOTES

1. United States Department of State, *Background Notes on North Korea* (June 1996), <http://www.state.gov/www/ background_notes/ North_korea_0696_bgn.html> (June 15, 1996).

2. Yong Soon Yim, "North Korean Military Doctrine," in Tae-Hwan Kwak, Wayne Patterson and Edward A. Olsen, eds., *The Two Koreas in World Politics* (Seoul: Kyungnam University Press, 1983), p. 127.

3. Because the story of the North Korean nuclear program is so recent, there are few primary sources available. There is a set of congressional hearings during which Clinton administration officials set forth the rationale for their policies. There are also several useful secondary sources. The first is an excellent, book-length study, Michael J. Mazarr, *North Korea and the Bomb: A Case Study in Nonproliferation* (New York: St. Martin's Press, 1995). Mazarr's study provides a very well-documented description of the drama through the end of 1994. Another valuable narrative of that period is Susan Rosegrant and Michael D. Watkins, *Carrots, Sticks and Question Marks: Negotiating the North Korean Nuclear Crisis,* Parts A and B, Case Studies C18-95-1297.0 and C18-95-1298.0 (Cambridge, MA: John F. Kennedy School of Government, Harvard University, 1995). A third source that updates the story through the end of 1996 is Don Oberdorfer, *The Two Koreas* (Reading, MA: Addison-Wesley, 1997). Subsequent developments are described in press reports.

4. Mazarr, *North Korea and the Bomb*, p. 15.

5. Oberdorfer, *The Two Koreas*, p. 252.

6. Mazarr, *North Korea and the Bomb*, p.16.

7. Oberdorfer, *The Two Koreas*, p. 89.

8. Ibid., pp. 68–74.

9. Mazarr, *North Korea and the Bomb*, p.25.

10. Quoted in ibid., p. 29.

11. Ibid., pp. 32–33.

12. Oberdorfer, *The Two Koreas*, pp. 250–51.

13. Ibid, p. 254.

14. Richard V. Allen, testimony, in Senate Committee on Foreign Relations, *North Korean Nuclear Agreement: Hearings before the Committee on Foreign Relations, United States Senate*, 104th Cong., 1st sess. (Washington, DC: U.S. Government Printing Office, 1995), p. 62.

15. Oberdorfer, *The Two Koreas*, pp. 255–60.

16. Allen, testimony, p. 62.

17. Oberdorfer, *The Two Koreas*, p. 267.

18. Mazarr, *North Korea and the Bomb*, pp. 83–94.

19. Ibid., p. 102.

20. Ibid.

21. Young Whan Kihl, "Compromise or Confrontation: Lessons from the 1994 Crisis," in *Peace and Security in Northeast Asia: The Nuclear Issue and the Korean Peninsula*, Young Whan Kihl and Peter Hayes, eds., (Armonk, NY: M.E. Sharpe, 1997), p. 183.

22. Oberdorfer, *The Two Koreas*, p. 282.

23. Rosegrant and Watkins, *Carrots Sticks and Question Marks* (Part A), p. 14.

24. Mazarr, *North Korea and the Bomb*, pp. 120–21.

25. Oberdorfer, *The Two Koreas*, pp. 285–86.

26. Mazarr, *North Korea and the Bomb*, p. 127.

27. Ibid., p. 132.

28. Oberdorfer, *The Two Koreas*, p. 293.

29. Ibid., p. 295.

30. Ibid., p. 297.

31. Mazarr, *North Korea and the Bomb*, p. 144.

32. Oberdorfer, *The Two Koreas*, p. 299.

33. Ibid., p. 300.

34. Mazarr, *North Korea and the Bomb*, p. 147.

35. Oberdorfer, *The Two Koreas*, p. 302.

36. Mazarr, *North Korea and the Bomb*, p. 150.

37. Ibid.

38. Oberdorfer, *The Two Koreas*, p. 303.

39. Ibid., p. 304.

40. Ibid., pp. 308–9.

41. Rosegrant and Watkins, *Carrots Sticks and Question Marks* (Part A), p. 46.

42. Oberdorfer, *The Two Koreas*, p. 315.

43. Ibid., p. 310; Rosegrant and Watkins, *Carrots Sticks and Question Marks* (Part A), p. 46.

44. Mazarr, *North Korea and the Bomb*, p. 160.

45. Rosegrant and Watkins, *Carrots Sticks and Question Marks* (Part A), p. 37.

46. For an excellent description of this incident, see Joe Wood and Philip Zelikow, *Persuading a President: Jimmy Carter and American Troops in Korea*, Case Study C18-96-1319.0 (Cambridge, MA: John F. Kennedy School of Government, Harvard University, 1996).

47. Oberdorfer, *The Two Koreas*, p. 318.

48. Mazarr, *North Korea and the Bomb*, p. 163.

49. Oberdorfer, *The Two Koreas*, p. 329.

50. Rosegrant and Watkins, *Carrots Sticks and Question Marks* (Part B), p. 3.

51. Ibid., p. 6.

52. Quoted in Mazarr, *North Korea and the Bomb*, p. 168.

53. Rosegrant and Watkins, *Carrots Sticks and Question Marks* (Part B), p. 9.

54. Ibid., exhibit 1.

55. Ibid.

56. Daryl M. Plunk, *The U.S.–North Korean Nuclear Agreement: A Six Month Report Card*, Asian Studies Center Backgrounder (Washington, DC: Heritage Foundation, 1995); "North Korea Jerks the US, South Korea in Nuke Talks," *Christian Science Monitor*, June 5, 1995, p. 1.

57. "North Korea Curtails Its Nuclear Program," *Christian Science Monitor*, September 21, 1995, p. 1.

58. "To Get US Attention, N. Korea Acts as if It's on Brink of War," *Christian Science Monitor*, April 9, 1996, p. 1.

59. Oberdorfer, *The Two Koreas*, p. 370.

60. Testimony of Charles Kartman, acting assistant secretary of state for East Asian and Pacific Affairs, United States House of Representatives, Committee on International Relations, *Testimony before the House International Relations Committee, Subcommittee on Asian and Pacific Affairs*, 106th Cong., 1st sess. (Washington, DC: U.S. Government Printing Office, 1997).

61. "KEDO Reactor Project Moves Through Protocols Toward Implementation," *Arms Control Today* 27, no. 3 (April 1997): 39.

62. U.S. Department of State daily press briefing, July 14, 1997.

63. "UNICEF Chief Says 80,000 North Korean Children May Die of Starvation," *New York Times*, August 9, 1997, sec. 1, p. 5.

64. "North Korea Initiates Huge Energy Project," *Washington Post*, August 19, 1997, sec. A, p. 18.

65. U.S. Department of State daily press briefing, August 22, 1997.

66. "Famine as a Political Weapon," *Washington Post*, November 8, 1997, sec. A, p. 23.

67. Alexander G. Higgins, "Koreas to Hold Peace Talks in March," Associated Press, December 10, 1997.

68. Marcus Noland, "Why North Korea Will Muddle Through," *Foreign Affairs* 76, no. 4 (July/August 1997): 114.

69. United States Senate, Committee on Foreign Relations, *Implications of the US–North Korea Nuclear Agreement, Hearing Before the Subcommittee on East Asian and Pacific Affairs of the Committee on Foreign Relations*, 103rd Cong., 2nd sess. (Washington, DC: U.S. Government Printing Office, 1994), p. 2.

70. Ibid., p. 9.

71. Rosegrant and Watkins, *Carrots Sticks and Question Marks* (Part B), p. 12.

72. Kathleen C. Bailey, "The Nuclear Deal with North Korea: Is the Glass Half Empty or Half Full?" *Comparative Strategy* 14, no. 2 (April 1995): 137.

73. Ibid.

74. United States Senate, *Implications of the US–North Korea Nuclear Agreement*, pp. 2–3.

75. Rosegrant and Watkins, *Carrots Sticks and Question Marks* (Part B), p. 12.

76. Ibid.

77. Mazarr, *North Korea and the Bomb*, p. 178.

78. Oberdorfer, The Two Koreas, pp. 335–36.

79. Leon V. Sigal, "Look Who's Talking Nuclear Diplomacy with North Korea," *Items* 51, no. 2–3 (June–September 1997): 31–36.

80. Rosegrant and Watkins, *Carrots Sticks and Question Marks* (Part B), p. 13.

81. Kjell Goldmann, *The Logic of Internationalism: Coercion and Accommodation* (London: Routledge, 1994), p. 165.

82. Alexander L. George, *Forceful Persuasion: Coercive Diplomacy as an Alternative to War* (Washington, DC: U.S. Institute of Peace, 1991), p. ix.

83. Ibid., p. 5.

84. Alexander L. George and William E. Simons, ed., *The Limits of Coercive Diplomacy* (Boulder, CO: Westview Press, 1994), pp. 16–20.

85. George, *Forceful Persuasion*, pp. 75–81.

86. Ibid., p. 84.

87. George and Simons, *The Limits of Coercive Diplomacy*, p. 293.

88. Michael Walzer, *Just and Unjust Wars*, 2nd ed. (New York: Basic Books, 1992), p. 85.

89. Margaret Gilbert, "Agreements, Coercion, and Obligation," *Ethics* 103, no. 4 (July 1993): 679.

90. Ibid., p. 691.

91. I. William Zartman, "Negotiation as a Joint Decision Making Process," in *The Negotiation Process: Theories and Applications*, I. William Zartman, ed. (Beverly Hills, CA: Sage, 1978), p. 70.

92. Ibid., p. 73.

93. Kent Greenawalt, "Shortfalls of Realism, Shared Social Values, and Authority: The Problem of Political Coercion," *Journal of Religion* 73, no. 4 (October 1993): 543.

94. Michael W. Morris, Damien L. H. Sim and Vittorio Girotto, "Time of Decision, Ethical Obligation, and Causal Illusion: Temporal Cues and Social Heuristics in the Prisoner's Dilemma," in *Negotiation as a Social Process*, Roderick M. Kramer and David M. Messick, eds., (Thousand Oaks, CA: Sage, 1995), p. 212.

95. Leonard Greenhalgh and Deborah I. Chapman, "Joint Decision Making: The Insepara-bility of Relationships and Negotiation," in Kramer and Messick, eds., *Negotiation as a Social Process*, p. 167.

96. Fred Charles Ikle, *How Nations Negotiate* (New York: Harper & Row, 1964), pp. 3–4.

97. Martin Patchen, *Resolving Disputes Between Nations: Coercion or Conciliation* (Durham, NC: Duke University Press, 1988), p. 231.

98. Roderick M. Kramer, Pri Pradhan Shah and Stephanie L. Woerner, "Why Ultimatums Fail," in Kramer and Messick, eds., *Negotiation as a Social Process*, p. 306.

99. Charles Lockhart, *Bargaining in International Conflicts* (New York: Columbia University Press, 1979), p. 181.

100. Ibid., p. 333.

101. P. Terence Hopmann and Theresa C. Smith, "An Application of a Richardson Process Model: Soviet–American Interactions in the Test Ban Negotiations 1962–1963," in I. William Zartman, ed., *The Negotiation Process*, p. 152.

102. Patchen, *Resolving Disputes Between Nations*, p. 342.

103. Robert E. Bedeski, "KEDO and the Pursuit of Non-Proliferation on the Korean Peninsula," paper presented at the Fourth Annual CANCAPS conference, Calgary, Alberta, Canada, December 14–15, 1996, p. 1.

104. Sigal, "Look Who's Talking Nuclear Diplomacy with North Korea."

8

Sheathing the Sword of Justice

The cases in the preceding chapters confirm that the realists are right: the use of violence or coercion by states remains a central aspect of international politics. In the cases, states have sought to advance national objectives or to promote political change by threatening mass annihilation, employing overwhelming military force, imposing economic sanctions, secretly manipulating elections, planning or tolerating assassinations and plotting coups. In the cases we have examined, the justifications for force and coercion have varied in quality. In most instances, the arguments were found to be weak rationalizations for a realist viewpoint that continues to dominate the behavior of states.

But the cases also show that the just-war tradition, with its bias against violence, can illuminate moral choices regarding violence and coercion. They suggest a growing recognition on the part of policy makers and citizens that although coercive practices are part of international reality, they are not desirable in themselves. Rather, the cases show an increasing dissatisfaction with realist arguments and a greater role for moral argumentation in international politics. This development, nascent as it is, seems to reflect a sense that there are core human values at stake. To the extent that respect for human life and integrity, and the establishment and protection of human freedom, are held to be core values, actions that violate these values carry a negative weight and must be justified.

CORE VALUES AND THE BURDEN OF PROOF

There is much skepticism regarding the notion of core values, but there is ample reason to accept that respect for life and promotion of freedom are in fact shared human values. Rushworth Kidder has found in interviews with "people of conscience" from virtually all major world cultures that these values, together with fairness, unity, tolerance and responsibility, come up continuously in their aspirations for humanity.[1] Philosopher Sissela Bok cites several examples of recent efforts to document shared values across cultures, including the 1993 United Nations World Conference on Human Rights, the 1993 World Parliament of Religions, Pope John Paul II's encyclical *Veritatis Splendor*, and the report of the Commission on Global Governance, *Our Global Neighborhood*. Though Bok is critical of many aspects of these efforts, it is noteworthy that they all identify respect for human life as a core value, and—despite differences in the interpretation of specific rights—they all acknowledge the goal of greater self-determination for people and societies.[2]

Bok derives several common values by examining the attributes that human societies must have in order to survive. She concludes that they require certain "minimalist values," among them "some form of positive duties regarding mutual support, loyalty and reciprocity."[3] She also identifies as typical of human civilizations some "negative duties to refrain from harmful action."[4] The implication of these findings is, again, that deviation from the positive duty to be mutually supportive and the negative duty to avoid harm must be justified.

Frances Harbour has found that a number of authorities cite a "shared core" of basic values, including approval of justice, beneficence, good faith, veracity and self-control, coupled with disapproval of murder and incest or rape. Because of the diversity of human civilizations, these basic values are mediated and expressed in a variety of specific rules and practices. For example, the basic value of the sanctity of life expresses itself through limitations on harmful activities and unauthorized killing. The specific limitations may differ from culture to culture. In the Semitic cultures, for example, one way in which the limits are characterized is through rules of warfare. The Christian value system spawned the just-war tradition, with its emphasis on specific questions and criteria, among them the principle of discrimination and protection of noncombatants. A similar concept exists in the Islamic tradition, but there is a difference in the definition of noncombatants. The Christian tradition regards as noncombatants those who are not part of regular or irregular military forces, a concept that is enshrined in international law, while the Islamic view has traditionally been that all males of fighting age are to be considered combatants.[5]

Thus, the shared values that Harbour identifies become a sort of foundation upon which secondary and tertiary systems of behavior and custom are built. Given the historical evolution of the modern nation-state system from the political center of western Europe, it is not surprising that most of the modern rules regarding the relations of states reflect the mediation of the core values through the Western traditions. The recurring use of the just-war tradition in debates about the use of force in international politics is therefore both a reflection of shared human values and a historical phenomenon that reflects the origins of the modern international system of states. These aspects of the tradition mean that it is perfectly reasonable to use its criteria as standards of justification for force and coercion, despite the fact that other traditions do not share all of its specific tenets.

We may not be able to prove with rigor that avoidance of harm and protection of freedom are universal values, but it is reasonable to assume that most people would agree that proposals to use violence and coercion internationally are weighty matters that must be discussed and argued. There is some empirical evidence to support this, at least among American opinion leaders. A comprehensive study of their attitudes toward war and peace found overwhelming rejection of the notion that warfare can be justified to achieve national advantage or to convert others to American beliefs by force, and widespread support for the notion that war should be a last resort after other measures have failed.[6] In surveying the conclusions from these case studies, then, it is reasonable to assume that the burden of justification falls on those who advocate violence and coercion, and that most Americans, if not most of the world's people, would agree with that criterion.

ETHICAL TRADITIONS AND POLITICAL DEBATE

The cases discussed in this book concern controversial issues, and there is no shortage of differences of opinion regarding what should have been done about them. The cases present examples of arguments that come from the entire range of ethical traditions, from nationalistic realism to cosmopolitan pacifism.

Realist arguments were presented in the most extreme form in Saddam Hussein's assertion of his right to invade Kuwait in the Iraqi national interest and to redress putative historical injustices. The fact that Kuwait was universally recognized as an independent state, not as a province of Iraq, did not deter him. Rather, he disregarded arguments about sovereignty and right in a reprise of the arguments of the Athenian generals in the Melian Conference. President Nixon's behavior regarding Chile, and the statements of his national security adviser, Henry Kissinger, also demonstrated a reliance on the realist tradition. This was particularly true of Nixon's decision to expand his covert action program to encompass the violent overthrow of the Chilean government and Kissinger's stated contempt for the Chilean electoral process.

President Kennedy and his key advisers also adopted an extreme realist posture with respect to Cuba. His focus was on the U.S. national interest, and he did not hesitate to use force, stealth and economic pressure to promote his concept of U.S. requirements. In doing so, he resorted to extreme, disproportionate measures, including attempted assassination, in emulation of Machiavelli's prince. President Reagan demonstrated a realist's preoccupation with power in his decision to build up U.S. military forces. And his characterization of the former Soviet Union as an "evil empire" put him in the same category as realists Kennedy, Nixon and Bush, who attempted to portray their opponents as essentially malevolent.

Yet Reagan also had a streak of Kantian idealism in his vision of a nuclear-free world. That he sought to achieve it through a controversial strategic defense program does not invalidate his commitment to reducing and eventually eliminating the nuclear threat. Thus, curiously, Reagan shared the goals of the nuclear pacifists of the Pax Christi movement, though not their view of how to achieve them.

Arguments in the Kantian idealist tradition came from Ramsey Clark and other critics of the Gulf War, who held that the actions of the United States were unjustified and disproportionate. Similarly, former President Carter showed himself firmly in that tradition when he counseled conciliatory measures toward North Korea. Paradoxically, in the case of Burundi, cosmopolitan liberals were more adamant than realists in promoting the use of force. While Boutros-Ghali and the leaders of nongovernmental organizations (NGOs) urged an international intervention to halt genocide, realists in power in key nation-states hesitated because of the lack of a clearly defined national interest in the area.

Though the extremes of realism and liberalism are most clearly visible in the cases, there were also instances in which the more moderate traditions were employed. Proponents of continued economic sanctions against Iraq, as well as opponents of the embargo against Cuba, used detailed analyses of the effectiveness of past sanctions to underscore their points. Ambassador Robert Gallucci made a classic "act utilitarian" argument in explaining and defending the nuclear agreement with North Korea. It was the best approach available, in his view, to reduce the nuclear threat while providing mutual benefit to both sides. Critics of the agreement also used utilitarian arguments, but these were of the "rule utilitarian" variety. Congressional critics expressed concern about the precedent of "rewarding" nuclear proliferation, and officials of the IAEA worried that the international regime for controlling proliferation would be weakened by the agreement.

The explicit use of just-war arguments was seen in Bush's rationale for the Gulf War. In retrospect, he seems to have made a strong case with respect to the *jus ad bellum*, although his actions regarding the *jus in bello* are more questionable. The American Catholic bishops, of course, were the most explicit in their recourse to the just-war tradition in the debate over nuclear deterrence. Their arguments were sober, sophisticated and specific. Conscious of the political complexity of their proposals, the bishops did not hesitate to speak their minds while leaving the implementation to political leaders. In the end, it was Ronald Reagan, a unique blend of realist and liberal, who demonstrated the political skill (and luck) to begin the process of real reductions in nuclear weapon arsenals.

The cases show that in general, the realists failed to provide sufficient justification for the use of force and coercive measures. Saddam's rationalizations were decisively rejected by the international community. The just-war tradition would condemn his goals and his actions as wholly inconsistent with the principles of just cause and intention. Nixon's cavalier attitude toward Chile's sovereignty was inconsistent with the values of respect for life and freedom, and his willingness to employ the most violent and disruptive tactics violated the principles of proportionality and discrimination. Similarly, Kennedy's support of assassination plots against Castro raises troubling questions about his intentions and judgment, and his intensification of economic sanctions demonstrates an insensitivity to the impact of his actions on ordinary people.

On the other hand, the critiques of the idealists often seemed disconnected from reality. Ramsey Clark's arguments condemned the United States and the coalition while ignoring Saddam's responsibility for the Gulf War and his violation of international norms. The nuclear pacifists surely knew that the American people did not support unilateral disarmament initiatives, though perhaps they thought that their arguments would help to tilt the balance of opinion toward eventual reductions in the nuclear threat. In the Burundi case, the arguments of Boutros-Ghali and the NGO leaders generally fell on deaf ears. They seriously underestimated the ability of the realist leaders of most states (Canada excepted) to compartment their thinking and turn away in denial from human tragedy.

Utilitarian debates, while useful in illuminating the facts and considerations at stake, fell victim to their own inherent weakness, the sheer complexity of the issues under discussion. Arguments about the effectiveness of sanctions, the efficacy of deterrence and the future behavior of states regarding their treaty obligations depend on a systematic and complete marshaling of facts that is exceedingly difficult in international politics. The utilitarian argument about the obligation to intervene in Burundi to forestall genocide bogged down in debates over the details of implementation before it was overtaken by rapid and confusing developments in Burundi and the region. The cases show the challenge of making consequentialist moral arguments in a chaotic environment where consequences are nearly impossible to predict with confidence.

Though employed explicitly in only a few cases, the arguments of the just-war tradition seemed, in contrast, to be moderate and convincing. The cases showed that the vocabulary and concepts of the tradition were meaningful in illuminating the issues at stake in the nuclear debate and the Gulf War. The analyses also showed that they can help to clarify the actions of states and to suggest alternatives that better conform to the goal of preserving life and freedom.

THE JUST-WAR TRADITION IN THE MODERN ERA

It is reasonable to ask, however, whether the just-war tradition continues to be relevant to modern international politics. The history of the tradition suggests that this is so. The principles of the just-war tradition have survived profound changes in the international system. Conceived in the waning days of the Roman Empire, notions of *jus ad bellum* and jus *in bello* have been reexamined and refined in subsequent eras. Aquinas revisited Augustine's principles in the Middle Ages and found that they illuminated issues related to the warfare then being conducted among rival sovereigns, as well as the roving bands of mercenaries that plagued Europe. Vittoria and Suárez extended the tradition into the Age of Exploration, helping to clarify principles related to the use of force against indigenous peoples in the lands being colonized by Europeans. With the Peace of Westphalia in 1648, and the establishment of the modern nation-state system, many of the tenets of the just-war tradition found their way into positive international law, and in the twentieth century were embodied in international agreements such as the Geneva Convention.

The Cold War period saw a decline in the explicit use of the just-war tradition, as the polarization of the international system into clashing ideologies promoted a sort of moral absolutism that justified virtually any means to ensure survival against a foe who was assumed to be both immoral and determined. Thus the infamous Doolittle Report counseled the use of extreme measures to counter what was seen as a threat to the survival of democratic forces worldwide. As this threat was seen more accurately over time, however, the arguments of the just-war tradition began to resurface, first in debates over nuclear deterrence, then in the Gulf War and most recently in arguments about humanitarian intervention.

The tradition is certainly durable, but important questions remain. First, given the enormous destructiveness of modern weapons, does it make any sense in the modern era to talk about a "just war?" Second, whether or not large-scale war can be justified, can the tradition shed light on other situations involving international coercion, such as covert political action, economic sanctions, humanitarian intervention and coercive diplomacy? The cases analyzed in this book suggest that both of these questions can be answered in the affirmative.

Just-War and Modern Weaponry

A significant challenge to the just-war tradition arose during the Cold War, as authorities pondered whether the destructiveness of nuclear weapons invalidated all justification for warfare in the modern era. In the wake of the Gulf War, commentators have once again raised the issue of the tradition's continued validity. Three major objections have been put forward. The first is the argument, from pacifist commentators, that the tradition is incompatible with basic Christian values (and values held widely in other ethical traditions) regarding the sanctity of life. The second is that some important aspects of modern warfare are absent from the framework of the just-war tradition. The last is that the tradition fails to provide clear guidance, because it contains elements that are vague and potentially contradictory.[7]

With regard to the pacifist critique, the major elements were summarized in chapter 3. The underlying premise is that modern war is so destructive that it is fundamentally different from the wars of the past. Because, in this view, modern war is a phenomenon involving entire populations and all of a nation's resources, it cannot be limited. It is thus inherently disproportionate to any just objective, except perhaps a pure defense against continuing aggression.[8]

John Langan notes that this objection raises the possibility of a significant revision of the tradition to include the notion that defensive war against ongoing aggression should be "a remote peripheral exception" to a general condemnation of warfare that would remain at the center of the just-war framework.[9] He agrees that it is always appropriate to condemn warfare as a reflection that something terrible has happened in human affairs, but refuses to extend the condemnation to the just-war tradition itself. Recognizing that conflict in human affairs is inevitable, he suggests that even in the modern era, the tradition provides useful questions that try to address the international community's response to a breakdown of peace and a violation of its minimal standards.[10]

To the second objection, that the tradition is incomplete, Langan notes that commentators focus on uses of the tradition that ignore relevant aspects of history. Some critics have accused Western policy makers in particular of ignoring historical facts that bear on their responsibility for the tensions that lead to conflict in the modern world. Langan agrees that it is valuable to look at the arguments about war in the broadest framework. He contends that this is clearly within the boundaries of the just-war tradition. Just cause requires a broad historical understanding of the circumstances that lead to a potential conflict. Assessment of just intention is illuminated by historical facts that bear on the moral character, policy objectives and past behavior of the protagonists. And historical notions of justice and injustice have a bearing on considerations of proportionality as well.[11]

The final objection is that the tradition in indeterminate. It lacks, critics say, criteria that allow for measurement and that are widely agreed upon. As Langan puts it:

The meaning of such terms as "just cause" and "legitimate authority" is subject to dispute. The measurement of proportionality is subject to challenge, both by those who wish to attend to different values in the situation and by those who regard the notion as an incoherent relative of utilitarianism. The theory itself gives very little guidance about how to make decisions in clouded situations where one affirms both the justice of the cause and the disproportion of the means.[12]

The lack of clear, measurable criteria in the just-war tradition is obvious and not surprising. Though the tradition is itself part of a broader approach that emphasizes the potential to discover universal truths through "right reason," authorities have for centuries stressed the difficulty of reaching correct judgments of right and wrong, especially in complex political situations. The just-war tradition's lack of clear answers is at once a weakness and a strength. It would be wonderful, albeit utopian, to have a "checklist" that leaders could use in deciding to go to war. But issues of war and peace are simply too complicated for such a treatment The just-war tradition recognizes this, and that recognition is a positive element. Rather than providing measurable criteria to achieve some sort of Platonic ideal of perfect peace and justice, it presents difficult questions, in the Aristotelian tradition of philosophical inquiry into reality in search of practical wisdom.

The cases in this book reinforce the conclusion that in dealing with modern warfare, the just-war tradition has weaknesses, but also considerable strengths. Both were evident, for example in the clash between the Reagan administration and the American Catholic bishops over nuclear deterrence. The advent of weapons of mass destruction has posed a profound challenge for the just-war tradition. In the debate on their pastoral letter, some members of the Bishops' Conference, especially those associated with Pax Christi, advocated unilateral disarmament and nuclear pacifism. Their position underscored the fact that the just-war tradition's principles of proportionality and discrimination were developed in earlier ages, when the potential to destroy life on a massive scale was not envisioned. These critics rightly questioned whether such criteria made any sense at all when applied to the issue of nuclear war.

On the other extreme, some members of the administration contended that the United States should attempt to "prevail" in a nuclear war, a goal that was eventually incorporated into U.S. nuclear doctrine. They claimed that through improvements in weapons technology and investment in defensive measures, the United States could "survive" nuclear attack and reconstitute itself as a viable civilization. Thus, they implicitly claimed that the just-war criteria could apply to nuclear war, if the alternative to war was destruction of Western civilization and its values.

Moderates on both sides rejected these positions and embraced the vision of a world free of nuclear weapons, but as an ultimate goal rather than an immediate imperative. Both Reagan and the bishops were uncomfortable with the moral burden of nuclear deterrence. They recognized that a nuclear war must be avoided at all cost and that it was extremely unlikely that such a war could be controlled. In effect, both protagonists realized that nuclear war would be disproportionate, indiscriminate and uncontrollable, and that a strategy that sought to deter aggression by relying on the threat of nuclear war was morally untenable in the long run. Thus, they shared the view that deterrence should be replaced by something more consistent with the sanctity of life. But because of their differing perspectives, and because the just-war tradition does not provide clear answers about weapons and strategy, they advocated different approaches, the bishops counseling a gradual shift to conventional deterrence and Reagan a reliance on strategic defense.

The case of the Gulf War showed the continuing relevance of the tradition, especially the questions associated with the *jus ad bellum*. The criterion of just cause helped to underpin the decision to counter Saddam's aggression. The intentions of President Bush and other coalition leaders were murky and diverse, but they certainly included the laudable goal of restoring Kuwait's sovereignty. The principle of competent authority (as well as political reality) dictated the formation of the coalition and the need to wage the war under the umbrella of United Nations resolutions. Last resort required that measures short of force be attempted before the war, and the fact that there was disagreement simply underscored the importance of this criterion to the debate and decision. The principle of probability of success dictated the formation of a large and powerful military force, while proportionality imposed limits on the employment of certain measures, especially weapons of mass destruction.

The conduct of the war raised serious questions. However, the analysis indicated that even with the destructive power of modern weaponry, it is still possible to use the principles of proportionality and discrimination to evaluate the combatants' actions. That the coalition, as well as Iraq, did not fare well in some aspects of the evaluation is not a weakness of the just-war tradition, but rather a sign of human fallibility. In sum, the argument that modern means of warfare have invalidated the just-war tradition is belied by the cases.

Extending the Tradition

The second area that the cases investigated was the applicability of just-war arguments to coercive actions other than war. This requires that we expand the tradition's emphasis on the sanctity of life to include a reverence for the potential of human beings to define themselves and their communities in freedom. This of course is firmly in the Western Enlightenment tradition that emphasizes the inalienable rights of "life, liberty and the pursuit of happiness" And as we have seen, Kidder's work suggests that such rights are the aspiration of a variety of world cultures. Extending the just-war tradition to include a bias against coercion is a logical step.

Again, the cases showed that this step can be taken. The examination of the U.S. secret interventions in Chile showed that concepts of the just-war tradition are useful in evaluating covert political action. Application of the tradition's criteria showed that while both the 1964 and 1970 operations were questionable, the former was certainly "more justified" than the latter. The just-war tradition provides not only a yardstick by which to measure the decisions of presidents Johnson and Nixon, but also a set of guidelines by which to evaluate future proposals. The latter effectively refute the extreme realism of the Doolittle Report and suggest that covert action should become a rarer and more constrained tool of American foreign policy.

The analysis of the embargo against Cuba showed that just-war principles, especially proportionality, discrimination and probability of success, can help to illuminate decisions on economic sanctions. In the case of Cuba, the sanctions were morally questionable from the outset because they were embedded in an overall policy framework that advocated sabotage and even assassination to threaten the Castro regime economically and politically. The policy approach was clearly disproportionate. The extension of the embargo to food and medicines, and the attempted extraterritorial application of the Helms–Burton Act, indicate a broadening of the effort that is inconsistent with the principle of discrimination. And the fact that sanctions have not achieved the desired result after almost four decades indicates that the standard of probability of success has not been met. Significantly, the low probability of meeting U.S. goals was known to key officials from the beginning, but was disregarded in their zeal to overthrow Castro.

The case of North Korea provided an interesting example of the usefulness of the tradition in evaluating a mixed strategy of coercion and conciliation. Prominent in the assessment was the principle of last resort. The North Korean case demonstrated the value of a step-by-step approach to resolving international disputes, with coercive measures held in reserve until needed. It also underscored the utility of the principle of competent authority, illustrated by the international community's consensus on the goal of constraining North Korea's nuclear ambitions that eventually brought even China in line with U.S. objectives and tactics. This case also showed how the lack of clarity regarding policy objectives can contribute to delay, confusion and risk, even when the overall goal is a just one.

It is clear, then, that the just-war tradition can be applied to a variety of issues dealing with international coercion, but only if it is properly understood as a tradition of questions, rather than as a rigid theory that purports to provide direct answers. The tradition begins with the notion of the sanctity of life and, following from that, a strong bias against warfare. The just-war tradition requires those who advocate war to probe deeply into the situation they face, their motivations, their authority to use force, the likelihood that they will achieve just goals, the cost of violence and the alternatives they should consider. These are little more than commonsense questions that anyone facing an ethical dilemma should consider.

It is equally clear that the just-war tradition must continue to evolve, as it has since the time of Augustine, if it is to be useful to modern policy makers. Over the centuries, authorities in the tradition have changed their views about the answers to some of the questions, and have suggested new areas for investigation. These modifications have been influenced both by a dialogue within the tradition and by changes—some evolutionary, some revolutionary—in the international system itself. With respect to just cause, for example, the majority of commentators now focus on repelling aggression as the principal justification for the use of force. Walzer allows for exceptions, but these can be seen as an extension of the concept of repelling aggression to include responding to actions within a state's borders when they violate fundamental values of community and humanity. Similarly, the concept of competent authority has evolved in recent years so that most nations accept, if only reluctantly, that some form of collective authority is required for the decision to go to war.

The Question of Obligation

A particularly difficult issue for the just-war tradition is that of humanitarian intervention. The problem is not only to justify the right to employ force in the face of the tradition's bias against war, but also to confront the problem of the obligation to preserve life, even when there is a significant moral cost to doing so. The just-war tradition deals with the justification of force. It does not directly confront the question of when, if ever, the use of force is a positive international obligation. Yet the Burundi case showed in ample detail that exactly that argument is made by officials of international organizations and NGOs, and even by some leaders of nations. While we surely could construct a deontological rationale regarding an obligation to rescue, the most direct and powerful argument is the utilitarian one: if it is in our power to prevent something very bad from happening, and we can do so without sacrificing something of comparable moral significance, then we ought to do it.[13]

Since the end of the Cold War, humanitarian intervention has eclipsed nuclear deterrence in the literature on ethics and international affairs. Yet the emphasis is still primarily on the justification of intervention rather than the obligation to intervene. But it is increasingly urgent to examine the nature of international obligation, and to prepare the means to intervene when obligation arises. As discussed in chapter 4, there is now an emerging view that the erosion of state sovereignty, chaos and centrifugal tendencies within nation-states are threatening the viability of the nation-state system.[14] The just-war tradition, with its emphasis on the maintenance of sovereignty and its bias against force, is generally used to argue in support of the current international system. Yet the experience of failed states like Somalia and the former Yugoslavia shows that force is now used not only to defend state sovereignty but also to restore or reshape it. The Burundi case further suggests that there are certain human tragedies, primarily genocide, whose prevention or reversal is so important that it not only overrides the presumption of state sovereignty, but may actually create an obligation for the international community to intervene over the objections of a sovereign government. It is essential that this growing problem be incorporated into the debate over intervention and the justification of force.

The Just-War Criteria: A Tentative Revision

The cases analyzed in this book suggest that the just-war tradition is applicable to modern warfare, and that it can be adapted to illuminate a number of other issues related to coercion in international politics. They also suggest, however, that modest revisions in some of the criteria may be necessary. The following is an outline of some possible refinements.

- Just Cause and Just Intention: The enormous destructive power of modern warfare, as demonstrated by the nuclear policy and Gulf War cases, argues for raising the barriers to war.

This means reexamining the causes that can justify it. Clearly, naked aggression, as in the case of Iraq's invasion of Kuwait, can occasion a forcible response, as Walzer argued in his legalist paradigm. But we should be wary of some of his "revisions." Preemptive war in the modern era should be exceedingly rare, and undertaken only when there is clear evidence of unacceptable risk. Similarly, intervention in internal conflicts should be approached warily. On the other hand, Walzer's proposal that rescuing people from massacre be a just cause does not go far enough. As the Burundi case suggested, this may sometimes be a positive international obligation, and force may be not only justified but also morally required. There must be explicit recognition of the fact that, in the real world, intentions are never pure. But it is important to identify all of the goals that a policy might seek to achieve and to weigh each in moral terms in order to derive a net assessment.

- Competent Authority: In the modern era, individual nation-states should try to avoid unilateral resort to force. This is especially true for the United States and the other powerful states whose considerable military capability carries a concomitant responsibility for caution. Just as prudent leaders seek outside counsel, so prudent states seek support in the international community for weighty decisions. Given the existence of the United Nations Charter, regional defense treaties and emerging norms of collective action, the burden of proof under this criterion should be on states that advocate unilateral use of military force.

- Last Resort: While the use of military force should always be deferred if possible, the cases indicate that there may well be moral problems with other policy instruments, especially covert action and economic sanctions. Even coercive diplomacy, to the extent that it relies on credible threats of violence, raises ethical questions. This criterion should then be refined to encompass a continuing requirement to use the least harmful categories of action possible, and within those categories to choose the least harmful techniques, preferring nonlethal covert action to lethal, and economic sanctions targeted on leaders and their policies to general ones aimed at populations.

- Probability of Success: The sheer complexity of the problems emerging in the post-Cold War world defies ready calculations of the probability of success. Given this uncertainty, it is understandable that nations overcompensate and use overwhelming force, large-scale intervention or severe sanctions in order to ensure that they prevail. Measures to promote victory are not prohibited by this criterion; rather, they are required of a just protagonist. But nations must be cautious, in the application of these measures, that they do not, as was the case in the Gulf War, violate other standards of proportionality and discrimination in their drive to ensure success.

- Proportionality and Discrimination: The destructive power of modern nuclear weapons, and the consensus that they cannot be controlled in warfare, argue that nuclear warfare can never be a proportionate response to an international threat. Similarly, lethal biological agents and many chemical weapons are unacceptable under these criteria. So too is any long-term policy of deterrence based on the threat of using weapons of mass destruction. It is also inappropriate to threaten, as the Clinton administration has done, to use one category of such weapons to deter the use of others. Effective elimination of the biological and chemical weapons threat must rest on strengthening international regimes of control and on conventional deterrence, rather than on the threat of nuclear retaliation.

THE JUST-WAR TRADITION AND THE POLICY AGENDA

There is no agreed organizing principle for American foreign policy at the turn of the millennium, and no common label for the current historical period. With the end of the Cold War, President Bush suggested that we were entering a "New World Order" characterized by growing respect for the rule of law. That vision, sadly, has not been realized.

During the Cold War, the ideological competition against communism and the military competition against the Soviet Union provided a framework for the conduct and evaluation of U.S. policy. Now that the Soviet threat has dissipated, there is a conceptual and practical vacuum. The United States needs a way to frame coherent policies, but, as Stanley Hoffman observes, "Coherence requires at least two things: a clear sense of what the dangers are—an ordered and graduated list of the unacceptables so to speak; and an awareness of the fact that the pursuit of any one value, be it peace or distributive justice at the expense of other values, liberty or of the necessities of the contest, military balance, for instance leads to calamities."[15]

The just-war tradition suggests that the vacuum could be filled by a new organizing principle based on core human values. The basic goals of U.S. foreign policy would be to promote international respect for human life and freedom. The "unacceptables" would be those developments and trends that most threaten these core values. And the just-war tradition, with its emphasis on justification, right intentions, authority, proportionality and discrimination, provides a continuing reminder of the need to achieve balance among potentially conflicting policy goals.

What would an American foreign policy look like if it adhered more closely to the standards of the just-war tradition? There is no unequivocal answer because, as we have seen, the tradition is one of questions and guidelines rather than of specific answers. We can, however, speculate about the content of a policy program based on the underlying principles of respect for life and the promotion of freedom.

Principles of U.S. Policy

To begin with, such a program would have a strong bias against unilateral intervention. It would be cosmopolitan in its orientation, with strong support for international organizations. Coercive policies and instruments would continue to be used, but with greater caution and attention to principles of proportionality and discrimination. Only the clearest violations of international norms would merit the more violent policy responses, and weapons of mass destruction would never be used. The preference would be for negotiated solutions, multilateral if possible, even if these appeared somewhat more risky than the use of force.

There would be strong support for the rule of law. But, in recognizing that positive international law may not always be enforceable, nor always be responsive to human needs, the United States would be prepared to depart on occasion from a strictly legalistic approach. This might involve, for example, seeking an accommodation that, as in the North Korean nuclear case, falls short of the desires of "rule utilitarians" regarding enforcement of international norms. It might also include rapid intervention in a humanitarian emergency, in advance of formal international approval.

The United States would maintain sizable and capable military forces, and would undertake their continuing modernization both for national security and for use in internationally sanctioned contingencies. The United States would support improvements in the United Nations' system for identifying peacekeeping requirements, as well as in the organization's authority to raise peacekeeping forces.

The United States would accept its responsibility for international peacekeeping as well as the limits of its authority. In establishing foreign policy priorities, the United States would be guided by two principles. First, it would continue to take the lead in areas of the world where it has historically exercised leadership and where its previous actions leave a legacy of responsibility for the current situation. (Cuba and Chile are prime examples.) Second, it would be prepared to commit its resources throughout the world to prevent or counter particularly dangerous or outrageous situations, including the acquisition of weapons of mass destruction by despotic leaders, the collapse of government structures and endangerment of populations, and widespread abuses of human rights, especially genocide.

U.S. leaders would seek to moderate their rhetoric in crisis situations. They would ponder information on the political pressures facing their adversaries, their psychological motivations and their needs. While not bending to inappropriate pressure, they would recognize the utility of dialogue—open or secret—as well as coercion.

With respect to nuclear weapons, U.S. policy would be based on the recognition that any use of weapons of mass destruction is morally unacceptable. Moreover, it would accept that deterrence is morally questionable but is a fact of international life. It would continue to give the highest priority to preventing nuclear war, to supporting reductions in offensive nuclear forces and to exploring defensive systems. It would give serious attention to identifying the minimum level to which nuclear forces could safely be reduced, given the current holdings of nuclear powers and the possibility of further proliferation. It would dismantle and destroy, by mutual agreement if possible, weapons that are particularly threatening to deterrence, such as highly accurate submarine-launched missiles with multiple warheads. It would take steps to implement President Reagan's pledge to share internationally the fruits of any breakthroughs in defensive technology.

Limiting the proliferation of weapons of mass destruction—nuclear, biological and chemical—would also command the highest priority. The United States would continue to work for international regimes to control such weapons. At the same time, it would seek bilateral or multilateral agreements that, as in the case of North Korea, recognize the legitimate interests of threshold nuclear powers as well as the potential threat they pose to international stability. Such a policy would be firmly grounded in the understanding that decreasing reliance on nuclear weapons for deterrence requires that the underlying causes of the insecurities that face states must be addressed, even as further reductions are being negotiated.

In certain cases, such as Iraq, which has demonstrated blatant disregard for international norms, the United States would continue to take the lead in arguing for coercive measures. Even in these cases, however, the United States should have the courage to engage these countries in dialogue about their needs. In cases of clear recalcitrance, the limited use of military force, with careful and discriminate targeting, would be considered. In addition, the illegitimate proliferation of weapons of mass destruction and associated technologies would be one of a very small number of areas in which covert action would be authorized.

In using its conventional military forces abroad, the United States would shun unilateral warfare in favor of broad regional or international coalitions, even if this meant giving up some operational control of its forces. It would insist that force be used only in a just cause and for good intentions, and that clear war aims must be established. It would honor the importance of "fighting well," and not abandon legitimate aims for political or public relations gains.

Human rights would be a major theme of U.S. policy, but promotion of rights would be accomplished primarily by diplomacy, example and education. The stress would be on disseminating information about basic political rights, rather than forcing American values onto other societies. The exceptions would be situations in which the most fundamental rights were being violated in ways that shock international sensibilities: specifically, genocide. Responses to such outrages would be recognized as both a categorical imperative and a utilitarian goal, and as such would command a priority as high as nuclear deterrence or nonproliferation. In such cases, the United States would take the lead to intervene and halt the killing, and to collaborate with national and international organizations to build democracy and respect for life, and to tackle underlying economic and social inadequacies over the long term.

Trade policy would be based on the assumption that free trade, like free exchange of ideas, promotes human rights and development. Trade sanctions would be employed less frequently, in recognition of the fact that they violate the categorical imperative that people are to be treated as ends in themselves and the Pauline principle that no good can come out of evil. U.S. policy would follow the "condition of business principle," refusing normal trade relations to those who engage in horrendous abuses of human rights. The practice of invoking trade sanctions out of frustration or moral outrage would be replaced by a more calculated policy that weighed the likely effectiveness of sanctions against the harm that they may do to the innocent. Preference would be given to multilateral regimes rather than unilateral embargos, and to controls that impact directly on decision makers rather than on the broad population.

Covert action would be employed only rarely. Preference would be given to overt policy instruments, and the need for secret operations would have to be justified rigorously. The prohibition against assassination would be incorporated into legislation. The United States would abandon its practice of trying covertly to overthrow foreign governments, unless those governments posed an immediate and significant threat to international stability. Even then, proposed covert actions would have to meet high standards with respect to the probability of success and the means employed. (History suggests that even covert actions that achieve short-term success may lead to long-term problems, as in Iran and Guatemala.) Stealth would be used primarily to counter stealth; covert operations would generally be confined to countering clearly identifiable threats from illicit activity such as drug trafficking and weapons proliferation.

Regional stability in key areas would continue to command U.S. attention. American policy would recognize a special obligation to promote stability in areas close to home, defined geographically or in terms of history or trade relations. In other areas, the United States would look primarily to regional powers to ensure stability, but would be available to assist key allies and international organizations with logistical support and humanitarian aid. As noted above, in cases where instability results from massive human rights abuses, the United States would not shrink from leadership.

The Case Studies Revisited

With these principles in mind, we can take another look at the case studies. None of the stories is complete. In every case, there are continuing challenges to U.S. policy and to international stability. Indeed, by the time this manuscript sees print, the stories will have evolved to new stages. But the formal aspects of the just-war tradition will remain helpful, regardless of how the material aspects of the cases change. They suggest actions that the United States could take in the future that would help to bring the cases nearer to a just resolution.

With respect to nuclear deterrence, the United States would take its cue from the agendas established by the Catholic bishops and Joseph Nye, and work to improve conventional deterrence, enhance crisis stability and pursue arms control negotiations. While recognizing that deterrence is necessary in the foreseeable future, it would work to reduce reliance on nuclear weapons in the long run. The United States would use diplomacy and economic incentives to press for early Russian ratification of the START II Treaty. It would also increase its collaboration with Russian authorities to stem the potential outflow of nuclear materials and related advanced weapons. It would further refine its nuclear employment policy and identify the smallest number of weapons required to ensure deterrence now and in the future, with perhaps a dozen nuclear-armed nations, some of which would harbor aggressive ambitions. The United States would seek to engage these states in both bilateral and, if possible, multilateral dialogue aimed toward eventual agreements on reducing or eliminating their nuclear arsenals. This would require some political compromises, and the acceptance that these states—Libya and Iraq, for example—merit such treatment despite their reprehensible international behavior. The North Korean precedent is instructive in this regard.

The United States would also continue to work cautiously on defenses against ballistic missiles. If such defenses prove to be feasible, it would organize international regimes to discuss the phased diffusion of defensive technologies in coordination with reductions in offensive arsenals.

In its policy toward Iraq, the United States would continue to press for cessation of prohibited weapons programs. It would explore diplomatic options, legal sanctions such as expelling Iraq from the United Nation, or the more precise targeting and enforcement of sanctions, using military force only as a last resort. Moreover, the

United States would accept its responsibility for the unsettled situation at the end of the Gulf War. It would cease unilateral efforts to overthrow Saddam Hussein, but would be alert to the growth of any domestic opposition and ready to assist a democratic movement if it establishes that it is representative of the Iraqi people's will. (There is no moral barrier, as noted in chapter 5, to providing information and encouragement to democratic forces, especially if this is done as part of an overt strategy, but it would be problematic to foster opposition, as some have suggested, based on small groups that claim to represent the popular will.[16])

The United States would collaborate with other members of the UN Security Council to craft a coherent strategy of coercive diplomacy to reduce the threat from Saddam's weapons of mass destruction. This would require, as suggested above, a willingness to enter into direct talks, and to provide carrots as well as sticks. These could include mutually beneficial economic relations and recognition of Saddam's authority in Iraq. The United States would offer to participate in a program to rebuild Iraq's infrastructure, contingent on satisfaction of international demands regarding cessation of nuclear, biological and chemical weapons programs.

In Central and East Africa, instability and violence continue. Burundi has a new constitution, and dialogue among the warring parties has deepened. President Clinton's trip to Africa has underscored U.S. interest in the continent, but in a foreign policy based on just-war principles, more concrete steps would be taken. The United States would continue to press its African Crisis Response Initiative, but would also make a serious commitment to improving the United Nations' rapid response capability. It would consult regularly and share information with officials of international and nongovernmental organizations, and be prepared to provide airlift and logistical support for an intervention if Hutu–Tutsi violence in the region escalates. For the long term, it would work with governments of the region to craft a development strategy that includes both economic infrastructure and nation-building.

The United States would recognize its responsibility for the societal problems that followed the overthrow of Allende in Chile, and accelerate its efforts to include Chile in a hemispheric trade pact that would enhance opportunities for economic prosperity. The U.S. government would do its part to help repair the rifts in Chilean society by sharing information on the abuses of the military regime and helping to close the books on the thousands who were "disappeared" for opposing that regime.

The United States would end the embargo against Cuba and begin the process of building enduring political and economic ties for the post-Castro era. (The visit of the pope in January 1998 provides an appropriate rationale for reexamining the U.S. sanctions policy.) It would carry through with its obligations under the "agreed framework" with North Korea, keeping a wary eye on that country's activities, especially with regard to nuclear programs. (This would require the administration to resolve the continuing issue of funding for the energy resources that it has promised under the framework.) It would continue to promote aid and economic relief for both North and South Korea, helping them to achieve the economic and political preconditions for eventual reunification.

JUSTICE AND AMERICAN LEADERSHIP

As the cases and the proposed policy approaches suggest, justice demands that more explicit attention be given to limiting the use of coercive measures to situations in which they are both necessary and controllable. It is unrealistic to expect this to happen overnight. The cases show that there is still a strong tendency in U.S. policy to use force to achieve national aims. In their survey research, Brunk, Secrest and Tamashiro found that "relatively few Americans embrace the strict just-war tradition in its pure form."[17] On the other hand, they found an overwhelming majority to be concerned about the moral dimensions of warfare. They argue that

When morality and political practicality clash, people's attitudes about international conflict fall along a spectrum characterized by three modal possibilities. . . . Among American elites, the clergy tend toward the strict just-war position, and military officers tilt in the better safe than sorry direction. Journalists and foreign service officers are found between these two extremes, while members of Congress are particularly crosspressured.[18]

This assessment suggests that moral progress is possible. The key to moving American decision-making more toward the just-war position is to make the moral arguments more visible in the press, the foreign affairs bureaucracy and the Congress. (In the American system, military officers, despite their preferred opinions, will support a political consensus on the use of force.) The conclusions of the survey research aside, the case studies in this book suggest that this has been happening. Just-war arguments were largely absent in decision-making regarding the Cuban embargo and covert action in Chile, but they have been made explicit and have had demonstrable impact in the cases of nuclear strategy and the Gulf War. In the debate over intervention in Burundi, there was clear attention to the need to justify the use of force, and in the case of the North Korean nuclear program, it was recognition that the use of force could have disproportionate and indiscriminate effects that helped make the Clinton administration receptive to former President Carter's compromise approach.

Institutional Changes

Thus, there is reason to be optimistic about the trend in the quality of debate on coercive measures in American foreign policy. But this trend is not yet embodied in any formal procedures, nor is adherence to the principle that coercion must be justified a key quality that voters consider in picking their leaders or that the leaders consider in making appointments.

There are specific changes that could be made in staff procedures that would bring the decision-making process closer to just-war standards. For the executive branch, each incoming president establishes a foreign affairs decision system, organizes various committees and appoints key officials to positions on the National Security Council staff and to the departments and agencies. One possibility, then, is that some of the just-war criteria could be incorporated into the system by presidential directive. As noted in chapter 2, President Clinton has revised the directive that establishes criteria for using nuclear forces. Chapter 5 suggested that some key questions, derived from just-war criteria, could be incorporated into the process for reviewing covert action programs. Recently, the Department of State has begun a review of policy regarding economic sanctions that could well include, at least tacitly, some standards related to probability of success, proportionality and discrimination.

In order for any such procedures to be effective, however, political leaders must pay attention to them and give them prominence in their decision-making. In other words, they must act with prudence, in the sense that Aristotle and Aquinas counseled. This responsibility begins, in the American system, with the president. But it also extends to the Congress, especially members of the most important committees that deal with military, diplomatic and intelligence matters, as well as to senior officials of the national security bureaucracy. In effect, there is no system of procedures that will guarantee justice in international politics apart from the moral character of the policy makers.

The Character of Leaders

In the final analysis, it is the capacity of decision makers to confront moral ambiguity that counts. Policy makers must from time to time face a contradiction between their personal values and the demands of office, the problem of "dirty hands" that inevitably accompanies public life. Public officials feel pressure to lie, deceive or harm in order to carry out the dictates of their position, and in a democratic system, they can rationalize their choices as reflecting the will of the people.[19] The cases in this book have demonstrated how easily such rationalizations can lead to unwise or unjust decisions, to deception and violence that are, in the final analysis, both unnecessary and disproportionate. In order to cope with the dirty hands dilemma, public officials must feel moral discomfort, and not glee, in doing harm. They must be psychologically integrated and ethically sensitive, skilled in moral reasoning as well as in political maneuvering. This applies to advisers (for example, Colin Powell in the Gulf War case) as well as to policy makers.

This book is not the place to debate the "character issue" in American politics. But we need not delve into allegations regarding illicit campaign contributions, conflict of interest or alleged sexual improprieties to raise concerns about the integrity of leaders, especially when they hold devastating coercive power. Chester Bowles decried the moral bankruptcy of the Kennedy administration's decision-making in the wake of the Bay of Pigs fiasco, quite apart from subsequent questions that were raised about the president's character. Yet it seems unlikely that a president could compartment his actions sufficiently that there would be no significant relationship between his values regarding personal relationships and his decisions on matters of state. Indeed, were he to do so, we could reasonably ask whether he was sufficiently integrated a person to hold such weighty responsibilities.

Integrity, in the sense of "wholeness," is an essential quality of leadership that must be earned. "Integrity is the way of a lifetime, not of an instant. While one admirable, ethical action deserves praise, it does not convert a lifetime of political self-service into a career of integrity."[20] The importance of training, experience and consistency in moral outlook was evident to Aristotle:

It is the way that we behave in our dealings with other people that makes us just or unjust. . . . Some people become temperate and patient from one kind of conduct in such situations, others licentious and choleric from another. . . . So it is a matter of no little importance what sorts of habits we form from the earliest age—it makes a vast difference, or rather all the difference in the world.[21]

It is unreasonable to insist on moral perfection in leaders. But it is not absurd to insist that they demonstrate moral progress. Aristotle observed that "Moral goodness is the result of habit."[22] The field of moral psychology has established that over the course of a lifetime individuals grow in their attention to moral issues and their capacity to make moral judgments.[23] All human beings are capable of learning from mistakes, failures and even immoral actions. Most of the world's religious and moral traditions note, however, that this is no easy task. (Augustine described in detail his agonizing journey from corruption to enlightenment in the *Confessions*.[24]) To experience moral growth, individuals must acknowledge their shortcomings (at least to themselves and close confidants), commit themselves to change and seek the help that they need to do so.[25]

Such openness to growth, however, is rare. Unethical practices by political leaders usually lead them to dissemble and cover up their errors. As Bok notes, the danger that by lying, one hurts oneself, is identified as a problem in many of the world's ethical traditions.

Psychological barriers wear down; lies seem more necessary, less reprehensible; the ability to make moral distinctions can coarsen; the liar's perception of his chances of being caught may warp. These changes can affect his behavior in subtle ways; even if he is not found out he will then be less trusted than those of unquestioned honesty. . . . Paradoxically, once his word is no longer trusted, he will be left with greatly decreased power—even though a lie often does bring at least a short-term gain in power over those deceived.[26]

It is reasonable to argue, then, that character counts. In that regard, there is great value to responsible investigative journalism, and even to some limited negative campaigning, to the extent that they help to make visible the totality of a candidate's behavior and character traits. Such information is necessary if voters are to consider the candidate's potential, as they should, in light of the standards of normative prudence.

How might voters do this? With Aristotle and Aquinas, they might begin by considering the following traits of a prudent leader:

- Deliberateness: Has the candidate demonstrated the capacity to connect ends with means and resolve ethical dilemmas? Has he or she shown an awareness of the moral dimensions of political issues and the capacity to refrain from rushing to judgment?

- Self-Control: Has the candidate demonstrated self-sacrifice and a capacity to delay gratification? Is the candidate tolerant of differences, or single-minded in the pursuit of passionate attachments?

- Good sense: Does the candidate demonstrate a sympathetic understanding of the impact of his or her actions on others? Has the candidate shown a sense of fairness, forgiveness and magnanimity toward allies and opponents alike? Has he or she acknowledged past shortcomings and shown the capacity to grow in moral awareness and ethical actions?

- Knowledge of particulars: In past positions of authority has the candidate shown the ability to master the details of a complex situation? Is he or she a "quick study" who has the capacity to get to the heart of an issue?

- Experience: What is the candidate's previous experience in leadership, politics and foreign affairs? Has the candidate shown an awareness of complexity and a sense of proportion in previous decisions?

- Good ends: What is the candidate's motivation for seeking office? Has he or she shown a genuine appetite for public service rather than a consuming ambition for power?

- Memory: Does the candidate understand the relevance of the past to current decisions? In public statements and policy decisions does he or she cite historical evidence and trends accurately and effectively?

- Intelligence: Does the candidate show the ability to grasp difficult situations and to analyze them logically? Does he or she have a mastery of economics and military affairs as well as politics?

- Teachableness: Has the candidate shown a willingness to seek the opinions of others and an openness to criticism? Has he or she sought advice from opponents as well as from a close circle of advisers?

- Prevision and Circumspection: Based on past performance, does the candidate seem to be aware of the consequences of action or inaction? Has he or she shown the ability to apply moral principles to specific situations?

- Caution: Has the candidate shown an awareness of evil while avoiding the demonizing of opponents? Has his or her personal and professional conduct shown the ability to resist attractions of evil, as well as a rejection of egotistical righteousness?

- Acumen: How wisely has the candidate performed under pressure? Has he or she shown the ability to avoid indecisiveness while still giving important issues sufficient reflection prior to acting?.

Finding candidates for high office who demonstrate these qualities will be well nigh impossible. Human beings are not angels, as the philosophers in the natural law tradition recognized. The cases demonstrate both the strengths and the flaws of past and current leaders. Eisenhower fostered deliberateness in decision-making but fell victim to a narrow conception of U.S. national interest. Kennedy grew in his capacity for deliberation and teachableness, but demonized his opponents and was prone to passionate attachments to disproportionate policies.   Nixon had remarkable geopolitical insights but acted rashly and defensively when challenged. Reagan had a flair for political leadership and a vision of a more peaceful, nuclear-free world, but failed to supervise his administration effectively and undercut support for his goals through immoderate rhetoric. Bush summoned considerable courage in responding to Iraqi aggression and showed political acumen in forging a coalition, but became dependent on a narrow circle of advisers and failed to follow through on his objectives. Clinton showed a willingness to compromise and take risks in the case of North Korea, but failed to act resolutely when confronted by genocide in Africa. Critics accuse Clinton and other recent presidents of being more sensitive to public opinion as measured by "tracking polls" than to moral responsibilities and effective leadership.

Thus, recent history shows that normative prudence is a difficult trait for leaders to develop. Perhaps former President Carter has come closest to becoming a prudent leader, in the period since he left office. Without the power (and responsibilities) of the presidency, Carter has provided leadership at home with respect to homelessness and other issues related to human dignity, as well as abroad in helping to forge policies in such troubled areas as Haiti and North Korea. This is in sharp contrast to his performance in office, which was characterized by inconsistency and confusion when facing major challenges in Afghanistan, Cuba, Iran and the former Soviet Union.

The fact that perfection is not readily at hand, however, is no reason to be pessimistic. The cases suggest that there is a perceptible trend toward more prudent decision-making regarding the use of force, as well as other coercive measures, in American policy. If individuals can experience moral growth, is it possible that nation-states may grow as well? Groups and communities certainly show differing patterns of moral sensitivity.[27] Some observers argue that views on the acceptability of war have changed profoundly, as evidenced by a consensus that force must be justified.[28] This suggests that moral progress by states is certainly a possibility, and the increasingly prominent place of the just-war tradition in arguments about international coercion is a hopeful sign. With continued attention to the core values of respect for life and freedom, and careful scrutiny of elected leaders and senior political appointees, it is entirely possible that continued progress can be made.

CONCLUSION

The just-war tradition is alive and well. For a tradition to be alive means that it is growing and adapting to meet new challenges while retaining its essential character. The just-war tradition is a tradition of balance and moderation. While firmly within the deontological category of ethical argumentation, it is nonetheless enriched by attention to circumstances and likely outcomes. These characteristics continue to make it well suited to issues of war and peace, the march of military technology notwithstanding.

Moreover, as elements of a broader natural law tradition, the tenets of just-war can find a wider application in international politics. The road map that they provide is especially needed at this juncture in human history. Hehir's analysis raises the possibility that the international system is on the edge of a profound shift. In the jargon of the "new sciences" of chaos and complexity theory, it is a "complex system operating at the edge of chaos." Like other complex systems, it is characterized by "sensitive dependence on initial conditions," a degree of interconnectedness so pervasive that even small changes in one part of the system can cause extreme and unpredictable events elsewhere. This is the "butterfly's wing effect," based on the analogy with the global weather system that is so complex that a butterfly can flap its wings in Tokyo and cause rain in New York.

In a chaotic environment, consequentialist ethics becomes problematic at best. The inherent unpredictability of international developments and the outcome of any particular policy initiative makes utilitarian reasoning extremely uncertain. It may be that the principle of sovereignty that has informed decisions about international violence and coercion will be replaced by some other more cosmopolitan, deontological view. Yet, to ignore in the meantime the consequences of a state's actions would be irresponsible in the extreme, and to engage in unbridled pursuit of national interest would be even more irresponsible in an increasingly interdependent world. This implies a gradual, cautious movement from a decision-making framework centered on nation-states to one that is more cosmopolitan in its vision.

In this situation, the just-war tradition has much to recommend it. Firmly grounded in a sense of duty to preserve life, it provides a method for evaluating threats to international order in terms of the just causes for using force. The tradition is also is cognizant of the existence of human greed and violence, and of the necessity of prevision and analysis before taking action. Thus it underscores Hoffman's counsel to consider the interrelationships among goals, and the linkage of means and ends. The challenge for both scholars and policy makers is to extend the tradition's scope to cover emerging international concerns, and to enhance its explicit use as a tool for policy evaluation.

Areas for Exploration

In pursuing this goal, it is important that scholars and officials continue to debate the justification of humanitarian intervention, and also to investigate the conditions that might create an obligation to intervene. They should also reopen the debate on the moral dimensions of nuclear deterrence, with emphasis on ethics and deterrence in a world of multiple nuclear powers. There should be more systematic investigation of the ethical aspects of economic sanctions and trade policy, with an explicit recognition of two significant factors: that there are some regimes with which nations simply should not do business, and that political rights are not promoted when basic economic rights are denied. Coercive diplomacy should be a topic for moral scrutiny. This should look first at the problem of threats and coerced agreements, and also at the problem of rewarding misbehavior or even evil actions by states.

On a more pragmatic level, since moral progress is a function of self-knowledge, there is a need for more case studies of international coercion in a just-war framework. Pursuing this exploration is an urgent task. The resurgence of interest in the just-war tradition offers an unparalleled opportunity to integrate moral sensitivity more closely with political-decision making.

NOTES

1. Rushworth Kidder, *Shared Values for a Troubled World* (San Francisco: Jossey-Bass, 1994), pp. 314–20.

2. Sissela Bok, *Common Values* (Columbia: University of Missouri Press, 1995), pp. 29–41.

3. Ibid., p. 13.

4. Ibid., p. 15.

5. Frances V. Harbour, "Basic Moral Values: A Shared Core," *Ethics and International Affairs* 9 (1995): 162–169.

6. Gregory G. Brunk, Donald Secrest and Howard Tamashiro, *Understanding Attitudes About War* (Pittsburgh: University of Pittsburgh Press, 1996), p. 85.

7. John P. Langan, S.J., "Just-War Theory After the Gulf War," *Theological Studies* 53, no. 1 (March 1992): 99.

8. Ibid., p. 100.

9. Ibid., p. 103.

10. Ibid., p. 102.

11. Ibid., p. 104.

12. Ibid., p. 105.

13. Garrett Cullity, "International Aid and the Scope of Kindness," *Ethics* 105, no. 1 (October 1994): 103.

14. J. Bryan Hehir, "Intervention: From Theories to Cases," *Ethics and International Affairs* 9 (1995): 1–13.

15. Stanley Hoffman, *Duties Beyond Borders: On the Limits and Possibilities of Ethical International Politics* (Syracuse, NY: Syracuse University Press, 1981), p. 196.

16. Richard Perle, "No More Halfway Measures," *Washington Post*, February 8, 1998, sec. C, p. 1.

17. Brunk, Secrest and Tamashiro, *Understanding Attitudes About War*, p. 197.

18. Ibid., pp. 196–97.

19. Peter French, "Dirty Hands," in *Essentials of Government Ethics*, Peter Madsen and Jay M. Shafritz, eds. (New York: Meridian, 1992), p. 243.

20. Joel L. Fleishman, "Self-Interest and Political Integrity," in *Public Duties: The Moral Obligations of Government Officials*, Joel L. Fleishman, Lance Liebman and Mark H. Moore, eds., (Cambridge, MA: Harvard University Press, 1981), p. 62.

21. Aristotle, *Ethics*, J.A K. Thompson, trans. (London: Penguin Books, 1953), p. 92.

22. Ibid., p. 91.

23. Lawrence Kohlberg, *Essays on Moral Development, Volume II: The Psychology of Moral Development* (New York: Harper & Row, 1984), p. 44. Carol Gilligan, while accepting the concept of moral development, has argued that Kohlberg's developmental theory devalues the ways in which women reach moral judgments. See Gilligan, *In a Different Voice: Psychological Theory and Women's Development* (Cambridge, MA: Harvard University Press, 1993).

24. *The Confessions of Saint Augustine*, John K. Ryan, trans. (New Yor:, Doubleday, 1960).

25. Arnold D. Hunt, Marie T. Crotty and Robert B. Crotty, *Ethics of World Religions* (San Diego: Greenhaven Press, 1991).

26. Sissela Bok, *Lying: Moral Choice in Public and Private Life* (New York: Pantheon Books, 1978), pp. 25–26.

27. Richard W. Wilson, "Moral Development and Political Change," *World Politics* 36, no. 1 (October 1983): 59.

28. Robert E. Osgood and Robert W. Tucker, *Force, Justice and Order* (Baltimore: Johns Hopkins University Press, 1967), p. 196.

Selected Bibliography

ETHICS AND COERCION: A FRAMEWORK FOR EVALUATION

Airaksinen, Timo. "An Analysis of Coercion." *Journal of Peace Research* 25, no. 3 (September, 1988): 213–27.

Aquinas, Thomas. *Summa Theologica*. Translated by Joseph Rickaby, S.J. London: Burns and Gates, 1892.

Aristotle. *Ethics*. Translated by J.A.K. Thompson. London: Penguin Books, 1953.

Augustine. *The City of God*. Translated by Marcus Dods. New York: Random House, 1950.

Beitz, Charles. "Nonintervention and Communal Integrity." *Philosophy and Public Affairs* 9, no. 4 (Summer 1980): 385–91.

Bentham, Jeremy. *Introduction to the Principles of Morals and Legislation*. Edited by J. H. Burns and H.L A. Hart. London: Methuen, 1970.

Brown, Seyom. "On Deciding to Use Force in the Post Cold War Era: Ethical Considerations." Paper presented at the Conference on Ethics, Security and the New World Order, National Defense University, February 11–12, 1993.

Coll, Alberto R. "Normative Prudence as a Tradition of Statecraft." *Ethics and International Affairs* 5 (1991): 33–51.

Donnelly, Jack. "Human Rights: The Impact of International Action." *International Journal* 43, no. 2 (Spring 1988): 241–63.

Doppelt, Gerald. "Statism Without Foundations." *Philosophy and Public Affairs* 9, no. 4 (Summer 1980): 398–403.

Fowler, Mark. "Coercion and Practical Reason." *Social Theory and Practice* 8, no.3 (Fall 1982): 329–55.

Hobbes, Thomas. *Leviathan*. Edited by Michael Oakeshott. (Oxford: Basil Blackwell, 1960).

Hoffman, Stanley. *Duties Beyond Borders*. Syracuse, NY: Syracuse University Press, 1981.

Kant, Immanuel. *Perpetual Peace*. New York: Liberal Arts Press, 1957.

Kennan, George. "Morality and Foreign Policy." *Foreign Affairs* 64 (Winter 1985/86): 205–18.

Koontz, Theodore J. "Noncombatant Immunity in *Just and Unjust Wars*." *Ethics and International Affairs* 11 (1997): 55–82.

Laberge, Pierre. "Humanitarian Intervention: Three Ethical Positions." *Ethics and International Affairs* 9 (1995): 15–35.

LaCroix, W. L. *War and International Ethics: Tradition and Today*. Lanham, MD: University Press of America, 1988.

Luban, David. "The Romance of the Nation-State." *Philosophy and Public Affairs* 9, no. 4 (Summer 1980): 392–407.

Machiavelli, Niccolò. *The Prince*. Translated by Paul Sonnini. Atlantic Highlands, NJ: Humanities Press International. 1966.

Mill, John Stuart. "On Utilitarianism." In *The Philosophy of John Stuart Mill*. Edited by Marshall Cohen. New York: Modern Library, 1961.

Morgenthau, Hans. *Politics Among Nations: The Struggle for Power and Peace*. New York: Alfred A. Knopf, 1954.

Nardin, Terry, ed. *The Ethics of War and Peace: Religious and Secular Perspectives*. Princeton: Princeton University Press, 1996.

Nardin, Terry, and David Mapel, eds. *Traditions of International Ethics*. Cambridge: Cambridge University Press, 1992.

Niebuhr, Reinhold. *Moral Man and Immoral Society: A Study in Ethics and Politics*. New York: Scribner's, 1932.

_____. *The Children of Light and the Children of Darkness*. New York: Scribner's, 1944.

Pennock, J. Roland, and John W. Chapman, eds. *Coercion*. Chicago and New York: Atherton, 1972.

Phillips, Robert L., and Duane L. Cady. *Humanitarian Intervention: Just War vs Pacifism*. Boston, Rowman and Littlefield, 1996.

Ramsey, Paul. *War and the Christian Conscience*. Durham, NC: Duke University Press, 1969.

Regan, Richard J. *Just War: Principles and Cases*. Washington, DC: Catholic University Press, 1996.

Rosenbaum, Alan S. *Coercion and Autonomy*. New York: Greenwood Press, 1986.

Rosenthal, Joel H. *Righteous Realists*. Baton Rouge: Louisiana State University Press, 1991.

Rothgeb, John M., Jr. *Defining Power: Influence and Force in the Contemporary International System*. New York: St. Martin's Press, 1993.

Smith, Michael Joseph. "Growing Up with *Just and Unjust Wars*." *Ethics and International Affairs* 11 (1997): 3–18.

Thucydides. *The Peloponnesian War*. Translated by John H. Finley, Jr. New York: Modern Library, 1951.

Walzer, Michael. "The Moral Standing of States." *Philosophy and Public Affairs* 9, no. 3 (Spring 1980): 209–29.

_____. *Just and Unjust Wars*. 2nd ed. New York: Basic Books, 1992.

Weber, Max. *Political Writings*. Edited by Peter Lassman and Ronald Speirs. Cambridge: Cambridge University Press, 1994.

Wertheimer, Alan. *Coercion*. Princeton: Princeton University Press, 1988.

THE ETHICS OF NUCLEAR DETERRENCE: THE REAGAN ADMINISTRATION VERSUS THE AMERICAN CATHOLIC BISHOPS

Cameron, J. M. *Nuclear Catholics and Other Essays*. Grand Rapids, MI: William Eerdman, 1989.

Castelli, Jim. *The Bishops and the Bomb*. Garden City, NY: Image Books, 1984.

Documents of Vatican II. New York: America Press, 1966.

English, Raymond, ed. *Ethics and Nuclear Arms*. Washington, DC: Ethics and Public Policy Center, 1985.

Feeney, Margaret. *Sword of the Spirit: Just War? Papal Teaching on Nuclear Warfare with a Scientific Commentary*. Hinkley, UK: Walker, 1958.

Gates, Robert M. *From the Shadows*. New York: Simon & Schuster, 1996.

Goodpaster, Andrew J. *Nuclear Weapons and European Security*. Washington, DC: Atlantic Council, 1996.

John XXIII, Pope. *Pacem in Terris*. New York: America Press, 1963.

Kaplan, Fred. *The Wizards of Armageddon*. New York: Simon & Schuster, 1983.

King, Robert L. "Rhetoric of Morality, Rhetoric of Manipulation." *Cross Currents* 34, no. 4 (Winter 1984–85): 455–72.

McGray, James W. "Nuclear Deterrence: Is the War-and-Peace Pastoral Inconsistent?" *Theological Studies* 46, no. 4 (December 1985): 700–10.

McNamara, Robert S. "The Military Role of Nuclear Weapons: Perceptions and Misperceptions." *Foreign Affairs* 62, no. 4 (Fall 1983): 57–80.

Murray, John Courtney, S.J. *Morality and Modern* War. New York: Council on Religion and International Affairs, 1959.

National Conference of Catholic Bishops. *The Challenge of Peace: God's Promise and Our Response. A Pastoral Letter on War and Peace in the Nuclear Age*. Washington, DC: US Catholic Conference, 1983.

Newhouse, John. *Cold Dawn: The Story of SALT*. New York: Holt, Rinehart and Winston, 1973.

Nye, Joseph S., Jr. *Nuclear Ethics*. New York: Free Press, 1986.

Okin, Susan Moller. "Taking the Bishops Seriously." *World Politics* 36, no. 4 (July 1984): 527–54.

Scheer, Robert. *With Enough Shovels: Reagan, Bush and Nuclear War*. New York: Random House, 1982.

Shall, James V., S.J., ed. *The Bishops' Letters: Out of Justice, Peace, Joint Pastoral Letter of the West German Bishops; Winning the Peace, Joint Pastoral Letter of the French Bishops*. San Francisco: Ignatius Press, 1984.

Shultz, George P. *Turmoil and Triumph: My Years as Secretary of State*. New York: Scribner's, 1993.

Talbott, Strobe. *Deadly Gambits*. New York: Alfred A. Knopf, 1984.

Tellis, Ashley J. "Nuclear Arms, Moral Questions, and Religious Issues." *Armed Forces and Society* 13, no. 4 (Summer 1987): 599–627.

Winters, Francis X. "After Tension, Detente: A Continuing Chronicle of European Episcopal Views on Nuclear Deterrence." *Theological Studies* 45, no. 2 (Winter 1984): 343–51.

ETHICS AND MILITARY FORCE: GEORGE BUSH AND THE PERSIAN GULF WAR

Baker, James A. *The Politics of Diplomacy*. New York: G.P. Putnam's Sons, 1995.

Baumann, Paul. "Limits of the Just War." *Commonweal* 118, no. 5 (March 8, 1991): 149–50.

Clark, Ramsey. *The Fire This Time: U.S. War Crimes in the Gulf*. New York: Thunder's Mouth Press, 1992.

DeCosse, David E., ed. *But Was It Just? Reflections on the Morality of the Persian Gulf War*. New York: Doubleday, 1992.

El-Baz, Farouk, and R. M. Makharita, eds. *The Gulf War and the Environment*. Lausanne, Switzerland: Gordon and Breach Science Publishers, 1994.

Freedman, Lawrence, and Efraim Karsh. *The Gulf Conflict 1990–91*. Princeton: Princeton University Press, 1993.

Gordon, Michael R., and Bernard E. Trainor. *The Generals' War: The Inside Story of the Conflict in the Gulf.* New York: Little, Brown, 1995.

Hallett, Brien, ed. *Engulfed in War: Just War and the Persian Gulf.* Honolulu: University of Hawaii, 1991.

Hehir, J. Bryan. "Baghdad as Target: An Order to Be Refused." *Commonweal* 117, no. 18 (October 26, 1990): 117–18.

———. "Just Cause? Yes." *Commonweal* 119, no. 4 (February 28, 1992): 8–9.

Hendrickson, David C. "In Defense of Realism: A Commentary on *Just and Unjust Wars.*" *Ethics and International Affairs* 11 (1997): 19–53.

Johnson, James Turner, and George Weigel, eds. *Just War and the Gulf War.* Washington DC: Ethics and Public Policy Center, 1991.

Langan, John P. "An Imperfectly Just War." *Commonweal* 118, no. 11 (June 1, 1991): 361–65.

McMahan, Jeff, and Robert McKim. "The Just War and the Gulf War." *Canadian Journal of Philosophy* 23, no. 4 (December 1993): 501–41.

Menos, Dennis. *Arms over Diplomacy: Reflections on the Persian Gulf War.* Westport, CT: Praeger, 1992.

Mervyn, David. *George Bush and the Guardian Presidency.* New York: St. Martin's Press, 1996.

Powell, Colin L. *My American Journey.* New York: Random House, 1995.

Renshon, Stanley A., ed. *The Political Psychology of the Gulf War.* Pittsburgh: University of Pittsburgh Press, 1993.

Schwarzkopf, H. Norman. *It Doesn't Take a Hero.* New York: Bantam Books, 1992.

Sifry, Micah L., and Christopher Cerf, eds. *The Gulf War Reader: History, Documents, Opinions.* New York: Times Books, 1991.

Smock, David R., ed. *Religious Perspectives on War.* Washington, DC: United States Institute of Peace, 1992.

Tucker, Robert, and David Hendrickson. *The Imperial Temptation.* New York: Council on Foreign Relations, 1992.

U.S. News & World Report. *Triumph Without Victory.* New York: Times Books, 1992.

Vaux, Kenneth L. *Ethics and the Gulf War: Religion, Rhetoric and Righteousness.* Boulder, CO: Westview Press, 1992.

Watson, Bruce W., ed. *Military Lessons of the Gulf War.* London: Greenhill Books, 1991.

Whicker, Marcia Lynne, James P. Pfiffner and Raymond A. Moore, eds. *The Presidency and the Persian Gulf War.* Westport, CT: Praeger, 1993.

Woodward, Bob. *The Commanders.* New York: Simon & Schuster, 1991.

Zahn, Gordon C. "An Infamous Victory." *Commonweal* 118, no. 11 (June 1, 1991): 366–68.

THE LIMITS OF HUMANITARIAN OBLIGATION: THE INTERNATIONAL COMMUNITY AND THE CRISIS IN BURUNDI

Andreopoulos, George, ed. *Genocide: Conceptual and Historical Dimensions.* Philadelphia: University of Pennsylvania Press, 1994.

Barry, James A. "President Who Feels Others' Pain Should Aid Burundi." *Christian Science Monitor,* September 27, 1996, p. 19.

Booker, Salih. "United States Should Do the Right Thing." New York: Council on Foreign Relations, September 27, 1996.

Cullity, Garrett. "International Aid and the Scope of Kindness." *Ethics* 105, no. 1 (October 1994): 99–127.

Donaldson, Thomas. *The Ethics of International Business*. New York: Oxford University Press, 1989.

DuPreez, Peter. *Genocide: The Psychology of Mass Murder*. London: Boyars/Bowerdean, 1994.

Elfstrom, Gerard. "On Dilemmas of Intervention." *Ethics* 93, no. 4 (July 1983): 709–25.

Fein, Helen, ed. *Genocide Watch*. New Haven: Yale University Press, 1992.

Fishkin, James S. *The Limits of Obligation*. New Haven: Yale University Press, 1982.

Harriss, John. *The Politics of Humanitarian Intervention*. Herndon, UK: Books International, 1995.

Hehir, J. Bryan. "Intervention: From Theories to Cases." *Ethics and International Affairs* 9 (1995): 1–13.

Himes, Kenneth R. "Just War, Pacifism and Humanitarian Intervention." *America* 169, no. 4 (August 14, 1993): 10–15.

James, Susan. "The Duty to Relieve Suffering." *Ethics* 93, no. 1 (October 1982): 4–21.

Johnson, James Turner. "Just War Tradition and Low Intensity Conflict." Paper presented at the Low Intensity Conflict Symposium, Naval War College, April 9–10, 1992.

Kegley, Charles W. "International Peacemaking and Peacekeeping: The Morality of Multinational Measures." *Ethics and International Affairs* 10 (1996): 25–45.

Lemarchand, Rene. *Rwanda and Burundi*. London: Pall Mall Press, 1970.

_____. *Burundi: Ethnocide as Discourse and Practice*. Cambridge, MA: Woodrow Wilson Center Press, 1994.

Marin, Michael. *The Road to Hell: The Ravaging Effects of Foreign Aid and International Charity*. New York: Free Press, 1997.

Matthews, Jessica. "Power Shift." *Foreign Affairs* 76, no. 1 (January/February 1997): 50–69.

Minear, Larry, and Thomas G. Weiss. *Mercy Under Fire: War and the Global Humanitarian Community*. Boulder, CO: Westview Press, 1995.

Prendergast, John. *Frontline Diplomacy: Humanitarian Aid and Conflict in Africa*. Washington, DC: Center of Concern, 1996.

Shue, Henry. "Mediating Duties." *Ethics* 98, no. 4 (July 1988): 687–704.

Singer, Peter. "Famine, Affluence and Morality." *Philosophy and Public Affairs* 1, no. 3 (Spring 1972): 229–43.

United Nations. *Report of the Secretary General on the Situation in Burundi*. S/1996/116. New York: United Nations, February 15, 1996.

_____. *Report of the Secretary General on the Situation in Burundi*. S/1996/335. New York: United Nations, May 3, 1996.

United States Department of State. *Burundi: Human Rights Practices, 1996*. Washington, DC: U.S. Government Printing Office, 1996.

Weiss, Thomas G. "UN Responses in the Former Yugoslavia: Moral and Operational Choices." *Ethics and International Affairs* 8 (1994): 1–22.

Wheatly, Margaret. *Leadership and the New Science*. San Francisco: Berrett-Koehler, 1992.

CAN COVERT ACTION BE JUST? LESSONS FROM U.S. INTERVENTION IN CHILE

Beitz, Charles R. "Covert Intervention as a Moral Problem." *Ethics and International Affairs* 3 (1989): 45–60.

Bok, Sissela. *Lying: Moral Choice in Public and Private Life*. New York: Random House, 1978.

_____. *Secrets: On the Ethics of Concealment and Revelation*. New York: Pantheon Books, 1982.

Bundy, William P. *A Tangled Web: The Making of Foreign Policy in the Nixon Presidency* New York: Hill and Wang, 1998.

Colby, William E. "Public Policy, Secret Action." *Ethics and International Affairs* 3 (1989): 61–71.

Hulnick, Arthur S., and Daniel W. Mattausch. "Ethics and Morality in United States Secret Intelligence." *Harvard Journal of Law and Public Policy* 87, no. 1 (Spring 1989): 509–22.

Johnson, Loch K. "On Drawing a Bright Line for Covert Operations." *American Journal of International Law* 86, no. 2 (April 1992): 284–309.

Leary, William M., ed. *The Central Intelligence Agency, History and Documents*. University: University of Alabama Press, 1984.

Lilla, Mark. *The Two Oaths of Richard Helms*. Case Study C14-83-525.0. Cambridge, MA: John F. Kennedy School of Government, Harvard University, 1983.

Phillips, David Atlee. *The Night Watch*. New York: Ballentine Books, 1977.

Ranelagh, John. *The Agency: The Rise and Decline of the CIA*. New York: Simon & Schuster, 1986.

Reisman, W. Michael, and James E. Baker. *Regulating Covert Action*. New Haven: Yale University Press, 1992.

Report of the Twentieth Century Fund Task Force on Covert Action and American Democracy. New York: Twentieth Century Press, 1992.

Shulsky, Abram N. *Silent Warfare: Understanding the World of Intelligence*. Washington, DC: Brassey's, 1991.

Treverton, Gregory. *Covert Action: The Limits of Intervention in the Postwar World*. New York: Basic Books, 1987.

United States Senate. *Staff Report of the Select Committee to Study Government Operations with Respect to Intelligence Activities: Covert Action in Chile, 1963–73*. 94th Cong., 1st sess. Washington, DC: U.S. Government Printing Office, 1975.

United States Senate Select Committee to Study Governmental Operations with Respect to Intelligence Activities. *Alleged Assassination Attempts Involving Foreign Leaders*, 94th Cong., 1st sess. Rept 94-465. Washington, DC: U.S. Government Printing Office, 1975.

THE ETHICS OF ECONOMIC WARFARE: THE UNITED STATES AND CASTRO'S CUBA

Bender, Lynn Darrell. *The Politics of Hostility: Castro's Revolution and United States Policy*. Hato Rey, Puerto Rico: Inter American University Press, 1975.

Bonsal, Philip W. *Cuba, Castro and the United States*. Pittsburgh: University of Pittsburgh Press, 1971.

Capitanchik, David B. *The Eisenhower Presidency and American Foreign Policy*. London: Routledge and Kegan Paul, 1969.

Clagett, Bruce M. "Title III of the Helms–Burton Act Is Consistent with International Law." *American Journal of International Law* 90, no. 3 (July 1996): 434–40.

Cuba Collection. Washington, DC: National Security Archive, 1997. Microfiche.

Damrosch, Lori Fisler. "The Collective Enforcement of International Norms Through Economic Sanctions." *Ethics and International Affairs* 8 (1994): 59–75.

Daoudi, M. S., and M. S. Dajani. *Economic Sanctions: Ideals and Experience*. London: Routledge and Kegan Paul, 1983.

Eisenhower, Dwight D. *Peace with Justice* . New York: Columbia University Press, 1961.

_____. *The White House Years: Waging Peace, 1956–1961*. New York: New American Library, 1965.

Falk, Pamela S. "Eyes on Cuba: U.S. Business and the Embargo." *Foreign Affairs* 75, no. 2 (March/April 1996): 14–18.

FitzSimmons, Louise. *The Kennedy Doctrine*. New York: Random House, 1972.

Fontaine, Roger W. *On Negotiating with Cuba*. Washington, DC: American Enterprise Institute, 1965.

Garfield, Richard, and Sarah Santana. "The Impact of the Economic Crisis and the U.S. Embargo on Health in Cuba." *American Journal of Public Health* 87, no. 1 (January 1997): 15–19.

Hersch, Seymour M. *The Price of Power: Kissinger in the Nixon White House*. New York: Simon & Schuster, 1983.

Hufbauer, Gary C., and Jeffrey J. Schott, assisted by Kimberly Ann Elliott. *Economic Sanctions Reconsidered: History and Current Policy*. Washington, DC: Institute for International Economics, 1985.

Kirkpatrick, Anthony F. "Role of the United States in Shortage of Food and Medicine in Cuba." *Lancet* 348 (November 30, 1996): 1489–91.

Kline, John M. *Doing Business in South Africa: Seeking Ethical Parameters for Business and Government Responsibilities*. Case Study in Ethics and International Affairs, No. 11. New York: Carnegie Council on Ethics and International Affairs, 1995.

Lowenfeld, Andreas. "Congress and Cuba: The Helms–Burton Act." *American Journal of International Law* 90, no. 3 (July 1996): 419–34.

Marks, Frederick W. *Power and Peace: The Diplomacy of John Foster Dulles*. Westport, CT: Praeger, 1993.

May, Ernest, and Richard Neustadt. *Thinking in Time: The Uses of History for Decision Makers*. New York: Free Press, 1986.

McDougal, Myers S., and Florentine P. Feliciano. *Law and Minimum World Public Order: The Legal Regulation of International Coercion*. New Haven: Yale University Press, 1961.

Morici, Peter. "The United States, World Trade and the Helms–Burton Act." *Current History* 96 (February 1997): 87–88.

Morley, Morris H. *Imperial State and Revolution: The United States and Cuba, 1953–1986*. Cambridge: Cambridge University Press, 1987.

Paterson, Thomas G. *Contesting Castro: The United States and the Triumph of the Cuban Revolution*. Oxford: Oxford University Press, 1994.

Pierce, Albert C. "Just War Principles and Economic Sanctions." *Ethics and International Affairs* 10 (1996): 99–113.

Plank, John, ed. *Cuba and the United States: Long Range Perspectives*. Washington, DC: The Brookings Institution, 1967.

Rabe, Stephen G. *Eisenhower and Latin America: The Foreign Policy of Anticommunism* Chapel Hill: University of North Carolina Press, 1988.

Rusk, Dean. *The Winds of Freedom*. Boston: Beacon Press, 1963.

Smith, Earl T. *The Fourth Floor: An Account of the Castro Communist Revolution*. New York: Random House, 1962.

Smith, Robert F. *The United States and Cuba: Business and Diplomacy, 1917–1960*. New York: Bookman Associates, 1960.

Smith, Wayne S. "Cuba's Long Reform." *Foreign Affairs* 75, no. 2 (March/April 1996): 99–112.

Sorensen, Theodore C. *Kennedy*. New York: Harper & Row, 1965.

United States Department of State. *Foreign Relations of the United States, 1958-1960,* Volume 6: *Cuba.* Washington, DC: U.S. Government Printing Office, 1961.

_____. *Foreign Relations of the United States,* Volume 10, *Cuba: 1961–1963* <http://www. state.gov/www/about_state/history/frusX/index.html>.

Wall, James M. "U.S. Cuba Policy Is Obsolete." *Christian Century* 111, no. 25 (September 7–14, 1994): 803–4.

Welch, Richard E., Jr. *Response to Revolution: The United States and the Cuban Revolution, 1959–61.* Chapel Hill: University of North Carolina Press, 1985.

COERCION AND CONCILIATION: THE UNITED STATES AND THE NORTH KOREAN NUCLEAR PROGRAM

Bailey, Kathleen C. "The Nuclear Deal with North Korea: Is the Glass Half Empty or Half Full?" *Comparative Strategy* 14, no. 2 (April 1995): 137–48.

George, Alexander L. *Forceful Persuasion: Coercive Diplomacy as an Alternative to War.* Washington, DC: U.S. Institute of Peace, 1991.

George, Alexander L., and William E. Simons, eds. *The Limits of Coercive Diplomacy.* Boulder, CO: Westview Press, 1994.

Gilbert, Margaret. "Agreements, Coercion, and Obligation." *Ethics* 103, no. 4 (July 1993): 679–706.

Goldmann, Kjell. *The Logic of Internationalism: Coercion and Accommodation.* London: Routledge, 1994.

Greenawalt, Kent. "Shortfalls of Realism, Shared Social Values, and Authority: The Problem of Political Coercion." *Journal of Religion* 73, no. 4 (October 1993): 537–58.

Ikle, Fred Charles. *How Nations Negotiate.* New York: Harper & Row, 1964.

Kramer, Roderick M., and David M. Messick, eds. *Negotiation as a Social Process.* Thousand Oaks, CA: Sage, 1995.

Kwak, Tae-Hwan, Wayne Patterson, and Edward A. Olsen, eds. *The Two Koreas in World Politics.* Seoul: Kyungnam University Press, 1983.

Lockhart, Charles. *Bargaining in International Conflicts.* New York: Columbia University Press, 1979.

Mazarr, Michael J. *North Korea and the Bomb: A Case Study in Nonproliferation.* New York: St. Martin's Press, 1995.

Oberdorfer, Don. *The Two Koreas.* Reading, MA: Addison-Wesley, 1997.

Patchen, Martin. *Resolving Disputes Between Nations: Coercion or Conciliation.* Durham NC: Duke University Press, 1988.

Plunk, Daryl M. *The U.S.–North Korean Nuclear Agreement: A Six Month Report Card.* Asian Studies Center Backgrounder. Washington, DC: Heritage Foundation, 1995.

Rosegrant, Susan, and Michael D. Watkins. *Carrots, Sticks and Question Marks: Negotiating the North Korean Nuclear Crisis.* Parts A and B. Case Studies C18-95-1297.0 and C18-95-1298.0. Cambridge, MA: John F. Kennedy School of Government, Harvard University, 1995.

Sigal, Leon V. "Look Who's Talking Nuclear Diplomacy with North Korea." *Items* 51, no. 2–3 (June-September 1997): 31–36.

United States Senate, Committee on Foreign Relations. *Implications of the US–North Korea Nuclear Agreement, Hearing Before the Subcommittee on East Asian and Pacific Affairs of the Committee on Foreign Relations,* 103rd Cong., 2nd sess. Washington, DC: U.S. Government Printing Office, 1994.

_____. *North Korean Nuclear Agreement: Hearings Before the Committee on Foreign Relations, United States Senate,* 104th Cong., 1st sess. Washington, DC: U.S. Government Printing Office, 1995.

Wood, Joe, and Philip Zelikow. *Persuading a President: Jimmy Carter and American Troops in Korea.* Case Study C18-96-1319.0. Cambridge, MA: John F. Kennedy School of Government, Harvard University, 1996.

Zartman, I. William, ed. *The Negotiation Process: Theories and Applications.* Beverly Hills, CA: Sage, 1978.

SHEATHING THE SWORD OF JUSTICE

Bok, Sissela. *Common Values.* Columbia: University of Missouri Press, 1995.

Brunk, Gregory G., Donald Secrest, and Howard Tamashiro. *Understanding Attitudes About War.* Pittsburgh: University of Pittsburgh Press, 1996.

Fleishman, Joel L., Lance Liebman and Mark H. Moore, eds. *Public Duties: The Moral Obligations of Government Officials.* Cambridge, MA: Harvard University Press, 1981.

Gilligan, Carol. *In a Different Voice: Psychological Theory and Women's Development.* Cambridge, MA: Harvard University Press, 1993.

Harbour, Frances V. "Basic Moral Values: A Shared Core." *Ethics and International Affairs* 9 (1995): 162–69.

Hunt, Arnold D., Marie T. Crotty and Robert B. Crotty. *Ethics of World Religions.* San Diego: Greenhaven Press, 1991.

Kidder, Rushworth. *Shared Values for a Troubled World.* San Francisco: Jossey-Bass, 1994.

Kohlberg, Lawrence. *Essays on Moral Development, Volume II: The Psychology of Moral Development.* New York: Harper & Row. 1984.

Langan, John, S.J. "Just-War Theory After the Gulf War." *Theological Studies* 53, no. 1 (March 1992): 95–112.

Madsen, Peter, and Jay M. Shafritz, eds. *Essentials of Government Ethics.* New York: Meridian, 1992.

Osgood, Robert E., and Robert W. Tucker. *Force, Justice and Order.* Baltimore: Johns Hopkins Univrsity Press, 1967.

Wilson, Richard W. "Moral Development and Political Change." *World Politics* 36, no.1 (October 1983): 53–75.

Index

About the Author

JAMES A. BARRY is Visiting Associate Professor at George Mason University, where he teaches courses in International Politics, American Foreign Policy, and Ethics and International Affairs. Mr. Barry spent more than 30 years in government service. He was Deputy Chief of the Arms Control Intelligence Staff and Director of the Center for the Study of Intelligence, the CIA's "think tank" for critical assessments of the profession of intelligence.

ISBN 0-275-96092-7

90000>

EAN

9 780275 960926

HARDCOVER BAR CODE